Body - Space - Expression

Approaches to Semiotics
75

Editorial Committee

Thomas A. Sebeok
Roland Posner
Alain Rey

Mouton de Gruyter
Berlin · New York · Amsterdam

*Rudolf Laban in his workshop
at Dartington Hall ca. 1938/39*

Body - Space - Expression

The Development of Rudolf Laban's
Movement and Dance Concepts

Vera Maletic

Mouton de Gruyter
Berlin · New York · Amsterdam   1987

Mouton de Gruyter (formerly Mouton, The Hague)
is a Division of Walter de Gruyter & Co., Berlin.

Library of Congress Cataloging in Publication Data

Maletic, Vera, 1928 —
    Body, space, expression.
    (Approaches to semiotics ; 75)
    Bibliography: p.
    1. Laban, Rudolf von, 1879—1958. 2. Movement notation.
3. Dance notation. 4. Dancing-Philosophy. I. Title. II. Series.
GV1785.L2M35 1987   792.8′2′0924 [B]   86-32424
ISBN 0-89925-141-2 (alk. paper)

CIP-Kurztitelaufnahme der Deutschen Bibliothek

Maletic, Vera:
Body - space - expression : the development of Rudolf Laban's
movement and dance concepts / Vera Maletic. — Berlin ; New
York ; Amsterdam : Mouton de Gruyter, 1987.
    (Approaches to semiotics ; 75)
    ISBN 3-11-010780-5
NE: GT

Printed on acid free paper.

Typesetting: Asian Research Service, Hong Kong. — Printing: Druckerei Gerike
GmbH, Berlin. — Binding: Dieter Mikolai, Berlin. Printed in Germany.

Acknowledgements

This book has emerged from a lifelong exposure to the work of Rudolf Laban and is the culmination of seven years of research. Most influential in its shaping were two persons. My mother, Ana Maletic, gave me my first exposure to the master's ideas and endowed me with an unremitting curiosity to pursue a critical study of his opus. The late Lisa Ullmann, my second Laban teacher, gave me access to sources in the Laban Archives and geneously assisted with reviewing my translations of Laban's German texts. I would like to dedicate this book to both of them.

The motivation to engage in the research has been sparked by many students and professionals in the U.S.A. who are interested in Laban's theories. I am therefore grateful to my students and colleagues, both at The Ohio State University and the Laban/Bartenieff Institute of Movement Studies, for having given me the incentive to carry through this difficult task.

My thanks are also due to Professor Diane Woodruff, and Dr. Suzanne Youngerman who offered valuable suggestions for the first drafts of this book, as well as to Professors Odette Blum, Lucy Venable, and Judy Van Zile who commented helpfully on Chapter III. Helen Priest-Rogers kindly furnished me with information on the Berlin period around 1935, and Isa Partsch-Bergsohn discussed with me Laban's concept of Eukinetics as perceived by Kurt Jooss.

I am grateful to Nancy Grace for her editorial assistance. Her particular sensitivity to the content of the book and to my Central European English made the collaboration very enjoyable. My thanks also go to Kimberly Elam for her adaptation of Laban's drawings from his *Choreographie*.

Finally I would like to acknowledge all the persons and publishing companies who have granted me permission to publish sections from Laban's writings and related literature:

— The late Lisa Ullmann gave me permission to include two of Laban's unpublished manuscripts from the Laban Archives: "Film ueber die Harmonische Bewegung des Menschlichen Körper's" and an untitled manuscript in English from 1957. (Since her death in 1985, the materials from the Laban Archives have been deposited at the National Resource Center for Dance at the University of Surrey, U.K.)

— Laban's son Roland Laban, who is now the copyright carrier of all publications by Rudolf Laban and Lisa Ullmann, authorized the publication of the Laban materials cited in the book. These include not only sections from English publications but also my translations of quotations from Laban's

German books (*Die Welt des Tänzers*, 1920 — Walter Seifert Verlag; *Choreographie*, 1926 — Eugen Diedrichs Verlag; *Gymnastik und Tanz* and *Des Kindes Gymnastik und Tanz*, 1926 — Gerhard Stalling Verlag). I am greatly indebted to Roland Laban for his gesture of confidence.

— Two English publishers complemented Roland Laban's authorization: Falmer Press Ltd. gave me permission to publish a quotation from *A Vision of Dynamic Space*. Sections from *Effort, Modern Educational Dance, The Mastery of Movement on the Stage, The Mastery of Movement, Principles of Dance Movement Notation, Choreutics*, and *A Life for Dance* are reprinted by permission of Pitman Publishing Ltd., London.

— The permission to publish sections from articles in *The Laban Art of Movement Guild Magazine* has been granted by Su Johnston, the present editor of *Movement and Dance: Magazine of the Laban Art of Movement Guild*.

— Walter Sorell kindly gave me permission to reprint quotations from *The Mary Wigman Book*.

The photograph of Laban has been furnished by courtesy of Ellinor Hinks who from 1977 to 1985 assisted Lisa Ullman's work with the Laban Archives collections.

Preface

The significance of movement in the life and dance of our times has been investigated in depth by Rudolf Laban (1879-1958), the Hungarian-born choreographer and dance scholar. Laban outlined a comprehensive account of movement phenomena and of factors generating them. He defined common denominators of all types of movement, such as behavioral and symbolic, and provided the means of differentiating them through description, classification, and notation. A growing interest in Laban's theoretical framework can be discerned in several recent manifestations. The 1979 celebrations of the centenary of his birth paid tribute internationally to the increasing significance of his concepts in the field of human movement and dance. Laban's movement analysis as applied in his system of notation, theory of spatial harmonies and of the dynamic rhythm of movement and dance (Effort) is being introduced with greater frequency into college and university dance curricula; it is also being incorporated in research in dance anthropology, history, education, and therapy, as well as in psychology and nonverbal communication.

That studies and interpretations of Laban's work are scarce and that a complete presentation of his ideas, concepts, and classifications is not available may be due to several factors. In his English writings, Laban primarily focussed on particular aspects of movement, such as its spatial structure, dynamic rhythm, and notation; more encompassing are his untranslated German writings. Referring to the latter, Max Terpis (1946) points out Laban's reluctance to fix his findings as a method or system, thus preventing him from writing down systematically and clearly the results of his investigations. Laban himself stated in 1957 that he lacked interest in establishing personal methods or in replacing other existing methods. Albrecht Knust, commenting a year later on the difficulty of communicating and spreading Laban's ideas through his written opus, maintained that much of Laban's work is so advanced that present day language does not express it clearly. After an examination of his writings one may be inclined to agree with Terpis' and Knust's views.

Laban's early German texts, at times written in a rhapsodic style characteristic of his epoch, do not facilitate literal translation. Many of his English texts present no lesser challenge due to their Central European structure and style. Even concepts and terminology formed in England and selected from the English language require interpretative efforts. Some comparisons, however, reveal that terms used in the 1920's are more descriptive of Laban's process of classification, whereas the later English expressions constitute a clearer but more hermetic technical terminology. The dearth and/or onesidedness of critical studies on Laban's theoretical framework is greatly due to the lack of such comparative approaches. It is as though no scholar has yet gained the perspective necessary to discuss Laban's theories in a comprehensive way. For instance, studies, such as Sam Thornton's (1971) and Betty Redfern's (1973), are limited because they are exclusively based on Laban's English writings which are in turn examined against the background of British educational dance from the 50's and 60's. Erroneous views can be found in studies, such as those by Gordon Curl (1966-1969) and John Foster (1977). While Curl's premisesses are discussed in Chapter V of this text, Foster's tenets can be faulted for their lack of accuracy and selectiveness of sources which is coupled with conclusions drawn from opinions by authors who did not have access to Laban's complete opus nor to his teaching. The nucleus for a sounder and more complete evaluation of Laban's concepts can be found in Irmgard Bartenieff's essay on the roots of Laban's theory (1970), in articles by Sylvia Bodmer, Martha Davis, and Marion North in the Fall 1974 issue of *Main Currents in Modern Thought*, as well as in a recent essay by Alan Salter in the November 1984 issue of *Movement and Dance: Magazine of The Laban Guild*.

Ultimately, a critical study of Rudolf Laban will remain open-ended and in constant making and re-making; a definitive work may never emerge. Although one might attempt to act as mediator for the presentation of the developments and consolidation of Laban's key concepts, the many strands of his resources, explorations, and formulations invite even more active participation. The individual addressing Laban's work is almost compelled to bring, in part, his or her own meaning to the Laban opus. This has been my recurring experience in dealing with his framework from the point of view of the art 'of dance, dance pedagogy, and research; his opus assumes different meanings according to both one's own stage of development and the particular line of investigation. It is symptomatic that even a recent attempt to compose a definitive biography has proven thus far elusive. The only communication from John Hodgson, commissioned to undertake this task in the early 1970's, was his statement made in 1979 that there is not one man but a hundred men in Laban.

The intent of this present study, however, is to offer a multilateral examination of the origins and development of Laban's key concepts in movement and dance. Because it appears that there was a constant fluctuation between Laban's composing-directing-performing-teaching activities and his theoretical investigations, including the design of his notation, an investigation of the totality of his activities is attempted in Part One. Part Two presents the research leading to the evolution of his key-concepts, classification and notation. In Part Three, Laban's ideas and concepts are examined in relation to various cultural, artistic and philosophical paradigms. (The latter is expanded on in Appendix I.) Complementary to the text are survey tables providing a chronological account of the formulation of concepts and of their sources. (Annotated bibliographies of sources are included in the Appendix, as well as survey tables presenting interpretations of Laban's concepts by his students and collaborators, and an overview of the integration of his concepts into other theoretical frameworks.)

Resources used for this multilateral study include primary source materials, such as Laban's German and English books, articles, and his manuscripts from the Laban Archives as well as writings by Laban's contemporaries in Germany, and entries in German dance books. My own long-term exposure to the oral tradition of Laban-based teaching in Europe and personal contacts with Laban himself constitute another important resource. Research methods used include a comparative analysis in several directions: (a) comparisons are made of points of view found in Laban's five German books and several articles from the 1920's, and early 30's, as well as in writings by his student-collaborators of that time; (b) presentations of movement and dance concepts in these are compared with Laban's English publications from the 40's and 50's; (c) the persistence of some concepts in the oral tradition is juxtaposed to their absence in Laban's publications; and (d) Laban's ideas are examined in relation to various artistic, scientific, and philosophical views. All the comparative analyses presuppose translating one language to another which is not merely a reconstruction of a text but more accurately an act of interpretation in which the translator's backround and understanding merge with the outlooks of the author. (English translations of book-, article-, and piece-titles are indicated in parentheses. Only translated works and pieces performed in the U.K. and the U.S.A. are italicized.)

My interest in Laban's applied theory is of long duration. After Laban-based training in Yugoslavia and studies at the Laban Art of Movement Centre in England, I taught dance and dance theory in three different cultures: Yugoslavia, England, and America. While teaching and co-teaching with Laban's key students and collaborators at the Addlestone Laban Centre (and subsequently the Laban Centre for Movement and Dance at the University of London Goldsmith's College), I also classified Laban's multilingual manuscripts in his archives. A recent interdisciplinary doctoral study at The Ohio State University (U.S.A.) provided a broader conceptual framework for critical evaluation of Laban's contributions to the study of movement and dance. A grant from the OSU College of the Arts has facilitated additional information gathering and interviews.

As a member of the third generation of Laban-trained teachers, I have frequently been confronted with presentations of end-products of Laban's theories not always providing insight into the process by which he arrived there. The comparative analysis of his German books with English texts has shown some missing links and also clarified his search and process of concept formulation. This publication is addressed to professionals in the fields of movement, dance, and behavioral and social sciences, as well as to readers with a general interest in these disciplines; it is hoped that this historical perspective will expand their understanding of Laban's concepts and will further Laban research based on primary sources.

Contents

Acknowledgements   v
Preface   vii
List of Tables   xiv
List of Illustrations   xv

PART ONE: INTENTS – ACTIONS – REVERBERATIONS   1

Introduction   3
1879-1900 Childhood and Adolescence in Central Europe   4
1900-1907 The French Phase of Assimilations   5
1908-1919 The German-Swiss Phase of Explorations   6
1920-1937 The German Period of Gestation   8
1938-1958 The English Period of Consolidations   24
Coda   27
Biographical Signposts   37
Notes to Part One   39

PART TWO: THE EMERGENCE OF CONCEPTS, THEORIES
          AND CLASSIFICATIONS   49

Introduction   51
Notes to Introduction   56
Chapter I: *Theory of Space*   57
   Directional Orientation and Levels   58
   Shape-Form and Extension-Size   63
   Choreutics – Space Harmony   64
   Survey of Laban's Theory of Space   73
   Survey of Space Harmony – Choreutics   75
   Harmony of Movement   77
   Notes to Chapter I   79
Chapter II: *Development of Concepts of Dynamics,*
            Eukinetics and Effort   93
   The Beginnings   93
   Rhythm and Phrasing   94
   Emergence of Eukinetics   97

The Concept of Effort   99
The Effort Theory   101
Summary in Terms of Correlations of the Early Concepts
to Concepts Formulated in the 40's and 50's   104
Notes to Chapter II   106
Chapter III: *Formation of Laban's Movement and Dance
            Notation Principles*   113
Introduction   113
The Emergence of the Principles of the System   115
History of the System   119
Bodily Articulation   123
Relationship Aspects   125
Laban's Notation in Relation to His Other Theories   126
Notes to Chapter III   128
Chapter IV: *Composition: A Synthesis of Applied Theory*   139
"Film about the Harmonious Movement of the Human Body"   144
Notes to Chapter IV   146

PART THREE: INTEGRATION OF THE PAST AND
            PROJECTIONS INTO THE FUTURE   149

Introduction   151
Notes to Introduction   151
Chapter V: *Paradigms Underlying Laban's Concepts*   153
  — reference to dance reformers   153
  — sources of choreology   155
  — awareness of post-Cartesian and contemporary
    philosophical stands   162
  — turn of the century models and values in movement and
    dance education   164
Notes to Chapter V   167
Chapter VI: *Open-Ended Conclusions*   171
General Movement and Dance Classification   172
Spatial Relationship/Order of Movement —
Space Harmony/Choreutics   175
The Theory of Dynamics — Eukinetics-Effort   178
The Concept of Harmony or Effort-Space Affinities   180
Laban's Collaborators   181
Pointing to the Future   182
Notes to Chapter VI   184

APPENDIXES 187

Appendix I: *The Lived Body-Space-Expression*   189
Notes to Appendix I   199
Appendix II: *British Applications of Laban's Concepts:*
Survey Tables   203
Appendix III: *Integration of Laban's Concepts into Other*
Theoretical Frameworks: Survey Tables   215
Appendix IV: *Annotation of Laban's Writings Used in the Research*   219
Appendix V: *Annotated Bibliography of Selected German Sources*   229

Bibliography   239
Index of Names and Sources   247
Index of Concepts   257

List of Tables

Table 1. *Stability and Lability/Mobility*: Choronological Survey of
Concept Formation and Links with other Concepts   84

Table 2. *Theory of Space*: Choronology of Concept Formulation
and Sources and Links with other Concepts
Orientation: Directions and Levels   85
Shape – Form   85
Extension – Size – Kinesphere   86

Table 3. *Choreutics – Space Harmony*
A. Concepts   87
B. Choreutic Forms – Scales, Rings   88

Table 4. *Stability and Lability/Mobility*: Chronological Survey of
Concepts Formulation and Links with Spatial Concepts   90

Table 5. *Correlation of Dynamics of Movement and its Spatial
Placement* as presented in *Choreographie* and *Choreutics*   91

Table 6. *Harmony of Movement*: Choronology of Concept
Formulation and Sources   92

Table 7. *Theory of Dynamics – Eukinetics*: Chronology of Concept
Formulation and Sources   109

Table 8. *Effort*: I. Description of the Term, II. Motion Factors, 110
III. Attitudes, IV. Effort Elements, V. Ranking and Grading,   111
VI. Combinations of Motion Factors/Effort Elements   112
VII. Transitions and Mutations   112

Table 9. *Kinetography Laban/Labanotation*: Development of
Principles and Chronology of Sources
a)   Link with Body Concepts   133
b)   Link with Space Concepts   134
c)   Link with Stability-Mobility/Lability   135
d)   Link with Dynamics and Time Rhythm   136
e)   Link with Relationship Concepts   137

Table 10. *Bodily Aspects*: Survey of Classification and Sources   138
Relationship Aspects: Survey of Classification and Sources   138

List of Illustrations

Figures 1-4   61
  1. The Octahedron
  2. The Cube
  3. Three-dimensional Planes: Vertical, Sagittal Horizontal
  4. The Icosahedron and its Inner Structure

Figures 5-6   71
  5. Inclinations of the A-scale
  6. The Order of the A-scale

Figures 7-10   72
  7. Inclinations of the B-scale
  8. A Three-ring
  9. A Four-ring
  10. The Axis-scale

Figures 11-13   108
  11. The Effort Graph
  12. Effort contrasts
  13. Effort transitions

Figure 14. Mono- and Polylinear Sequences   116

Figure 15. Symbols for 27 Main Directions   117

Figure 16. Swallow-tail Writing   120

Figure 17. Bodycross Writing   120

PART ONE:

INTENTS–ACTIONS–REVERBERATIONS

Introduction

To elucidate the substance and impact of Laban's life and times, Part One deals primarily with biographical data. Each period of Laban's life contributed significantly to the growth and development of his ideas, concepts, theories, and classifications. Although not the main concern of this study, the historical overview functions to create a space-time frame for the research, to situate Laban's early activities and "manifestoes" in the cultural milieu of Central Europe during the nascent decades of the twentieth century. Because accounts of his life and work in England from 1938 until his death in 1958 are available in English, readers interested in a further examination of this period are referred to more recent sources.

Since Laban was forced to flee Nazi Germany and his work and publications were banned until the end of World War II, most of the biographical sources remain in German publications prior to 1938. An exception to this is Laban's autobiographical *Ein Leben für den Tanz* (*A Life for Dance*), published in 1935 and translated into English by Lisa Ullmann in 1975; this is to date the only German book by Laban available in English. Being a "lively interplay of fantasy and reality," the autobiography is clarified by Ullmann's extensive footnotes which frequently serve as interpretations providing geographical and historical background to Laban's narration.[1] Additional valuable insights into Laban's life from 1913 to 1917 are found in writings by Hans Brandenburg and Mary Wigman, and Laban's working life until the late twenties is described in accounts by John Schikowski, Werner Schuftan, Rudolf Lämmel and Martin Gleisner.[2] The 1929 issue of *Schrifttanz*, celebrating Laban's 50th anniversary, includes a three-page list of dates from his life and work, and a chronological guide was compiled by Ullmann for the 1958 Laban memorial issue of the *Dance Notation Record*.[3] Further source materials have been found in various articles by Laban, his disciples, and contemporary critics in German magazines, periodicals, and booklets of the twenties and early thirties, as well as in some historical works;[4] prospectuses of workshops, schools, institutes, and centres were also used.

In addition to the issue of *Schrifttanz* celebrating Laban's 50th anniversary, a special December 1929 issue of *Singhor und Tanz* also pays tribute to the master. This symposium of articles by Laban's former student-collaborators and writers on dance and theatre provides an excellent source of information on his contemporaries' perceptions and evaluations of his activities and achievements by the end of the twenties. Laban as a person, teacher, inventor, and reformer of dance comes alive for us through these writings. They also reflect his contemporaries' views of the purpose and meaning of dance which were greatly influenced by Laban and by the common assumptions of his time. Of particular interest are articles by the editor of *Schrifttanz*, Alfred Schlee, and the editor of *Der Tanz*, Joseph Lewitan – both furnish a critical appraisal of Laban's special contribution which evades all attempts to pigeon-hole him or to label his opus, even at that time of his working life.

1879–1900 Childhood and Adolescence in Central Europe

Rudolf Laban was born on December 15, 1879 in Poszony, Hungary, now Bratislava in Czechoslovakia. His childhood and adolescence were spent in different parts of the Austro-Hungarian Empire where his father served as a military governor. From a whole range of family names and nobility titles, including Attila and Varalja, he used "von Laban" until the 1930's, abandoning the "von" when he emigrated to England in 1938.

During his early childhood, he was encouraged by his mother to pursue athletic activities, a desire, as he explains in *A Life for Dance*, motivated by "her ambition . . . to turn me into a competent horseman, swimmer, and tennis player."[5] According to another personal account Laban also received his first introduction to rhythmic gymnastics from a dance teacher in Budapest.[6] In addition, his father's military career provided Laban with the opportunity to become acquainted with a variety of military "choreographies," such as troop formations in parades, march-pasts, musters, and occasional funerals. It appears that the image of a soldier was of great fascination for the young Laban. He would also accompany his father on his travels to various provinces of the south eastern parts of the Empire, and throughout these journeys, Laban was introduced to a variety of ritualistic traditions, ceremonials, and folk dances which significantly influenced his formative years and paved the way for his future endeavors. On his visits to the Balkans, the Adriatic coast, Bosnia and Herzegovina (today parts of Yugoslavia), young Laban was intrigued, in particular, by the ceremonies of the whirling Dervishes and ritualistic sword dances. In *A Life for Dance*, Laban credits these experiences with solidifying his dedication to the art of dance: "The thought of the magic in the dance held fast in my mind and my decision to give my life to the arts became irrevocable."[7]

Another significant influence on young Laban was an apprenticeship with a painter in approximately 1895/6. Laban confessed his intention to become an artist to this old friend, and the painter, in turn, set out to teach the boy to observe and interpret life, as well as how to value work and to diligently master the craftsmanship of art. This experience also led to Laban's experimentations with sequences of *tableaux vivants* (living pictures) which he eventually transformed into various group dance scenes; it also brought about his introduction to theatre set design.[8]

Laban's family, however, did not share his enthusiasm for an artistic career. His father encouraged him instead to become a military officer, and Laban did, in fact, attempt to follow his father's wishes, entering a reputable military academy in Wiener-Neustadt, Austria in 1899. But the regimen of military life did not suit Laban's temperament or his dreams. He left the school after one year, striking out for the more creative environment of Munich and Paris where he began his explorations of art, architecture, stage design, dance, and dance notation.

1900-1907 The French Phase of Assimilation

Laban arrived in Paris via Munich. Because he broke away from his family to embark on an artistic career, he was forced to support his studies and to travel in and out of Paris following various job opportunities such as drawing caricatures for journals, arranging and performing in small revue-type shows, and painting posters.[9] During this period, however, Laban studied a great many artistic disciplines and began shaping the artistic vision that would lead to the revolutionizing of dance and dance theory. He took movement lessons with Monsieur Morel, a student of Delsarte, familiarizing himself with ballet steps, and "from the frozen form language of the old ballet style" started drawing out the living sense of movement.[10] One can presume that he had the opportunity to study Feuillet's *Chorègraphie* at the Bibliothèque de L'Opéra, and this activity planted the seeds for the development of his dance notation. In his subsequent treatise on the theory and notation of the new dance, he actually pays tribute to Feuillet by adopting the title *Choreographie*.

It was also in Paris that Laban began to formulate plans for a dance theatre. Stimulated by his studies of architecture at the École des Beaux Arts, he first envisioned such a theatre, similar to drawings which he later included in *A Life for Dance*: a huge, arena-like building enclosing a central space for dancers and audience seating in ring-like formations around a cupola.[11] This vision was a powerful and long-lasting one, and some ten years later, while living in Switzerland, he created a cardboard model of the theatre in the round.[12] Laban's progressive architectural ideas, fed by his crucial years of artistic apprenticeship, led to equally creative projects such as a "kilometre-house" — a vision of an enormous dome-like cover without supporting pillars[13] — and of a building for the Chicago World's Fair in 1933-34, a project which unfortunately never materialized due to financial difficulties.

1908–1919 The German-Swiss Phase of Explorations

Laban left Paris in 1908 and settled for a while in Munich. Besides jobs, such as painting posters and mounting numerous festivals during carnival time,[14] he was able here to explore more intensely his ideas of freeing both the dancer and the dance, and to bring dance to the layman as well as to the professional. As a result, he began a more consistent exploration of the ideological basis for and the creation of the dance, and by 1910 he had founded his first dance company and school. Driven by the desire to liberate dance from all extraneous influences, particularly those of music and drama, Laban created the principle of "free" or "absolute" dance.[15] The fundamental means of expression for dance were to be drawn from the rhythm of bodily movement and its spatial and dynamic components. Laban believed that dance could only establish an association with its sister arts if it need not rely so heavily on musical rhythm, mood, and structure or on a story line derived from poetry. With such a foundation in place, Laban was then able to start experimenting with the inter-relationship of dance-sound-word (Tanz-Ton-Wort). This triad did not aim at a fusion of heterogeneous aesthetic elements, as does a Wagnerian *Gesamtkunstwerk*, but was to be rooted in the expressive powers of gesture, song, and speech.[16]

In the process of thus freeing the material of dance, Laban also encouraged his students to work in less physically restricted environments. He wanted his students to experience a new way of life – a way of dancing in the open air, free of solid material boundaries. Therefore, from 1911 to 1914, his workshops, schools, and performance activities were divided between winter months in Munich and summer months in Ascona's Monte Verità, a health farm and cosmopolitan center on the Lago Maggiore in Switzerland.[17]

During this time, Laban captivated the imaginations of numerous talented individuals, many of whom first studied under him and later collaborated with him in teaching, idea development, and staging dances. Among his student-collaborators, the most outstanding were two former pupils of Émile Jacques-Dalcroze: Suzanne Perrottet and Mary Wigman; others included Käthe Wulff, Maja Lederer, and Dussia Bereska.[18] Wigman, perhaps the most renowned of his pupils, was encouraged by the painter Emil Nolde to join Laban; she did so in 1913 and became the "guinea pig" for his first sequences exploring the spatial harmonics of dance. For Wigman, Laban's approaches and main preoccupations of this period "provided for his students the experience of free improvisation, freeing . . . the creative forces."[19] A great variety of artistic stimuli were explored besides free dance improvisation:

the rhythm and meaning of spoken word, musical harmony, drumming accompaniment or moving and playing percussion instruments, costumes and sets. "Laban's countless experiments . . . would be worthy to be studied by directors of operas and plays who could draw from them a plentitude of new stimuli."[20] But most significantly for Wigman, Laban "liberated dance from its slave-like association with music, and reinstated its independence and beauty of an absolute language. He pursued movement in its smallest detail and proved that its liberated material can be brought into an organically unified compositional form."[21]

While at Monte Verità, Laban also directed the "School for the Arts," which, as well as summer workshops from 1915 on, was staffed by Mary Wigman, Suzanne Perrottet, and Maja Lederer; each was in charge of the movement section, sound and music section, and speech section, respectively. The school and workshops, open to young people who intended to train in the performing arts, emphasized "works of arts which are rooted in the unity of those expressive powers given to man naturally — without the aid of extra-human materials — in the triad of dance-sound-word."[22] More specifically, the prospectus for the "School of the Arts" articulated three approaches to the teaching of arts:

1. technique: body exercises, vocal, instrumental, and speech exercises;
2. the experience and practice of the arts — individually or in groups;
3. the compositional aspect of the arts.

At the beginning of World War I, Laban was in Switzerland and remained there until the end of the war. While in Zürich, his keen interest in the expressive power of movement and dance led him to delve further into the dynamic rhythms, spatial structure, and harmony of dance. Addressing himself both to the performing dance artist as well as to the layman in communal dance activities, Laban gradually developed his theory and practice of Space Harmony and its notation. During this period, he also had time to "study choreology [research into the art of movement] and all that is connected with it."[23] The first outline of the manuscript for his *Die Welt des Tänzers* (The Dancer's World) was also conceived at this time and comprised Laban's statement of belief in the universal significance of dance. The book, published in 1920, was written in five *Gedankenreigen* — rounds of thought similar in form to *Reigen*.[24] It is indicative of the rapid development of Laban's creative insights that eight years later he felt that he did not quite stand behind everything he had written in this book.[25]

Further activities in Zürich included visits to and participations in the first Dada manifestations. Laban's presence at several such events are noted in Dada publications; H. Ball, H. Richter, and W. Verkauf, for instance, comment on his appearance at the Cabaret Voltaire events. Richter also describes the choreographic participation of Laban's students Suzanne

Perrottet, Käthe Wulff, and Sophie Taeuber in the last Dada performance in Zürich in 1919.[26]

In keeping with his democratic vision of dance, Laban contributed choreography for layman dances in numerous festivals in Germany and Switzerland during this period. In addition, he managed to produce several performance pieces with his professional students. In 1914, he composed a dance-drama in collaboration with writer-poet Hans Brandenburg on the basis of Brandenburg's tragedy *Der Sieg des Opfers* (Victory Through Sacrifice).[27] His *Die Grünen* (The Green Ones) consisted of scenes from a larger work – *Die Erde* (*The Earth*, 1914), and *Der Spielmann* (The Fiddler) which he choreographed in 1916 and was his full length work; he also composed musical accompaniment for both *Die Grünen* and *Der Spielmann*.[28] One can gain a closer insight into this period from an 1921 article by Mary Wigman. She describes Laban's technical and theoretical investigations as occurring simultaneously with his projects for the large dance choir work *Die Erde*. Conceived when he was eighteen years old, Laban started its realization in 1914 when, as referred to above, only one of its sections, *Die Grünen*, was produced. Wigman comments that the idea of the work could be seen as an emergence of a new mythology based on the idea of relationships between the crystalline, plant and animal worlds. Laban's sketch-books were filled with choreographic notes and sketches for sets and costumes. Movers in red represented souls of animals, the blueish-white ones the spectres of crystals, and the green ones the spirits of plants.[29] Also overwhelming was the richness of musical motives which Laban created with the dance. Wigman maintains that the experience of producing the work with the available human material, however, brought about a turning point in Laban's activities. Realizing that inspiring talented people to dance did not suffice, "he understood that a work of art, conceived in an unified way, could only be done by people trained in a unified way. He had to form on his own his great instrument – the dance group – by finding a language which could be learned by all, and by establishing laws which could, in their clarity and simplicity, unite the most varied dance talents on a common basis . . . . The human orchestra had to be educated not only to dance, but also to understand the dance."[30] This brought Laban to embrace even more intensly dance education through "the foundation of the laws of dance harmony and the theory of spatial tensions."[31]

1920–1937 The German Period of Gestation

The decade and a half from 1920 to 1937 represents Laban's most fecund period – the evolution of his most intense activities and achievements in several concurrent areas. While the publication of his first four books (*Die Welt des Tänzers*, 1920; *Choreographie*, 1926; *Gymnastik und Tanz*, 1926; *Des Kindes Gymnastik und Tanz*, 1926) presents in part the initial formulations of his theory, Laban's lengthy search for a universal movement and dance notation attained its final solution. At the same time, his directing and composing pursuits in dance as an art form and dance for layman gained momentum. It is as though his experiences and insights during his Zürich residency prompted him to establish first a dance workshop and a dance group, and subsequently a school to train dancers — performers, choreographers, teachers — on the basis of his own principles.

In 1920, Laban founded the *Tanzbühne Laban* (Dance-Theatre Laban) in Stuttgart and co-directed it with Dussia Bereska. As a workshop for his dance theatre, he trained a group of twenty-five dancers; among the most outstanding of these students, who also became his collaborators and/or respected professionals in their own rights, were Kurt Jooss, Jens Keith, Edgar Frank, Herta Feist, and Albrecht Knust.[32] Simultaneously, Laban was also engaged as producer and ballet master at the Mannheim National Theatre, and in 1921, he drew twenty dancers from his own group to perform together with twenty members of the theatre ballet company. Here Laban created his first version of the Bacchanalia of Wagner's *Tannhäuser*, and among his own pieces, the dance-play *Die Geblendeten* (The Deluded) and *Epische Tanzfolge* (Epic Dance Suite), "the first choral work in a new style," with music by Frederich Wilckens.[33]

In 1923, Laban transferred his activities to Hamburg where the *Kammertanzbühne Laban* (Chamber-Dance-Theatre Laban) was founded, led by Dussia Bereska. Between 1924 and 1926, the ensemble toured Germany, Austria, Italy, and Yugoslavia. New students, dancers and subsequent collaborators who trained in this period included Sylvia Bodmer, Ruth Loeser, Julian Algo, Lotte Wedekind, Aino Siimola, Herman Robst, Martin Gleisner, and Gertrud Snell.[34]

The repertory of the company was expanded to include such works as *Der Schwingende Tempel* (The Swinging Temple), an oratorio-like work "of five *Reigen* lasting altogether three hours";[35] *Faust Part II* and *Prometheus* (1922), two works accompanied by speech-choirs;[36] *Die Gaukelei* (Jugglery), a dance drama with social overtones;[37] *Casanova*, a dance comedy;[38] *Don Juan* (1925), a dance drama by Gluck with Laban's choreography;[39] *Die Nacht* (The Night), a dance play about "violent storms and evil spirits of our time," with music derived from jazz written on the basis of Laban's notes for meter and rhythm;[40] *Narrenspiegel* (The Fools Mirror) (1925), a dance play for Laban's chamber dance theatre;[41] the *Ritterballet* (Ballet of the Knights), a ballet set to Beethoven's music and choreographed by Laban and Bereska.[42]

As did other reformers of modern dance, Laban was promoting the idea of dance for males. He explains in his autobiography that with the creation of *Don Juan* he had, after much struggle, finally succeeded in establishing the idea of the male dancer and the masculine style of dance.[43] Although he had an equal proportion of men and women assistant collaborators, the social tradition of patriarchy occasionally dominated his views, a fact evidenced by his statement that "the design of the art of dance – as all building – will remain predominantly a male endeavor."[44] The intent or "message" behind the creation of his dance works, however, was more extensive than the single need to propagate patriarchy. In *A Life for Dance*, his statement that "dance is an excellent medium for representing inner attitudes and conflicts" provided the foundation for all his choreographic endeavors.[45] In his creations of personalities, such as Agamemnon, Don Juan, and Casanova, Laban emphasized the embodiment of ethical values and attitudes. By disregarding the external influences, he focussed on representing the ethical qualities of the protagonist's inner disposition. This posture gave rise to dance-dramas of new dramaturgy, leading to new perceptions of life which inform us of the inner path taken by the character. It represents a turning to reality where the meaning of the development of the hero's true being can be found in the experience of his inner struggles. More generally, Laban believed that dance can mediate a direct communication to the heart, that it not only touches the feelings in a general way but that it also convinces.[46]

Concurrent with these choreographic activities was Laban's concern about central movement and dance issues. These are aptly illustrated in a talk he presented at the first German Dance Congress in Magdeburg (June 21-24, 1927) on the topic "Das Tänzerische Kunstwerk" ("The Dance as a Work of Art").[47] Excerpts from Laban's main points, numbered 1 through 9, are summarized as follows.

1. Dance as an art form requires the same link with tradition as does any other art form. A work of art should be formed on the basis of artistic laws; sheer intuition is not enough and that which arises out of improvisation is a natural manifestation – not art. All capacities of man, such as will-power, feelings, and intellect, are engaged in the forming of art.

2. Although the fundamental laws regulating the art of dance have been known for a millenium, they are at the present time forgotten. As a reminder, Laban points to choreology, choreosophy, and choreography. While choreology deals with the logic and balancing order of dance, choreosophy is the knowledge of the spiritual relationships of the dance content; choreography is the dance form itself.

3. The content of a dance work originates from the inner world, ranging from the drive for self preservation to virtues such as spirituality, truth, righteousness, and sacrifice.

4. The communication of dance content is derived from rhythmic-spatial

changes in the dancer's movement. The spectators perceive and understand the spiritual and instinctual components of the dance through their own sense of movement. Constructing an analogy with the experience of music, Laban explains that the perception of rhythmic-melodic tonal sequences in a piece of pure music, as different from programmatic music, generates the understanding of the feelings which underlie the work.

5. The form of the dance work is brought about by the type of movement used in a particular piece. The carrier of expression can be either a mimetic type of movement, which is stylized behavioral or functional movement, or pure dance movement consisting of ornamental fluctuations of balance; these may remain arabesque-like if the inner content is missing.

6. The dance design can be analyzed by means of choreology from the point of view of the dynamism of spatial directions building characteristic forms of design. They constitute a kind of language of dance which can in part be described by words, such as a gesture of adoration or a bacchantic turn. The study of choreography shows how sentences and poems can be built from such words gaining a dance sense. Dance structures can convey clearly to the viewer an inner experience and development of an inner drive which is anchored in a universal human experience. However, in order to communicate, a piece does not need to be an everyday action, or mime, or drama, but can be a dance.

7. Performance dance has nothing in common with body culture and harmonious movement. Those dance critics and writers, such as Fred Hildebrandt, who appear to promote dance through flowery descriptions of predominantly feminine bodies support dance illiteracy, missing out on any inner relationship with the language of dance. A cultural need for future dance works in which male dancers participate is obvious.

8. A clear composition and interpretation of the dance work is a condition *sine qua non* for further developments. It is as though we have no real art of dance. On one hand, we have just about differentiated social and performing dance, and on the other we still fight in form and content against the overtones of music and drama.

9. This does not mean that the art of dance should remain puritanically isolated. All of the arts can contribute to the enhancement of dance. Dance can also serve opera, plays, festivities, and other such manifestations. The contemporary art of dance has, however, no place of its own where it can be appreciated in its three-dimensionality; a circus may be far more appropriate than the proscenium theatre because the spatial design of the dance should be seen from above. We lack today a dance theatre not only from the point of view of an appropriate building but also from both the perspective of a well-trained ensemble, technically and expressively, and an educated audience.

Some of the above statements may appear surprising at first glance. Contrary to the general expectation that the reformer of the new dance would be an adversary of the ballet tradition, Laban called for a link with that tradition. Alfred Schlee, editor of *Schrifttanz*, reminds us of the astonishment Laban roused among his colleagues when he stated that "there is no old and new dance, there is only one art of dance."[48] Fritz Klingenbeck, Laban's assistant, comments as well that Laban's ideologies appeared perplexing, especially for many dance lovers who heard Laban reject ballet yet saw him introducing ballet techniques in his schools.[49] But to those familiar with *Choreographie*, it is known that Laban took the point of departure for his spatial order of the new choreography from the theory of ballet positions. Furthermore, Laban's clear delineation between the crafting of dance composition and intuitive movement improvisation, and between dance as an art form and other forms of body culture, may have surprised those who saw him as the creator of social dance activities for laymen.

Not all of his colleagues and critics, however, were baffled by Laban's apparently paradoxical stand. Hans Brandenburg, defining the forming of style as a simultaneous breaking (or widening) and establishing of boundaries, maintained that the new dance gained the possibility of style through Laban's work. In addition to Laban's creative theory and praxis, Brandenburg saw Laban's dance theatres, his involvement with the professional dance organizations, and, most of all, his dance notation, as building elements of style. Discussing Laban's attitude toward ballet, he believed that Laban did not break from but continued and deepened the ballet tradition. In Brandenburg's opinion, Laban's search for the grammar and syntax of the language of dance resulted in the discovery of laws of which ballet rules were only a part.[50]

Kurt Jooss described the dual attitude of Laban the artist and the "man of complicated modern sensibilities" toward the artificial formality of ballet at the beginning of the century – and of Laban the creator of a new dance theory who recognized "the essence of spiritual laws of ballet."[51] According to Jooss, Laban took the clear structure of ballet as the foundation for the new structure with its freedom and expressive power, thus unifying the Apollonian and Dionysian styles and fully reflecting the modernist spirit. For Jooss, Laban's dance was the dance of all "real" dancers, a dance which should not be the signal for war between the enemy camps of "ballet" and "modern" but a battle of dancers motivated by an inner enthusiasm to fight the army of unproductive art administrators.[52]

Despite such positive interpretations of Laban, his work still encountered a general resistance to change. Schlee points out that Laban had difficulty freeing German dance from its sterile isolation and its national limitations. He also records the dismay with which Laban's signal of war with artistic inflation was received.[53] Klingenbeck ascribes these difficulties to Laban's constant creation of something new. He saw Laban as the ingenious master who realizes ideas not thought of before and then leaves them to others to implement while he proceeds with newer visions: "Some may find it tragic that he [Laban] cannot pursue till the end all that which he himself inaugurated; but how could that be done by a single man who thinks already something new perhaps the opposite of what he thought before while others are trying to understand him?"[54]

The mercurial nature of Laban's genius did, in fact, attract as powerfully as it repelled and confused. One of his student collaborators, Käthe Wulff, argued that a frequent criticism made of Laban, the charge that he wanted too much and too many things and thus dispersed his energies, was not true. "The fact that nothing gets lost from his activities cannot be appreciated by those who expect to see achievements flow smoothly and in a visibly measurable fashion."[55] Mary Wigman saw him in a similar light. She envisioned him as "a great wanderer," one "who after entering an unknown country and having found what he wanted or what happened to meet his need, would soon leave it for the next one to be explored." Wigman believed that wherever he stayed, even if it were only for a short while, he left his traces. "He was forced," she explained, "to make many detours and probably enjoyed branching off the main road from time to time to investigate the more intimate side streets and bypaths. But the original direction of his research was never touched nor changed by such diversions. The essential nature of his work might be caught in one word: movement."[56]

As for the relationship between the theory and practice of dance, Laban dealt with this topic in his lecture-demonstration: "Problems of Dance," which he took on tour throughout Germany, Austria, and Switzerland in 1929. His presentation placed before his audiences a consideration of the problem extended to all areas of dance as well as his concern about dance as an independent discipline. The lecture-demonstration included slides with a chart titled "What is Necessary: Practically and Theoretically?"[57] in which Laban outlined the four major areas of dance. The first, *dance for layman*, was divided into two parts: recreational play and the formation of teachers. The latter, according to Laban, should mediate pedagogically gymnastic experiences in a rhythmically ordered play, beyond sheer body building; education through dance must touch all areas of experience and cognition. He then set forth a division for the *science of dance* and elaborated on the three areas which he had previously discussed before the 1927 Dance Congress: choreosophy — the theory of ethics and aesthetics of the new dance and dance education; choreology — the theory of the laws of dance events manifest in the synthesis of spatial and temporal experience; and choreography — the theory of movement articulation and notation for the purpose of recording educational exercises, as well as works of the art of dance. His third division, the *art of dance*, is communicated either through pure movement – where spatial structures and rhythmic characteristics predominate, and which is applied in solo, chamber and group dance – or through movement in unity with the art of speech and sound – which consists predominantly of movement expression in mimetic gesture, plays, and opera. Related to the art of dance was a fourth division, *dance pedagogy*, concerned with the training of professional dancers. Common to all the areas was the compositional formation of the works.

The area of *dance for layman* had been of interest to Laban long before he had put together the "Problems of Dance" lecture-demonstration. In fact, he had been creating and writing with unlimited gusto about other aspects of dance not discussed in his paper for the 1927 Dance Congress, namely social forms of dance such as festivities and movement choirs. Starting from a broad premise that the inner desire for beauty can be found everywhere in life, and that the spiritual components of art are the foundation for a festive culture, Laban perceived dance content in a variety of manifestations, fighting not only for the social significance of dance but also creating its social forms.[58] Free exercises which heighten an awareness of the body-mind unity in movement and participation in performances of plays of ritualistic-symbolic content were some of the potential festive activities envisioned by Laban. He felt that the spiritual upswing created through a balance between work and festivity should concern all organizers of popular entertainment and all educators of the young.[59] Festive dances could take the form of a dance-poem with its content growing out of a particular occasion, as did the celebration of the 150th anniversary of the Mannheim National Theatre which Laban staged in 1929. A festive play could also grow out of a special event and environment, such as the 1929 Vienna pageant for the crafts and trades directed by Laban.[60]

Not unlike choral signing and speech, choral dancing for large groups of laymen had already been inaugurated by Laban in Münich and Ascona. He and his colleagues developed it systematically as a dance form with its own appropriate gymnastic exercises and compositional forms. In the process, choral dancing gained a more organized form and a new name – movement choirs – during the 1920's. The *Zentralschule Laban* (Central-School Laban), founded in Hamburg in 1923, even featured a department for movement choirs.

Laban conceived of movement choirs as a medium providing an experience of togetherness, as community through dance: "Thousands of people can now experience the benefit of the rhythm and flow of dance, not only as spectators but also as active players in the joy of moving."[61] However, he emphasized that besides the shared experience of the joyful movement, the crucial task of the movement choirs was to maintain a sense of humanity in a dignified form. He saw choral movement not as one of the many ways to achieve body-mind education but as the only possible way — for adults and children alike.[62] Laban also realized that lay participation in these movement choirs led to greater appreciation of theatre dance, so his promotion of the dance form enabled him to solve several pedagogical problems at "one blow."[63]

Laban's first choir-work composition was *Lichtwende* (Dawning Light) performed in Hamburg in 1923 by eighty lay-dancers who also played percussion instruments. The dance drama *Agamemnon's Tod* (Death of Agamemnon), after Noverre, followed in the same year.[64] Together with Knust, who became the leader of the Hamburg *Bewegungschöre Laban* (Laban Movement Choirs), Laban created *Dämmernde Rhythmen* (Twilight Rhythms) in 1924.[65] The *Titan*, composed for a mass movement choir, was presented at the first German Dancer's Congress in 1927; the music was composed and conducted by Rudolf Wagner-Regeny.[66] The *Titan* was intended to show the power of community which Laban saw dormant in humanity. A subsequent performance of the piece, reproduced from notation scores by Knust in the Hamburg Zirkus Busch, moved Laban to write that the occasion was memorable for him "because it was one of the first proofs that a full-length work for many participants can be transmitted through notation."[67]

The culmination of Laban's activities with festival productions was his *Festzug des Handwerkes und der Gewerbe* (Pageant for the Crafts and Trades) for Vienna created in June 1929. The pageant consisted of an enormous procession with 10,000 performers on moving platforms; participants included dancers, actors, and members of various craft guilds, such as blacksmiths, tailors, furriers, shoe-makers, tanners, and bakers. Drawing from various occupational rhythms and traditions, Laban created movement and dance sections as part of the dance fabric of the pageant. This experience of having to establish contact with thousands of strangers, to witness professional infights and class hatred, made Laban strongly determined to provide the participants with not only an easing of tensions but also with meaningful recreation.[68]

During the same summer, rehearsals were under way for a large group dance titled *Alltag und Fest* (Everyday Life and Festivity) celebrating the 150th anniversary of the Mannheim National Theatre. Martin Gleisner, who also assisted with preparations, wrote the text which provided the frame for this movement play symbolizing the theatre expectations of the new generation. Approximately 500 young people from all walks of life performed this colorful movement and speech symphony in an open-air stadium.[69] Activities around both the Vienna and Mannheim events marked the beginning of Laban's interest and involvement with movement in work and the problems of industrialization which he would later tackle in the 1940's.

Because dance scores, similar to sheet music, were used in teaching and rehearsing various sections of these community events, Laban's invention of dance notation became a crucial tool in the production of movement choirs.[70] In his 1926 *Choreographie: Erstes Heft* (Choreography: Part One), he presents a clear outline of the spatial order of the new choreography as well as the first rudimentary outlines of his notation. Although he originally created the system within the context of his theoretical framework, he carefully nurtured its independence to achieve its universal application. In a promotional brochure for his Choreographic Institute (founded in 1926), he states that notation allows one, by means of "simple symbols," to record ballet and expressive dance styles, solo and group dances, dance plays, social dance, sequences from various gymnastic systems, and movement in both sport and work. The beauty of the system lies in the fact that its use does not require an expert knowledge of movement or dance, nor an acquaintance with his theory of harmony.[71]

Laban worked diligently on the system from 1924 until its publication in 1928. Day after day, he would come into his office, announcing to his assistant, Gertrud Snell, that he had finally dreamt the ideal solution. Consequently, Snell would have to repeatedly rewrite everything into the new "dream notation."[72] His attention to the task demonstrated a severely focussed persistence, and he would constantly redesign and reject and then begin again. As Mary Wigman recalled, "no error, no disappointment, no failure could ever keep him from pursuing this work."[73]

From 1926 to 1928, Laban poured his energies into the perfection of the system. During the winter of 1927/28, he worked almost exclusively on it, pushing everything else into the background in an attempt to complete his vision once and for all. Inspite of illness, he would work without a break, inventing new symbols, probing new methods, discarding a great deal, attempting to determine small nuances of movement, and always thinking ahead to the simplification of that which he had hardly yet invented.[74] By 1928 he completed and published the system, named Kinetography[75] (or Labanotation as it is known in the United States) and witnessed its recognition as an appropriate system at the second German Dance Congress held in Essen in June.[76] The booklet, titled *Schrifttanz: Methodik, Orthographie, Erläuterungen,* (*Script Dancing: Methodics, Orthography, Explanations*), can be seen as part two of *Choreographie* in that it presents the final version of the notation and marks the birth of Laban's system.

Several of Laban's presentations of his system of notation eventually gave rise in 1928 to the foundation of the Deutsche Gesellschaft für Schrifttanz (German Society for Script-Dance), a society for the development of dance literature from scores of notated dances serving as a basis for choreological research. From 1928 to 1931, the society produced a quarterly magazine called *Schrifttanz* (Script-dance or Written-dance) published by the Universal Edition in Vienna. In addition to articles, essays, critiques, and announcements, each issue included notation score supplements with extracts from choreographic works by Laban and his collaborators. For instance, in the first activity report of the society, one can find five consecutive notices about Laban's activities and those of his schools: an announcement about the reconstruction of the *Titan* from scores, notated at the Institute, is followed by information regarding plans for introductory student courses as well as Laban's series of lecture-demonstrations on notation for teachers of gymnastics and sports at the Berlin University. The magazine then reports on a promotional lecture for dance notation held by Laban in conjunction with performances of his Chamber-Dance-Theatre at a Berlin hotel, a Laban lecture in Plauen on the historical significance of the art of dance highlighted by a demonstration of Laban movement notation, and a list of notation courses organized at the Institute under Laban's direction for critics, musicians, artists, dancers, and lay persons. The magazine *Schrifttanz* was therefore another means of recording, commenting on, and promoting Laban's activities.

As a result of the on-going development of Laban's work with dance notation, festivals, movement choirs, and theatre dance, his schools in Germany began to serve an increasingly more integral and complex role in the dissemination of his theories. Several of the schools, those founded from 1921 to 1926, assumed a dual emphasis in response to Laban's multi-faceted activities. On one hand, they provided a training ground for the members of his groups for the new theatre dance, the Dance-Theatre Laban, and the Chamber-Dance-Theatre Laban, all formed between 1922 and 1924. On the other hand, Laban schools were also centers for movement choirs. The prospectus for Hamburg's Movement Choirs Rudolf von Laban, for example, lists two departments: the school of dance with full-time and part-time classes for the professional training of dancers and leaders of movement choirs, and a department for movement choirs, as mentioned earlier in this discussion. While Laban taught the choreographic master classes at the school, Albrecht Knust was in charge of the department of movement choirs which offered a variety of movement choir works for children and adults including dance plays and festivals.

The most significant event in the history of Laban schools, however, was the 1926 founding in Würtzburg of the Choreographic Institute Laban, which contained both the Central-School Laban and the Dance-Theatre Laban. Laban's work in the art and science of the new dance was the major concern of the Institute, and here research in theory, notation, and pedagogy was discussed and shared by Laban and his student-collaborators. The Institute was transferred to Berlin in 1927, and in 1929 it was joined with the Dance Department of the Folkwangschule in Essen under the direction of Kurt Jooss.

From its inception, Laban endowed the Institute with a far-reaching scope:

> [It is] a place for research, and for collecting choreographic knowledge . . . A place for the handing on of this knowledge to the growing generations of dancers and choreographers through clear contemporary practice; a place for collecting and publishing modern theatrical dance works; a place for the production . . . of old and new works of the art of dance . . . It is dedicated to the memory of the great dancers of the PAST: dedicated to the rising dancers of the FUTURE: and is operated in the PRESENT as a master's laboratory of choreology and the art of dance.[77]

The aim of the Institute was to form a new dance aesthetic and theory of dance within a two-part framework of theory and practice. The focus of the theoretical division was the research of choreological laws (laws of the science of dance), the development of notation, and the recording of old and new dances in addition to the training of dance notators and researchers. The practical division provided education for dancers, choreographers, and teachers of movement and dance. Common subjects included elements of choreographic movement training, introduction to form and expression, and lectures on the history and aesthetics of dance. Special subjects for dancers included dance technique, choreutics and eukinetics (the practical study of spatial form and rhythmic-dynamics, i.e., dynamic expression in dance), repertory, and performance. For choreographers, the Institute provided classes in the general theory of movement, dance notation, and the choreographic theory of harmony. Laban directed the Institute, assisted by Suzanne Ivers, and several of his master pupils were in charge of various specialty areas: Herman Robst conducted movement training; Dussia Bereska led classes for the Dance-Theatre Laban and in eukinetics; Ruth Loeser was in charge of the theory and practice of choreutics; and Gertrud Snell taught all the theoretical subjects including notation.[78]

After the 1929 merger with the Dance Department of the Folkwangschule Essen, Laban's Choreographic Institute and Central-School appear to have de-emphasized research in favor of gaining access to subsidiary courses in the departments of music and theatre to train dancers, choreographers, and movement and dance teachers. The curriculum was divided into foundation classes, classes for dancers, courses for dance teachers, a dance theatre studio, and Laban diploma courses. The latter could be taken by those who had successfully completed the initial two-year training followed by three additional one-month courses and at least two years experience in performance and/or teaching.[79] By 1930, areas of study, such as dance technique, had been redefined as the mastery of the body based on precomposed studies of modern dance; choreutics and eukinetics also referred to the study of harmonious movement sequences and their spatial and expressive relationships. Faculty for the department, now called the Tanz-schule Jooss-Zentralschule Laban (The Dance School Jooss – Central-School Laban), included Jooss, Sigurd Leeder, Lisa Ullmann,[80] Gertrud Snell, and others.[81]

Due to the rise of Nazism, Jooss and his collaborators left Essen in 1934 and transferred the school to Dartington Hall, England. As a result of a 10-year collaboration between Jooss and the artist and dancer Sigurd Leeder, the school was named The Jooss-Leeder School of Dance. The aims of the new school remained similar to those of the Essen school, namely the training of dancers and dance teachers. Courses in improvisation, dance styles and operatic dancing were added to those of dance technique, notation, composition and production, musical education, and teaching methods.[82]

Besides major schools – either under Laban's direction or in close collaboration with him – many other Laban schools and movement choir centers were formed throughout central Europe during the period between the two world wars. As of 1927, there were at least 28 accredited Laban schools founded in Germany, Czechoslovakia, and Switzerland.[83] The schools strove to maintain professional standards, and in the process the association of Laban schools required member school leaders to participate in yearly courses for further training and to submit a comprehensive activity report.[84]

In the early twenties, Laban continued to work with his dancers in resort areas near Stuttgart and Lübeck, such as Cannstadt and Gleschendorf. The summer residency in Bad Mergentheim in South Germany in 1927 was also important because it was there that Laban devised the final form of the principles of his system of notation.[85] Besides the dance company work, the summer workshops became summer schools and a forum for the Laban Diploma examinations; workshops, such as the one at Burg Lauenstein in South Germany, featured courses in dance-play directing, the theory of harmony, and notation for dancers, teachers, and laymen.[86] In 1930, the Laban summer course was organized in Bayreuth with introductory courses in the theory of harmony, notation, eukinetics, and a course in rhythm taught by Fritz Cohen.[87] Among the last summer workshops held in the thirties was the one in Mandelieu near Cannes, France, taught by Laban, Robst, and Kurt Graff from the Berlin Opera.[88]

The success and proliferation of the Laban schools was based to a great extent on Laban's personality. His charisma, brimming from a deep well of energy, was contagious and a potent motivating force for his pupils. Laban's power as a teacher was evident as early as 1913 in Ascona. At that time, Mary Wigman was the student most affected by and sensitive to the dynamics of Laban's personality. Wigman felt that Laban was more of a moving spirit

than a teacher, more of a guide toward a path which students had to in-
ternalize and formulate on their own, more of a leader with drum in hand,
inventing and experimenting. During the time Wigman studied with Laban,
he presented instructions primarily through improvisation evolving into dance.
He also encouraged drawing and poetry writing, and generally set students
free artistically to find their own roots and potentials. Wigman considered
him a great stimulator who handed out little criticism in the initial stages
of explorations, leaving students to struggle on their own for a clear dance
image. His subsequent pungent comments, however, were sometimes perceived as criticism without compassion. Laban could also at times appear as
a magician, "the lord of a dream-like and yet ever-so-real kingdom," and then
easily change from "the gallant knight into the grinning faun,"[89] but Wigman
also knew that he could be an exacting task master. During their 1913-19
collaborations to test Laban's theoretical findings, "every movement had to
be done over and over again until it was controlled and could be analyzed,
transposed, and transformed into adequate symbols."[90] In the process,
Laban's search for objectivity and Wigman's urge for "super-self expression"
led to occasional clashes. On the other hand, though, Laban's private work
with several sick persons revealed to Wigman the natural healing powers
inherent in body movement if correctly analyzed and applied in the right
measure.[91]

In the twenties, Laban's teaching style emphasized two specific features:
an intensity which compelled the student to unfold his or her utmost
potential, and a versatility in elucidating his teaching material. According to
Knust, a student-collaborator of Laban's at this time, Laban was able to adapt
his teaching methods to individual students and particular situations. At any
given time, he might choose to allow his students to grow freely and quietly,
while at another he would emphatically draw them out. He was just as likely
to one day foster personal movement, the next day to ask for an adaptation
to a partner or a group, and the day after that to require a complete merging
with a large uniform movement choir. Knust described Laban as a teacher
whose technique could sometimes be as awesome as a sacred act or ritual,
healing and soothing, while at other times his instructions were those of a
merciless overseer driven toward the greatest possible technical achievements. Ultimately, Laban vacillated between stimulating the imagination and
training the movement memory. Knust believed that the aims of Laban's
techniques were as manifold as the techniques themselves, and that Laban's
capacity of observation could be directed both toward the potential intent
of a particular movement phrase and to the general intents and characteristics
of a student's personality.[92] Lisa Ullmann, another Laban student during
the twenties who in the forties became his chief collaborator, considered
Laban capable of helping students to listen inward, to become aware of their

own particular heartbeats and breathing patterns. For Ullmann, the content of the course work became profoundly significant in Laban's hands as he consistently established links between the laws of harmony and life in its contemporary and historical manifestations.[93]

As sources indicate, Laban was enthusiastically involved in all areas of dance simultaneously. This multifaceted perspective extended as well to professional dance organizations, and prior to the Second World War, Laban devoted some time to administrative duties. He served as a member of the organizing committee of the first German Dance Congress in Magdeburg, sharing responsibilities with Anna Pavlova, Mary Wigman, Dr. Niedecken-Gebhard, and Oskar Schlemmer from the Bauhaus.[94] At this occasion, he also presided over the newly formed *Deutscher Tänzerbund* (German Dancer's Confederation) and led sessions on important professional matters such as social security benefits and copyright laws. Problems of professional training and plans for a dance academy were also discussed, and Laban and Wigman issued a statement that "the foundation of a German Dance Academy is urgently necessary, and we shall promote together the realization of this idea."[95] Five years later, in 1932, he was a member of the jury for the International Dance Competition in Paris. Although he was the only representative of modern dance, the first prize was unanimously awarded to *The Green Table* by Kurt Jooss. This work, remaining in the repertory of several ballet companies throughout the world, is a living example of a Laban-based tradition in choreography.

Additional activities during this period included Laban's acceptance of the position of Director of Movement and Dance at the Prussian Theatres in Berlin. While with the Theatres from 1930 to 1933, he vigorously opposed the star system in favor of ensemble team work.[96] As ballet master of the Berlin State Opera, Laban was able to appoint Suzanne Ivers, his assistant from the Choreographic Institute, to notate his dance productions.[97] In the same year, Laban was also invited to stage the Bacchanalia for Wagner's opera *Tannhäuser* in Bayreuth (Wagner's son Siegfried directed the opera, and Arturo Toscanini conducted the performance.). Assisted by Kurt Jooss, Laban found "a new way of using the traditional media" by linking Wagner's version of the nordic fantasy with contemporary stage forms.[98]

As already noted throughout this discussion, Laban published a great deal of material during the German period. In addition to the 1928 publication of his system of Kinetography, his social and educational ideas as well as further theoretical considerations formed the content of two major works published in 1926: *Gymnastik und Tanz* (Gymnastics and Dance) and *Des Kindes Gymnastik und Tanz* (Gymnastics and Dance for the Child).[99] His *Ein Leben für den Tanz* (*A Life for Dance*), the last book which he wrote in German, was published in 1935. Far from the standard autobiography in form and content, *A Life for Dance* is more precisely Laban's attempt to recapitulate his past dreams and achievements before his exile from Germany via France to England. One particulary interesting memory which he includes is an extensive account of a four-month visit in 1926 to the United States where he was especially intrigued by the rituals and dances of the American Indians but less impressed by movement and dance productions in Hollywood.[100]

Ultimately, Laban's German period of gestation marked a watershed in the development of dance as an independent artistic medium. He bequeathed to generations of dancers – to artists such as Kurt Jooss, Dussia Bereska, Gertrud Loeser, Jens Keith, Käthe Wulff, Edgar Frank, and Julian Algo – an entirely new way of perceiving dance. Kurt Jooss, for example, considered Laban's work during this period to have broken the old, narrow forms, a revolutionary phenomenon which he compared to the creation of the "new tonality," or atonality, and the twelve-tone musical system of the twenties. In contrast to Isadora Duncan's highly subjective points of view and Fokin's expansions of the ballet tradition, Jooss believed Laban's innovations to be young, full-blooded manifestations of modern man after the crisis of Expressionism.[101] Dance writer Fritz Böhme saw Laban in a similar light, describing him as a moment in the historical development of European dance in which dance as an art form became conscious of its material, dance as a cultural factor became more aware of its social connections, and dance as a product of historical movement became more informed about its actual past. The "idea Laban," Böhme argued, is not a creation of a new dance style or battle against an old style, or a new pedagogy or a new exercise system. What it actually is cannot be achieved only through technical exercises or imitation; it must be spiritually grasped and embodied by individuals.[102]

But it was Mary Wigman who articulated most powerfully Laban's contribution to dance. "All of us who dance today are indebted to Laban's work in every moment of our own creativity more than we can clarify," she declared.[103] "By means of his ingenial gift, unremitting search, inexhaustible energy, he succeeded to summarize the laws of dance movement into intelligible concepts." He gave to dance a structural foundation analogous to music harmony: "the spatial theory of movement and with it a point of departure, a basis for each dance creation."[104] Describing some specific dance elements forming the foundation that Laban gave to dancers in the late twenties, she wrote that "he taught us the essence of tension, the harmonic connection of swing sequences, and the unity of body and space."[105] His gymnastic system, based on the functions of the joints, tension, the relaxation of muscles, and other principles of natural body movement "was born out of his head for a new style of dancing and a new type of dancer."[106] For Wigman, Laban's work ultimately liberated dance from its slavish dependency on music and moved Laban closer to his ideal — the creation of a huge festivity which would draw together the participants and the audience in a strong common experience.

As of 1937, however, Laban had not been able to achieve the apotheosis of his ideal. Confronted with the rise of Adolf Hitler's Nazism, Laban's activities were abruptly brought to an end. The critical incident resulting in the suppression of his work arose during the preparations for the 1936 Olympic Games in Berlin. Several accounts of the events, including Laban's own memories, though differing in detail, do provide complementary and perspicuous information. Write-ups and publications preceding the events show how Laban, together with many other outstanding artists, was lured into the framework of Nazi spectacles. "It is especially timely that Laban's ideas of ritual be accepted today through the lay dancers and the movement choirs . . . . One thousand lay dancers are meeting in Berlin . . . without him and without the preparatory world of his ideas they would not exist," wrote the newly appointed editor of *Der Tanz*, describing the preparations for the festival at the Dietrich-Eckhard open-air theatre in Berlin.[107] Organized in June 1936 by the Reichbund für Gemeinschaftstanz (Reich League for Community Dance), one month before the Olympic games, Laban's mass movement choir was to crown this event. The League in its inaugural booklet titled *Wir tanzen* (We Dance) presents Laban as "the great master of modern German Dance [who] created the form of the modern community-dancing, the so-called Gemeinschaftstanz," and it places his work in the context of Nazi ideology.[108] In fact, notation scores for Laban's "Vom Tauwind und der neuen Freude" ("From the Thowing Wind and the new Joy") and its four sections — combat, reflection, joy, and consecration — were sent out by Knust to movement choir leaders in thirty German towns. Rehearsals from June 13-20 brought all the parts together accompanied by symphonic and choral music composed by Hans Claus Langer and selected passages from Nietsche's *Zarathustra*. The final event was, however, censored. Laban himself commented on this turn of events in a 1954 letter to the members of the Art of Movement Guild:

> They [the festival participants] studied their parts and came together in a dress rehearsal before 20,000 guests in a large arena. Everybody, including the audience, was most enthusiastic, except some representatives of the then Nazi government. The performance never took place because it was prohibited and so were all my other activities.[109]

It appears that the realization of mutual incompatibility was also triggered by Laban's role in the International Dance Festival, another dance event preceding the opening of the games. The Festival had originally been planned as a competition, and Laban, who presided over the jury, decided against the awarding of prizes.[110] Lotte Auerbach, a Laban student from Germany, reports that Laban found it impossible to agree with Dr. Goebbels, German's

Minister of Propaganda, who ordered Laban to act as adjudicator and present the first prize to a German group.[111] Apparently in retaliation for Laban's defiance, the government banned the performance of Laban's piece for the opening of the Dietrich-Eckhard theatre. Horst Koegler, a dance critic and the author of *In the Shadow of the Swastika: Dance in Germany, 1927-1936*, also describes the crowning event of the opening of the newly built Olympic Stadium on August 1. The pageant called "Olympic Youth" joined many artists such as Werner Egk and Carl Orff (music), Hans Niedecken-Gerbhard (theatre production), Mary Wigman, Palucca, and Harald Kreutzberg (dance) in a collaboration. Laban was to direct some major scenes but was replaced by Dorothee Günther. Koegler maintains that "when Laban saw those ten thousand moving and dancing people he seems to have felt like Goethe's sorcerer's apprentice. What he had envisaged as a noble festivity of man . . . was perverted into a mass-manipulated spectacle of politically castrated people."[112]

Laban's work, in toto, was declared to be in opposition to the state. He was confined to the small village of Staffelberg, and his work was prohibited and censured throughout Germany. Fortunately, an invitation to the Congress of Aesthetics in Paris in 1937 allowed him to leave the country.

1938–1958 The English Period of Consolidations

In January 1938, Laban emigrated to England where his former collaborators offered him hospitality. Kurt Jooss and his wife, the dancer Aino Siimola, along with Sigurd Leeder and Lisa Ullmann, had already left the Folkwangschule in Essen in 1934 to establish the Jooss-Leeder School at Dartington Hall. Under the care of the Jooss' and Lisa Ullmann, Laban began to regain his health which had suffered severely after his work was forbidden by the Nazis — the destruction of his more than twenty years of activity in Germany had been a devastating blow to him.

Laban's English period, which started just before the eruption of World War II, continued until his death at the age of 79. While at Dartington Hall, Laban lectured and worked on the manuscript of *Choreutics*, a sequel to *Choreographie* and an elaboration on the applied theory of Space harmony; it was published posthumously in 1966. Due to the beginning of World War II and the subsequent evacuation of the defense area in the south of England, however, Laban and Ullmann moved in 1940 to various places such as London and Wales, finally settling in Manchester in 1942. Throughout that time, they established contacts and collaborations with training colleges for teachers and with the Ling Physical Education Association. Lecture-demonstrations, conferences, and courses were also organized and marked the beginnings of Modern Educational Dance as well as Educational Gymnastics in England.

In 1941, Laban began to collaborate with Frederic Charles Lawrence, a management consultant in industry. The war had restricted the filming of time and motion studies, and, as a result, the need to retrain women for jobs customarily held by men had reached a crisis situation. Lawrence invited Laban to record industrial processes and to assist with work study problems. The outcome of this collaboration was *Effort*, a book published jointly by Laban and Lawrence in 1947.

A year earlier, Lisa Ullmann had founded the Art of Movement Studio where Laban lectured and continued his research until his death. The formation of the Studio was primarily the result of Ullmann's activities and contacts with English Education Authorities. The Studio, which opened in Manchester, gained recognition in 1949 from the Ministry of Education, and authors such as Valerie Preston, Warren Lamb, and Marion North trained there. In 1953, the Studio moved to Addlestone in Surrey, and in 1954 it became incorporated in the Laban Art of Movement Centre, an educational trust.

In contrast to Laban centres in Germany, the focus of the Art of Movement Studio shifted from theatre to education. The prospectus of the Centre from the 1950's includes a description of five areas of activity: the art of movement in education, movement in work, movement in rehabilitation, the art of movement in recreation, and movement training for the stage. In addition, short courses in special aspects of movement research were provided by the movement research foundation. "The work of the studio," as Laban described it, "is based on the observation as well as on the practical experience gained in teaching adults and children: the students are gradually led to appreciate the dual need of practice and observation and to apply this approach in their work after they leave . . . Throughout their course, the students become increasingly aware of the world of values embedded in the harmony of movement and of how such awareness can be communicated to others."[113] Coupled with training courses leading to the Art of Movement Studio Certificate (two years) and the Art of Movement Studio Diploma (three years), several other courses were established during the 1950's and 1960's. Two types of one-year training courses for teachers in England and Wales were subsidized by the Department of Education and Science: a "special course" of advanced study for teachers, lecturers, and advisers who had taught for at least five years, and a "supplementary course" for any qualified teacher who wanted to specialize in movement education and dance. A two-year training program for future teachers — approved by the Department of Education and Science — was also offered and complemented by a one-year course for teacher training in the London colleges.

All courses covered practical work and theory. The aim of the study was the appreciation and practice of physical movement as a medium of expression for the individual, as a means of communication, and as a discipline for the development of the individual as a member of the human community. The primary focus throughout the training was the awakening and development of the creative faculty, the kinesthetic sense, and the capacity for participation in group actions. Areas covered in various courses included body training; Effort and the rhythm of exertion and recovery; shape of gesture and bodily carriage; harmony of movement, or the relationship of dynamics, stresses, and spatial patterns in bodily actions; movement observation; methods of recording: Kinetography Laban and Effort notation; group relationships; theory and practice of movement education; and subsidiary studies of music, drama, art, national and period dance, anatomy and physiology.[114]

In the late 1940's and 50's, the Centre also organized Laban summer schools and housed a collection of Laban's manuscripts in German, French, and English dating from the time of his emigration to England — the so-called "Laban Archives." In the mid-seventies, the Centre became associated with the University of London Goldsmith's College and moved to its campus. Under the name of the Laban Centre for Movement and Dance, it has since taken up new directions.

Additional Laban organizations founded after the Second World War included the Laban Art of Movement Guild which came into being in 1945 offering annual conferences and later featuring weekend courses for its members — primarily teachers and lecturers in dance and physical education. In the early 1950's, information about various regional dance groups was first disseminated by a newsletter which grew into *The Laban Art of Movement Guild Magazine*; in 1983, its name was changed to *Movement and Dance: Magazine of The Laban Guild*.

During the last two decades of his life, Laban's activities encompassed observations and analysis of work processes as well as lecturing at the Art of Movement Studio; he also collaborated with the Esmé Church Theatre School and Children's Theatre in Bradford. His publication efforts at this time included *Modern Educational Dance* (1948) and *The Mastery of Movement on the Stage* (1950), both reflecting his concerns with dance education and the performing arts. Laban continued teaching, lecturing, and developing his theories after the Art of Movement Studio (that is, he and Lisa Ullmann) moved to Addlestone in 1953. The last book he published was *Principles of Dance and Movement Notation* in 1954. He also collaborated with Ullmann on the revised edition of *The Mastery of Movement*, which was published posthumously in 1960. Laban died on July 1, 1958 in Weybridge, Surrey, England, undergoing a lung emboly.[115]

Coda

Laban was a man of great complexity. He made so many seminal contributions in so many diverse areas of dance that it is difficult to label him according to established categories, such as dancer, choreographer, teacher, inventor, researcher, creator, theoretician, or even pioneer, trailblazer, stimulator, and initiator. What is certain is that both he and his work inspired and caused controversy. It is also certain that the significance of his work and its impact on dance cannot be denied. He left to generations of movement and dance professionals an oeuvre with seemingly unlimited possibilities for interpretation and implementation. And in response to this wealth of material, dance critics, historians, dancers — throughout Laban's lifetime and up to the present day — have evaluated, reviewed, scrutinized, and, in general, attempted to put into their own words what Laban did and did not say.

Among the first dance books in which Laban is discussed is the second edition of Hans Brandenburg's *Der Moderne Tanz* (The Modern Dance) published in 1917. Having collaborated with Laban in München and Ascona, Brandenburg presents pertinent accounts of the issues of "free dance" and "dance, sound, word" which are particularly valuable since Laban did not write much on these subjects. Within his nine-page discussion, Brandenburg also attempts to delineate Laban's most fundamental movement concepts.[116]

A brief critical mention of Laban can also be found in Oskar Bie's *Der Tanz* (The Dance) from 1923. When referring to German schools, Bie maintains that Laban and Loheland[117] fostered body dance culture frequently imbued with literature and views of the world. Mary Wigman, who freed herself from these dogmatic circles, is seen by Bie as the most accomplished German dancer, the embodiment of the link between the ideal art of dance and the healthy body.[118]

The *Geschichte des Tanzes* (History of Dance) by John Schikowski and published in 1926 dedicates five pages to the "actual creator and founder of the modern art of dance Rudolf von Laban . . . who layed its theoretical and practical foundation and paved the way for its accomplishment."[119] Not unlike Brandenburg, Schikowski elaborates on the principles of "free dance"; however, his interpretation of Laban's movement concepts, while they cover the same ground, are presented with greater clarity. Schikowski draws from *Die Welt des Tänzers* and describes Laban the author as a person obsessed with the demon of dance and as a theoretician of ingenious partiality who reduced everything to the rhythmical movement of the body. He also furnishes information about the itinerary of Laban's activities and his choreographic works, and he evaluates Laban as dancer, choreographer, and teacher.[120]

Another extensive entry on Laban was composed by Werner Schuftan for his 1928 *Handbuch des Tanzes* (Handbook for Dance); the revised and enlarged French edition was published in 1938. Schuftan describes Laban as a fiery and restless spirit, constantly producing new ideas and projects. He maintains that, although unpredictable in responses, Laban's love for movement in all its living forms stood as a constant. He describes Laban as a man who relied on his trust in the natural development of things and did not project far ahead. Schuftan goes so far as to argue that regardless of one's acceptance of Laban's theories, the fact remains that without Laban there would be no new dance: furthermore, there would be no modern dance composers and percussionists. In the French edition, Schuftan is almost apologetic about the fact that he has to mention Laban's name in conjunction with every new reform – not only in dance theory and notation but also in architecture, specifically Laban's project for a theatre in the round.[121]

The most comprehensive account of Laban's theory is contained in Martin Gleisner's *Tanz für Alle* (Dance for Everybody), also published in 1928. A Laban student and collaborator, Gleisner dedicates a chapter to "Der neue Tanz und das Werk Rudolf von Laban" ("The new dance and Rudolf von Laban's work"). After discussing Laban's creation of the "absolute" dance, he expands on the way in which Laban developed his theory by drawing from dance tradition. Gleisner concludes by declaring that Laban built the foundation for the new dance form and dance pedagogy. He then follows this chapter with his own elaborations on Laban's ideas on dance for layman in movement choirs, on festivity and dance, and discusses the further development of movement choirs.[122]

Alfred Schlee, in his 1929 article "Wo steht Laban?" ("Where Does Laban Stand?") from *Der Tanz*, presents a substantial evaluation of Laban's achievements and temperament. Schlee comments that because one is never quite clear where Laban's development is leading, it is difficult to summarize the opus of his first fifty years in a conventional way.[123] Each new work which he created would show a new or different path from that which was expected. The new work would frequently appear abruptly jumpy, and only much later would one be able to grasp the consistency of the transformations – only to again be at a loss in front of the next creation. Laban's drive to push forward was so impulsive that he sometimes lost connection with a work before it was completed. He was unable to make up his mind and rely on a single success, preferring to kill off the triumph rather than acknowledge it. Schlee concludes that this rushing ahead with ideas before executing them is a flaw from which many a work suffers, a tendency which can be observed in other great musicians and painters, but he adds that Laban's case was more difficult because of the lack of tradition in dance.

The various phases Laban passed through in his development until 1929 co-existed side by side, and Schlee discerns these phases in Laban's earlier collaborators or students who were not able to follow his development. In some cases, the students would even surpass themselves under Laban's personal influence but would become stuck when his direct influence ceased. Or they would think that they were continuing Laban's work but were actually only covering a minute section of it. Many even gave evidence of what Laban had already overcome.

Schlee also explains that in Laban's theoretical work, he allowed caution to govern: only a little was published. But this "little" peaked in a master achievement — the new dance notation which would in itself be sufficiently significant to give the content to a whole life. Schlee noted, however, that the publication of the new and complex theory of movement harmony was still outstanding.[124]

Schlee believed that Laban stood at the same place where he had begun: on the peak of searching youth. Laban, who spoke in so many forms, remained true to himself. Schlee saw him as the great stimulator, the uncompromising champion, the enemy of all stagnation. Unchanged, Laban possessed the feeling for the necessity of the immediate and the future. He did not terminate his path, Schlee concluded — he promised a great deal which yet remains to be fulfilled.

In the same issue of *Der Tanz*, its editor, Joseph Lewitan, wrote a eulogy in praise of Laban's achievements, calling him a dance-tribune and a minister of the "inner and outer" affairs of dance.[125] Summarizing Laban's main points at the first German Dancer's Congress, Lewitan concludes that Laban's concept formulation (such as Eukinetics, Choreutics, types of dancers, chamber dance, kinetography and direction of movement choirs) is directed toward bringing discipline into dancers' opinions, fighting illussions of grandeur, and fitting parts into a whole — the art. If his work did not penetrate equally deeply into all directions, if in places there was not more given than a concept or direction — Laban's mission in dance reposed in expansions, he declared. Lewitan believed that a more intensive elaboration of the various paths Laban had shown would undoubtably follow. In Laban's creation of kinetography, however, Lewitan perceived the brilliance of success, and he summarizes Laban's principle message for his generation as follows:

Dancer submit yourself to the laws of your art. Transform your body into an instrument; above all transform your spirit and soul so that your body does not misuse the laws of art out of ignorance.

In the mid-thirties, due to the rise of Hitler and Laban's conflicts with the German authorities, written reviews of Laban began to disappear from German publications. While the anthology *Der künstlerische Tanz unserer Zeit* (The Art of Dance in Our Time), published in 1935, still included a portrait and a dance picture of Laban, the 1937 publication *Tänzer unserer Zeit* (Dancers of Our Time) omitted Laban's name entirely, even from the context of Mary Wigman's artistic biography.[126]

In America, however, several informative articles about Laban's work appeared in the late thirties. Helen Priest wrote two articles for *Dance Observer* (May and June 1937) about Laban's system of recording, and Irma Otte-Betz published three articles on all aspects of Laban's work in the same magazine (December 1938; January and March 1939). Defining Laban's work, Otte-Betz explains that it comprises three interdependent areas: (1) the dance "free in itself, yet ruled by certain laws of harmony – but not identical with them," (2) the physical education of the dancer, and (3) the theory of harmony which includes the spatial and rhythmic-dynamic aspects. She considers dance writing to be the fourth part of Laban's work and independent of the other three areas.[127]

Max Terpis, a former dancer and choreographer who also studied in Laban's school in Zürich and with Mary Wigman, pays tribute to the master in his book *Tanz und Tänzer*, published in 1946 in Zürich. He emphasizes the comprehensiveness of Laban's investigations: "There is not an area for this great all-embracing spirit where he did not search for dance relationships."[128] Terpis analyzes Laban's movement theory and concludes that it comprises all imaginable movements and movement possibilities of the human body. He notes that Laban observed with scientific interest the initiation and flow of each move which he analyzed and recorded, and that he saw the spirit, soul, and will as motoric powers. Terpis argues, however, that Laban did not systematically and clearly present in any of his books the results of his investigations, a phenomenon which he attributes to Laban's reluctance to fix his insights and knowledge as a "method" or "system." He adds that the extraordinary impulse which Laban gave to dance, his deep insights and completely new points of view, live mainly in the oral tradition and have already been assimilated by the dance practices of today.[129]

It is interesting to note that among the above-mentioned articles and book entries, very little mention and evaluation is made of Laban as a dancer and choreographer. Several accounts do exist, however, one of the earliest being Mary Wigman's reflections on Laban's activities as a performer and composer from 1913 to 1919. In *The Mary Wigman Book*, she vividly exemplifies his talent for improvisation and characteristation in her description of the scene of an Austrian regiment parading through the streets of Vienna with Laban handling props, sound, and gesture transformations. Laban's inclination to create fascinating events through improvisation and his lack of motivation to fix them in an artistic form is also mentioned. "Relentlessly in the constant flow of time, his inexhaustible imagination gives birth to every new form," she explains. "Perhaps he is not so much fulfilling as he is fructifying, inspiring."[130] Wigman concludes that Laban always needed and actually found people who would take up his ideas and put them to practical use.[131]

Herta Feist, referring to Laban's choreographic work in the 1920's and 1930's, reports that it caused both enthusiasm and upheaval. She remarks that either the spiritual content of his work or its style of performance would always be noticed, provoke vivid discussion, and frequently trigger strong opposition. The reaction, she suggests, resulted from the fact that Laban appeared to create a mirror of people's lives.[132] Her impressions are corroborated by Egon Vietta who writes that Laban achieved a breakthrough with his first experiments in producing dramas of antiquity in new ways: his introduction of the movement-choir revolutionized choreography after World War I.[133]

Albrecht Knust maintained that Laban's motivation for all of his subsequent activities as reformer, inventor, and educator sprang from his early disappointment in the audiences' lack of response to his early work, a reaction which Laban thought was due to a general lack of sensitivity to movement.[134] While Kurt Jooss saw Laban as a dancer first in all manifestations of his person, Hans Brandenburg believed that Laban's interest in dance concerned from its beginnings choreography, the seeking after of the syntax and grammar of the artistic language.[135] John Schikowski is critical of Laban as a performing dancer and of his actual choreographic structures, although he considers him a creator of fruitful dance ideas. He argues that the motifs which Laban profusely churned out within a single dance scene would suffice for the creation of an entire dance drama and that in his compositions the mimetic elements not only contribute but actually create the basis of the representations. Schikowski finds that even in Laban's larger compositions he was more of an ingenious stimulator than realizer. It was Mary Wigman, he contends, who brought the choreographic structure, initiated by her teacher, to its completion: Her "absolute dance" differed from Laban's "free dance" particularly in its structural unity of style; the boundary she created between dance and mime was also clearly delinated. Schikowski concludes, however, that such criticism does not diminish Laban's invaluable achievements in dance theory and pioneering practice.[136]

A somewhat different view of Laban's and Wigman's choreography can be found in a 1930 article by Fritz Böhme about representation and experience in dance. He writes that Laban's "Gaukelei" belongs to the genre of dramatic theatre dance. Its content is based on representation and mediates individual conflicts and actions in very general terms, such as the dramatic resolution of the problem of tyranny. Its form brings a confluence of rhythmic and gestural elements, and weaves the dancerly-mimetic elements with the rhythm of choral gesture; one can thus define it as a rhythmically heightened space mime. In contrast, he classifies Wigman's "Swinging Landscapes" as a lyric-epic dance suite which invites the emotional participation of extra-theatrical dimensions.[137]

In a 1935 article surveying the state of the art in German dance culture, Fritz Braur states that a new dance style was in the making and that its forerunners were the Laban-Wigman dance. A more conscious tightening of the link between the exemplary style of classical ballet with an equally valid style of the new dance is proposed. It appears that in this context, Laban was seen as a critical contributor to the making of the new German dance.[138]

The evaluation, interpretation, and criticism of Laban's ideas and creations illustrate that while there are differing appraisals of his performing and choreographing activities, the conclusions in regard to his theoretical framework were unanimously laudatory and support the opinion that he significantly changed the face of dance as we know it. He himself commented toward the end of his life that he achieved two or three "things" which he perceived earlier than anyone else:

1) I have reminded people of the existence of the world of movement and of its importance as it had been felt in ancient times in its great unity embracing all activities of man – from work to recreation – from art to therapeutic affairs – from education to science.

2) I have stated my belief that every age or period of history has to find its own expression, and not so much guided by single individuals – artists, teachers – than by their own conscience.

3) I have tried to collect some fundamental facts of movement as seen in nature – and also as found in tradition. Not, of course, the tradition of particular methods of training or taste, but the tradition of movement conscience which could help to reawaken and to strengthen our own.[139]

But Laban, no matter how revolutionary or global his theories may have sounded or still sound, was very much a product of his time. His work coincided chronologically and in part geographically with a variety of significant events which have shaped the spirit of the twentieth century Western world. Two world wars, preceded and followed by radical social changes, were the background for a multitude of movements in the arts, education, and behavioral science. And to better appreciate Laban's contributions and impact, one must finally come to see him as part of that world, as an actor in the milieu of Central Europe at the beginning of the twentieth century.

The performing arts tradition had already been revolutionized at the turn of the century through many ideas and realizations, such as Wagner's concept of the Gesamtkunstwerk, Ibsen's and Strindberg's dramaturgy, Appia's and Craig's theatre design, and Stanislavsky's directing. These were followed by Reinhardt's innovations, the Brecht-Weill theatre of social critique, Piscator's political theatres, and Kaiser's expressionist plays. Different points of view ranging from realism to symbolism and expressionism occurred in rapid succession, either clashing or existing simultaneously. Another important genre of performance, derived from various movements in the arts and architecture, was frequently mediated through dance, i.e. manifesto performances of the Italian Futurists, the Dadaist in Zürich and Berlin, the Surrealists in Paris, and the Bauhaus performances in Weimar and Dessau all of which were geared toward the new unity of art and technology. The German film industry also provided some valuable contributions in the late 1920's and early 1930's.

Although a clear distinction was made by Brandenburg between Laban's early dance-sound-word explorations and Wagner's idea of the Gesamtkunstwerk,[140] Laban acknowledged in the 1930's his debt to the master's movement drive. He was particularly impressed not only with Wagner as "a renewer and prophet of the arts of poetry and music" but also with his way of thinking in terms of movement, a mode of consciousness which made him "a decisive influence on the art of movement."[141] It appears, however, that Brandenburg's and Laban's statements are not contradictory because the latter led to a distinction between applied dance (such as in opera or festivals) and independent dance (such as in theatre dance works and Reigenwerk).[142] These particular Laban statements did, in fact, give rise to a recent examination by Jennifer K. Holbrook (1983) of Laban's and Wagner's positions.[143] Holbrook makes the valid observation that both artists were innovators extending in their own ways the boundaries of the permissible from inner forms of life. However, her analogy between Wagner's emphasis on the psychology and emotion of his characters and Laban's emphasis on inner attitudes is questionable.

By the same token, one can continue to draw many analogies between Laban and other modernist artists, an example being the comparison of Laban's dance-play *Die Nacht* (1927), a song of hatred against the "machine" man, to German expressionist playwright Georg Kaiser's *Gas I* and *II* (1918-1920), which present a nightmare picture of industrialization. On the other hand, analogies can also be made in terms of the use of the classical Greek chorus and protagonists; Laban frequently applied both concepts in works such as *Faust Part II* (1922) and *Agamemnon's Tod* (1923) as did another German Expressionist, Ernst Toller, in his *Man and Masses* (1919). (It is interesting to find that both Laban and Toller used a steep ramp of steps in their productions to enhance the dramatic action.) Further, the expressionist style of acting, particularly fostered by the director Leopold Jessner, with an overemphasis on gesture and facial expression, may be seen as echoed in performing styles of Laban and his dancers, as well as Wigman and Jooss.

Laban's preoccupation with defining and articulating the new sense of space may be seen as synchronous with similar concerns by the members of the Bauhaus — a community of artists and designers concerned with the fusion of art and technology. While Laban presented his spatial theories with drawings of the human figure within geometrical forms and photographs of dancers practicing his spatial scales in the icosahedron (1926), Oskar Schlemmer demonstrated on the Bauhaus stage in 1927 his stereometry of space, with dancers within a spatial linear web. In addition, Laban's project for a theatre in the round preceded the plans for a total theatre designed by the founder of Bauhaus – architect Walter Gropius. Laban's sketches and a cardboard model on which he worked between 1917-1919 coincided with Max Reinhardt's adaptation of the Zirkus Schumann for his *Grosses Schauspielhaus* in Berlin (1919). Gropius' project in the late 1920's for an adaptable theatre in the round, designed for the director Ervin Piscator, was never actually built. Laban's absence of comments with regard to Schlemmer, Gropius and the Bauhaus is a rather interesting omission since both Laban and Schlemmer were members of the organizing committee of the first German Dancer's Congress (1927). Furthermore, the Bauhaus stage workshops and festivities attracted not only the members of the Institute in Weimar and, later, in Dessau, but also local and neighboring community members. Schlemmer, however, refers only briefly to Laban in his letters and diaries.[144] His remarks about the 1932 dance competition in Paris are especially ambiguous. Although he felt that Jooss deserved the first award for *The Green Table*, he expressed great surprise at the quality of the production. He also suggested that the piece contained some common aspects with his *Gesture Dance* and that the basic steps of the warriers might be identified with his own *Space Dance*.[145]   A recent study by Elizabeth Mauldon discusses similarities and differences between Laban and Schlemmer.[146] In an attempt to examine the two artists against their cultural milieu, Mauldon emphasizes Laban's contacts with the Dada movement. While the common trends in the endeavors of both artists-theoreticians, such as the synthesis of organic and geometrical works, are well presented, Laban's distinction from Schlemmer's preoccupations with abstraction and formal principles is not clearly drawn from the perspective of Laban's activities in the 1920's and 1930's.

At the time of Laban's pre-World War I activities in Munich, the city was also the gathering place for expressionist painters. *Der Blaue Reiter* was formed there as a sequel to the earlier *Die Brücke* in Dresden. While Nolde and Kirchner, artists from the *Brücke*, expressed sociological, sexual, and religious subject matters, Marck and Kandinsky, from the *Blaue Reiter*, took an interest in rhythmical, almost dance-like, non-subject oriented compositions. Emil Nolde, in particular, was acquainted with Laban's performances since he urged Mary Wigman to work with the man who moved as she did and danced without music. The chamber dance theatre's performance of Laban's *Narrenspiegel* (1926), evincing some expressionistic overtones in its dances of life and death, inspired Ernst Kirchner to create a painting on the theme (1927). Although one can find that some of Laban's approaches to the subject matter and its choreographic and painterly treatment correspond with some expressionistic points of view, Laban himself argued against such manifestations. At the occasion of the pageant of the crafts and guilds in Vienna (1929), he let it be known that he strongly disliked several of the contributions offered by the painters and sculptors: "Expressionism was fashionable and there was no distortion and destruction in representation that was not used to replace a lost and healthy sense of form."[147] It is interesting to note that Alfred Schlee evaluates a dance encyclopedia entry from the late twenties which describes Laban as the main exponent of expressionism as a misjudgment. But it is a fact that Laban's work was already significant during the expressionist period and that at the same time Laban worked with Mary Wigman who became the proponent of the new German expressive dance — Ausdruckstanz. Here a clarification by the German dance critic Hedwig Müller is pertinent when arguing that "the word Ausdruckstanz is not a label for a single dance ideology or theory with a clearly defined technique and teaching method. Rather it is a collective term for some highly contradictory dance concepts, ranging from the truly expressionist to those making politically relevant statements. Expressionism itself occupied only a limited area in this broad spectrum of dance activities between the First World War and the coming to power of the National Socialists."[148] Laban, however, distanced himself from expressionism as a German national art form.[149] Ironically, though, his work met a fate similar to that of his expressionist contemporaries, men such as Emil Nolde who was forbidden to paint by the Nazis and saw his paintings confiscated as well.

As noted earlier, Laban had actual contacts with Dada manifestations in Zürich (1915-1919), but despite these, he left no comments concerning them. Hans Richter, however, does refer to Laban's revolutionary contributions to choreography, although the active participants and contributors to the Dada events were Laban's students and not Laban himself.[150] In a recent study Naima Prevots re-examines the issue of the Laban-Dada interactions and suggests that they must have proved a strong mutually reinforcing agent.[151] In fact her reference to a review on Sophie Taeuber, the young artist who studied dance with Laban "not as a chance game but as a creative game with variable rules that unfolds in time and space as a unique, moving, ephemeral sculpture,"[152] brings to mind not only Laban's movement scales, but also his manuscript titled "Raumspielpuzzle" (Spacegamepuzzle).[153] Although written after Laban's emigration from Germany, its intention of awakening the spatio-temporal awareness in a game-like fashion could be likened to some of the Dada emphases on chance.

We have noted that Jooss compared Laban's dance works with the breakthrough of "atonality." Arnold Schoenberg, the first composer to abandon tonality in 1908, was active in Vienna and subsequently was awarded a professorship at the Prussian Academy of Arts in Berlin. He had to relinquish this position in 1933 with the rise of the Nazi regime and then emigrated to the United States. Laban also held a position at the Prussian Theatre in Berlin at the same time (1930-33) but had to emigrate three years later. It is Laban's student Suzanne Perrottet who selected Schoenberg's pieces for her dance contributions at the last Dada event in 1919.[154] It also appears that Laban's musical collaborator, Rudolf Wagner-Regeny, composed by using the principle of atonality.[155]

In the field of dance Isadora Duncan's discovery of the solar plexus as the central spring for all motor power and Ruth St. Denis' striving toward spiritual values of dance were introduced to German audiences before World War I. Subsequent appearances of Serge Diaghileff's Ballet Russe exposed new concepts of the total theatre. Movement education at the turn of the century was reformed through multiple approaches, such as Bess Mensendieck's, Loheland's and Rudolf Bode's gymnastic systems, Emile Jacque-Dalcroze music education through movement and dance, and Rudolf Steiner's translations of poetry into dance. Apart from individual differences in the above gymnastic, rhythmic and eurhythmic systems, one can trace several shared beliefs and values which may have sprung from the need to counteract the reduced body-mind involvement in factory work. Laban's concern about gymnastics and dance, as well as movement choir activities show concurrent efforts in these directions. With regard to direct contacts with the key reformers in movement and dance one can only speculate. Laban might very well have seen Duncan in Paris or visited her school in Grunewald near Berlin (1904-1908), although no documentation exists to verify the conjecture. He might also have seen performances of the Ballet Russe in Switzerland or Germany, and Laban wrote that "Diaghileff and Fokine, and other prominent members of the Russian Ballet and other ballet groups, have encouraged me in the attempt to create a library of written dance."[156] Laban's creation of the "free dance" was also, in part, a response to Jacques-Dalcroze's ideas with which he must have been familiar via Wigman and Perrottet.

Further discussion of Laban's implicit and explicit debt to many of the above schools of thought, as well as the synchrony of his work with that of Carl Gustav Jung, will be developed in Chapter V. At this point, however, Laban is succinctly described by Alan Salter who concluded that "though Laban can, at various stages, be linked with various labels − Dada, Expressionism, Abstract or Metaphysical Art, even the Bauhaus − he remains his own man through an unremitting concern for the appropriateness of art and action to the human condition."[157]

Biographical Signposts

1879 December 15 born in Poszony (also referred to as Pressburg) now Bratislava in Czechoslovakia.

1890's impressions of military parades, folk dance tradition and rituals

1895/6 apprenticeship with a painter; experiments with *tableaux vivants*

1899-1900 attempt to train at the Military Academy at Wiener-Neustadt

1900-1907 studies in Munich and Paris

1908-1910 activities in Munich leading up to the forming of his first dance company and school and *Tanz-Ton-Wort* explorations

1911-1914 workshops, schools and performances in Munich and the "School for the Arts" at Monte Verità in Ascona on the Lago Maggiore; major students-collaborators Mary Wigman, Suzanne Perrottet

1914 outbreak of World War I

1914-1918 teaching, choreographing and performing in Zürich; new student-collaborator Dussia Bereska. First outline of "Die Welt des Tänzers."

1916 first performance of the full length work *Der Spielmann*, a dance fairy-tale, with choreography and music by Laban (Zürich)

1920 founding of the *Tanzbühne Laban* in Stuttgart (Direction Laban and Bereska); most outstanding students Kurt Jooss and Albrecht Knust. Publication of *Die Welt des Tänzers*

1921 ballet master at the Mannheim National Theatre; creates *Die Geblendeten, Epische Tanzfolge* and the Bacchanalia for Wagner's *Tannhäuser*

1923 establishes *Zentralschule Laban* and its department for movement choirs in Hamburg; founds the *Kammertanzbühne Laban* led by Bereska; new dancers and subsequent collaborators include Ruth Loeser, Sylvia Bodmer, Aino Siimola, Martin Gleisner and Gertrud Snell. Choreographic works for his dance theatre created between 1923 and 1927 include *Der Schwingende Tempel, Faust Part II, Prometheus, Die Gaukelei, Casanova, Don Juan, Die Nacht, Narrenspiegel*, and *Ritterballet*. Works for movement choirs include *Lichtwende, Agamemnon's Tod, Dämmernde Rhythmen*, and *Titan*.

1926 Publication of *Choreographie, Gymnastik und Tanz, Des Kindes Gymnastik und Tanz*; founds the *Choreographisches Institut Laban* in Würtzburg; makes a four-month visit to America

1927 Participates in the first German Dancer's Congress in Magdeburg: "The Dance as a Work of Art" lecture; member of the organizing committee; instrumental in forming the Deutscher Tänzerbund; Choreographic Institute Laban transferred to Berlin including *Zentralschule Laban* and *Tanzbühne Laban*.

1928 Publication of his system of Kinetography; formation of the society for Schrifttanz and the quarterly magazine *Schrifttanz*; Kinetography acknowledged as appropriate notation for theatre dance at the second German Dancer's Congress in Essen.

1929 Production of the *Festzug des Handwerkes und der Gewerbe* for the city of Vienna; production of *Alltag und Fest* for the 150th anniversary of the Mannheim National Theatre.

The *Choreographisches Institute Laban* joins the Dance Department of the Folkwangschule in Essen (directed by Kurt Jooss).

1930 Laban serves as Director of movement and dance at the Prussian Theatre in Berlin including the ballet master position at the Berlin State Opera until 1933. Invited to stage the Bacchanalia for Wagner's *Tannhäuser*

1932 Member of jury for the International Dance Competition in Paris: Jooss' *The Green Table* awarded the first prize

1933 Hitler appointed chancellor; Nazis establish blacklist of authors and works; Laban's activities are gradually restrained

1935 Publication of *Ein Leben für den Tanz*

1936 Final conflict with the Nazis surrounding preparations for the Olympic Games in Berlin. Laban confined to Staffelberg and all his activities and publications banned

1937 Attends the Congress of Aesthetics in Paris as a means to escape from Germany

1938 Emigrates to England and recuperates at Dartington Hall

1939 Writes the manuscript of *Choreutics*, (published posthumously in 1966), and lectures in the Joss-Leeder School

1940 Outbreak of World War II; due to the evacuation of South England Laban and Lisa Ullmann move to London and subsequently to Wales

1941 Begins collaboration with industrial consultant F.C. Lawrence

1942 Moves to Manchester

1946 Ullmann founds the Art of Movement Studio. Laban lectures at the Studio and collaborates with Esmé Church Theatre School and Children's Theatre in Bradford

1947 Publication of *Effort* co-authored with F.C. Lawrence as a result of observation and analysis of work processes

1948 Publication of *Modern Educational Dance* – concerned with education in British schools

1950 Publication of *The Mastery of Movement on the Stage* – concerned with the performing arts

1953 Moves to Addlestone, Surrey, near London

1954 Establishment of the Laban Art of Movement Centre as an educational trust incorporating the Art of Movement Studio

1956 Publication of *Principles of Dance and Movement Notation* – summarizing approaches to notation

1958 Died on July 1 in Weybridge, Surrey.

Notes to Part One

1. Rudolf Laban, *A Life for Dance*, "Translator's Preface," unnumbered.
2. Cf. Hans Brandenburg, 1917, 1929a, 1929b; Mary Wigman 1927, 1929, 1975; John Schikowski, 1926; Werner Schuftan, 1928, 1929, 1938; Rudolf Lämmel [1928] ; Martin Gleisner, 1928, [See annotated bibliography for titles and paginations].
3. Cf. *Schrifttanz*, Heft IV, 1929, pp. 73-75; *Dance Notation Record*, Vol. IX, Fall and Winter, 1958 , pp. 3-4.
4. *Die Tat, Monatschrift für die Zukunft Deutscher Kultur*, Leipzig, 1920-1927; *Die Neue Schaubühne*, Dresden, 5./6. Heft, September 1921, 3 Jahrgang; *Schrifttanz, Organ der Deutscher Gesellschaft für Schifttanz, Vierteljahresschrift*, Vienna, 1928-1931; *Der Tanz, Monatschrift für Tanzkultur*, Berlin, 1927-1936; *Singhor und Tanz, Fachblatt für Theatersingchor und Kunsttanz*, Mannheim, 1929-1930; *Die Schönheit*: Viertes und Fünftes Rhythmusheft XXII, Rudolf von Laban I, II, 1926; *Der Scheinwerfer, Tanz Sonderheft* Essen, 11/12 Heft, 1928; Liesel Freund, *Monographien der Ausbildungen für Tanz und Tänzerische Körperbildung*, Band I, Berlin, 1929; *Wir Tanzen*, Berlin 1936; Horst Koegler, *In the Shadow of the Swastika: Dance in Germany, 1929-1936. Dance Perspectives*, 57, Spring 1974. Hans Richter, *Dada: Art and Anti-Art*, London: Thames and Hudson, 1965.
5. Op. cit. p. 36.
6. Cf. Rudolf Lämmel, *Der Moderne Tanz*, Berlin-Schöneberg: Peter J. Oestergard Verlag, [1928] , pp. 13, 82.
7. Op. cit., p. 56; Laban's accounts of the impact the dancing Derwishes made on him can also be found in Mary Wigman, "Rudolf von Laban's Lehre vom Tanz," *Die Neue Schaubühne*, September 1921, p. 101, and in Lämmel, *Der Moderne Tanz*, p. 82.
8. Cf. *A Life for Dance*, pp. 10-13, 167.
9. Cf. *A Life for Dance* note on p. 47; caricature drawing is also mentioned in Lämmel's *Der Moderne Tanz*, p. 82.
10. Cf. Martin Gleisner "Conversations between Laban and Myself in 1926," *The Laban Art of Movement Guild Magazine*, No. 65, 1980, pp. 16-19, and Wigman (Op. Cit. in Note 7 above), p. 101.
11. Op. cit., Fig. 9, p. 186.
12. Cf. Käthe Wulff, "Aus Alten Briefen" ("From Old Letters"), *Schrifttanz*, Heft IV., 1929, p. 72; See Werner Schuftan, *Manuel de Danse* (Paris: Éditions Edgar Malfère, 1938), p. 175.
13. Cf. *A Life for Dance*, p. 164.
14. According to a personal communication from Laban to Ana Maletic in the 1930's, such festivals would frequently be financed by rich persons with an aspiration to perform. Laban would at times reach for shrewd solutions, such as suggesting: "I need a spectacular nymph behind this tree. . . ."

15. While Hans Brandenburg in *Der Moderne Tanz* (München: Georg Müller, 1917, pp. 36-41) and John Schikowski in *Geschichte des Tanzes* (Berlin: Büchergilde Gutenberg 1926, p. 138) use the term "free dance," Martin Gleisner in *Tanz für Alle* (Leipzig: Hesse and Becker Verlag, 1929, p. 92) refers to it as "Absolute dance."

16. This interpretation is drawn from Brandenburg (1917: pp. 40-41) and contradicts a recent premise developed by Jennifer Holbrook in "Laban, Wagner and the Gesamtkunstwerk," *Movement and Dance: Magazine of The Laban Guild*, no. 70, 1983, pp. 17-24.

17. Monte Verità (the mountain of truth) was a new life style colony initiated by Henry Oedekoven at the beginning of the century; it was also referred to as "Kuranstalt" (cf. *The Mary Wigman Book* pp. 40-41) and it became a meeting place for the intelligentsia, such as D.H. Lawrence, James Joyce, Martin Buber, Paul Cassierer, Carl Gustav Jung, Hans Arp, Hugo Ball and Oskar Schlemmer. Oedekoven also founded there a "Schule für Kunst," (School of the Arts) as an "individualistic cooperative." With Laban's arrival in 1913, the school became based on his new educational principles. (Cf. the prospectus of the school from 1913)

18. *Suzanne Perrottet* joined Laban in Ascona after studying with Jacques-Dalcroze. A performer and musician, she also taught in Laban's schools and workshops at Monte Verità and in Zürich between 1914-17. Perrottet was also actively involved with the Dada movement and participated in their events in Zürich (1916-19) with her own pieces set to Schönberg and Satie. (Cf. Richter, 1965: 69-70, 77-79). From 1919 Perrottet also co-directed a Laban school in Zürich.
    Mary Wigman (1886-1973) is a well known figure of the German *Ausdruckstanz* (expressive dance, which should not be identified with expressionist dance). A recent documentary film "Mary Wigman: When the Fire Dances Between Two Poles" (produced by Allegra Fuller-Snyder and Annette Maconald) includes several of her works, such as the "Witch Dance," and sequences of her teaching and discussing dance.
    Käthe Wulff began working with Laban in 1914 and in 1917 collaborated on a dance-building project. With Perrottet, she co-directed the Laban School in Zürich from 1919. Wulff was also among the "Laban Ladies" particularly active in the Dada performances. Together with Sophie Taeuber – another Laban student and abstract painter who married artist Jean Arp – she produced *Die Kaufleute* ("The Merchants") which they wrote down in Laban's notation. Wulff also performed the piece *Noir Kakadu* and recited poems by Huelsenbeck and Kandinsky. (Cf. Richter ibid.) In the twenties, Wulff headed a Laban school in Basel and also performed some interesting creations at the second German Dancer's Congress in Essen in 1928. (Cf. Fritz Böhme, "Laban's Offsprings," *Schrifttanz*, Heft VI, 1929, p. 68)
    Dussia Bereska joined Laban in 1916 and became his collaborator in

several areas of his activities. He refers to her in his autobiographical book as the brave and inspired colleague who had the idea of founding the chamber-dance-group and who helped with the organization and training of the group. "A wealth of delightful short dance-works were produced with her both participating and directing" (*A Life for Dance*, p. 106). Bereska directed the group and organized tours. Laban also acknowledged her contribution to the elaborations of principles of Kinetography. From 1929 to 1938, Bereska directed a Laban school in Paris and also prepared students for the Laban diploma. One of those students was Ana Maletic who subsequently founded a Laban-based school in Yugoslavia.

Maja Lederer was trained in music and drama. She sang in some of Laban's early productions and taught speech courses in Laban's work-shops and schools in Munich and Ascona. Lederer was also Laban's second wife and they had five children.

19. Mary Wigman, "Rudolf von Laban Zum Geburtstag," *Schrifttanz*, Heft IV, 1929, p. 65.
20. Mary Wigman, "Rudolf von Laban's Lehre Vom Tanz," *Die Neue Schaubühne*, September 1921, p. 105.
21. Ibid., Source in note 19 above.
22. Hans Brandenburg cited in the prospectus of the school.
23. Rudolf Laban, "Letter to Guild Members," *The Art of Movement Guild Magazine*, No. 15, 1954, p. 6.
24. *Reigen* has a double meaning: it can refer to a round dance in the folk-dance tradition, and it can also mean a work consisting of several parts.
25. Cf. Rudolf Lämmel, *Der Moderne Tanz*, [1928], p. 82.
26. Cf. Richter, 1964, pp. 31, 43, 45, 69-70, 77-80.
27. Cf. *A Life for Dance*, pp. 91-92.
28. Cf. Ibid., pp. 14-30; 68-74.
29. Cf. Mary Wigman, "Rudolf Von Laban's Lehre Vom Tanz, "*Die Neue Schaubühne*, Sep. 1921, pp. 102-103, and Rudolf Laban, *A Life for Dance*, pp. 14-30.
30. Mary Wigman Ibid.
31. Mary Wigman Ibid., p. 103.
32. Kurt Jooss (1901-1979) is widely known for his choreographic work (Cf. also Urs Leicht editor, *Jooss: Dokumentation von Anna und Herman Markard*, Köln: Ballett-Bühnen-Verlag, 1985). He started his choreographic apprenticeship with Laban in Mannheim, Stuttgart and Hamburg and in 1924 became a "movement regisseur at the theatre in Münster. As co-founder of the Folkwangschule in Essen — a pro-gressive school combining speech, music, and dance education, Jooss became the director of its dance department in 1928. Laban ac-knowledged Jooss' contribution to the principles of Kinetography. His famous ballet *Der Grüne Tisch* (*The Green Table*) grew out of

Jooss' endeavour to build a modern dance ensemble based on Laban's concepts. In his later works for the "Ballet Jooss" and in his Jooss-Leeder school at Dartington Hall in England, Jooss associated Laban's principles with a ballet technique base.

Jens Keith later became ballet master in Essen and a solo dancer at the Berlin State Opera. In his choreographic interpretations of Milhaud's *Salat*, "he aimed for a lively expressive theatre dance, and created a clear and inventive composition" (Böhme, 1929: 67). *Edgar Frank* also became a soloist at the Berlin State Opera.

Herta Feist founded her own school in Berlin in the late 1920's. After first producing Laban's works, she subsequently created her own pieces, drawing from psychological experiences. *Berufung* (Evocation) was her large choric mask-play, a dramatization of the idea of healing light (cf. Böhme, 1929: 67).

Albrecht Knust's contribution to the development of Laban's notation is well-known, particularly through his publications (see annotated bibliography). After a period of apprenticeship, Knust was placed in charge of the *Zentralschule Laban* in Hamburg and the section for the *Hamburger Bewegungschöre Laban* (the Hamburg movement choirs Laban). In 1930, together with Azra von Laban (Laban's daughter), he established the *Hamburger Tanzschreibestube* (Hamburg Dance Notation Bureau). As a result of his involvement staging Laban's and his own compositions for movement choirs, Knust developed writing rules and symbols for the notation of group movements. In 1935 he decided to dedicate all his activities to notation and founded the *Berliner Tanzschreibestube* (The Berlin Dance Notation Bureau). Among other students and collaborators, two persons who later promoted Laban-based work in America and worked with Knust in the 1935-36 period were: Irmgard Dombois – Bartenieff, the founder of the Laban Institute of Movement Studies in New York, and Helen Priest-Rogers, one of the founders of the Dance Notation Bureau in New York. From 1937 until the end of World War II, Kinetography, along with all Laban work, was banned and Knust continued to work secretly. He outlined the handbook and notated the first full-length ballet scores (*The Devil in the Village*) by Yugoslav-born choreographers Pino and Pia Mlakar. From 1951 until his death in 1978, Knust was in charge of Kineto-graphy at the Folkwangschule in Essen.

33. Cf. *Schrifttanz*, Hetf IV, 1929, p. 74, and *A Life for Dance*, p. 95.
34. *Sylvia Bodmer* was at that time noted for her expressive performances in Laban's *Gaukelei* and Jooss' *Tragödie* (cf. Böhme, 1929, p. 67). In the 1930's she codirected with Lotte Müller a Laban school in Frankfurt and later emigrated to England, forming the Manchester Dance Circle in 1940. See bibliography for publications.
    Ruth Loeser became Laban's partner in several dance recitals, and taught space harmony at the Choreographic Institute. She later became

ballet mistress in Düsseldorf. (Cf. Böhme, 1929, p. 68, and *A Life for Dance*, p. 99, note [3]).

Julian Algo was later appointed ballet master in Duisburg and subsequently in Scandinavia (Cf. ibid).

Lotte Wedekind became the director of one of the Laban schools in Berlin; she trained Lisa Ullmann, amongst others.

Aino Siimola, Estonian born dancer, became Jooss' wife and rehearsal assistant.

Herman Robst later taught at the Choreographic Institute Laban and at Laban's summer workshops.

Martin Gleisner, former actor, became one of the most active collaborators in developing and organizing Laban's movement choir idea. He founded and directed choir centers in Thüringen, Jena, and Berlin. Integrating movement-speech and singing in his own creations he also developed Laban's dance-word-sound idea. In the 1930's, he emigrated to various countries in Europe and subsequently came to America where he earned a living as a social worker and a teacher. Gleisner returned to Germany just before his death in 1980. See annotated bibliography for publications.

Gertrud Snell became Laban's assistant by focussing her energies on issues of dance notation and Laban's dance theory. In 1929 she compiled notes and drawings on Laban's spatial scales and other configurations which became the basis for part two of *Choreutics* (Laban's 1939 manuscript which was published posthumously in 1966). Snell taught at the Choreographic Institute and in the 1930's worked at the Paris Laban school. See annotated bibliography for publications.

35. Cf. *A Life for Dance*, p. 100; also see Gleisner's *Tanz für Alle* on p. 166 for photograph.

36. Cf. *A Life for Dance*, pp. 160-161 including extensive notes (15) and (16) about the background of both productions.

37. Cf. Ibid., pp. 96-98.

38. Cf. Ibid., p. 176.

39. Cf. Ibid., pp. 176, 182-183.

40. Cf. Ibid., pp. 43, 180-181.

41. First performed by the *Kammertanzbühne Laban* in Berlin, 1926; cf. ibid. pp. 3-13, and *Schrifttanz*, Heft IV, 1929, p. 75. It is interesting to find that the German Expressionist painter Ernst Kirchner made a painting titled *Dance for Laban's Narrenspiegel* in 1927 (Cf. Donald E. Gordon, *Ernst Ludwig Kirschner*, Cambridge, Mass: Harvard Univ. Press, 1968, p. 379).

42. Cf. *A Life for Dance*, pp. 180-182, and *Schriftanz*, Heft IV, 1929. p. 75.

43. Cf. *A Life for Dance*, p. 182.

44. Rudolf von Laban, "Das Tänzerische Kunstwerk," *Die Tat*, November 1927, p. 590.

45. *A Life for Dance*, p. 177.
46. Cf. Ibid., pp. 175-180.
47. *Die Tat*, November 1927, pp. 588-591.
48. "Nicht Stehen Bleiben!" ("Not to Remain Standing"), *Singhor und Tanz:*, Festnummer Laban, Heft 24, December 1929, p. 307.
49. Fritz Klingenbeck "Kleiner Rückblick" ("Brief Retrospective"), *Singhor und Tanz*, December 1929, p. 306.
50. Cf. Hans Brandenburg, "Laban als Stilreformer" ("Laban as Reformer of Style"), *Singhor und Tanz*, December 1929, pp. 297-298.
51. Cf. Kurt Jooss, "Rudolf von Laban und das Ballet" ("Rudolf von Laban and the Ballet"), *Singhor und Tanz*, December 1929, pp. 296-297.
52. Cf. Ibid.
53. Cf. Source in note (48) above.
54. Cf. Source in note (49) above.
    Singhor und Tanz, Dec. 1929, p. 306.
55. Käthe Wulff, "Aus Alten Briefen" ("From Old Letters"), *Schrifttanz*, Heft IV, 1929, p. 72.
56. *The Mary Wigman Book*, p. 32.
57. Cf. *Schrifttanz*, Heft I, 1929, p. 19 for chart.
58. Cf. Martin Gleisner, "Laban als Wegbahner des Tanzes für die Allgemeinheit" ("Laban as Initiator of the Dance for All"), *Singhor und Tanz*, December 1929, p. 301.
59. Cf. Rudolf von Laban, "Kultische Bildung im Feste" ("Cultic Education through Festivity"), *Die Tat*, Heft 3, 1920, pp. 161-168.
60. Cf. *A Life for Dance*, pp. 140-154, 174.
61. Ibid. p. 184.
62. Cf. Rudolf von Laban, "Vom Sinn der Bewegungschöre" ("About the Purpose of Movement Choirs"), *Schrifttanz*, Heft II, 1930, pp. 156-157.
63. Cf. Albrecht Knust, "Laban als Erzieher" ("Laban as Educator"), *Singhor und Tanz*, December 1929, pp. 304-305.
64. Cf. *Schrifttanz*, Heft IV, 1929, p. 74, and Martin Gleisner *Tanz für Alle* (Leipzig: Hesse & Becker Verlag, 1928), p. 174 for photograph.
65. Cf. *Schrifttanz*, Heft IV, 1929, p. 74, and Gleisner, 1928, p. 162 for photograph.
66. Cf. *A Life for Dance*, pp. 136-137, and Gleisner, 1928, p. 167 for photograph.
67. *A Life for Dance*, p. 180.
68. Laban's detailed description of the event can be found on pp. 142-151 of *A Life for Dance*. Cf. also Fritz Klingenbeck, "Der Tanzende Festzug," *Schrifttanz*, Heft 2, 1929, pp. 27-28.
69. The event is described in detail in an article "Rudolf von Laban: 'Alltag und Fest'" signed Dr. B. He refers to the sections "External polarities," "Dance of life," "Hymn to work," and "Festive march." Cf. Schrifttanz, Heft III, pp. 56-58. Cf. also *A Life for Dance*, pp. 152-154.

70. Cf. *A Life for Dance*, p. 152.
71. Cf. Prospectus of the Choreographic Institute Laban in Berlin announcing the course taught by Laban from May 21 — June 15, 1928.
72. Cf. Gertrud Snell-Friedburg, "The Beginnings of Kinetography Laban," *The Laban Art of Movement Guild Magazine*, No. 63, 1979, pp. 11-13.
73. *The Mary Wigman Book*, p. 38.
74. Cf. Fritz Klingenbeck, "Kleiner Rückblick," *Singhor und Tanz*, Dec. 1929, p. 306.
75. Cf. Chapter III.
76. Cf. *Schrifttanz*, Heft IV, 1929, p. 75, and *A Life for Dance* pp. 185 note (19).
77. Flyer of the Choreographic Institute, Würtzburg, 1926.
78. Information compiled from prospectus of the Institute from 1927/28, and from "Das Choreographische Institut Laban," Laban's article in *Monographien der Ausbildungschulen für Tanz und Tänzerische Körperbildung*, Band I. (Berlin: Leo Alterthum Verlag, 1929), pp. 11-14.
79. Cf. Ibid.
80. *Lisa Ullmann* (1907-1985) trained with two Laban teachers in Berlin — Herta Feist and Lotte Wedekind, and between 1927 and 1929 gained the Laban Diploma under the master's guidance. From 1930-1940 she co-taught with Jooss and Leeder, first at the Folkwangschule in Essen and from 1934 at the Jooss-Leeder School at Dartington Hall in England. Besides teaching choreutics, eukinetics and dance notation, Ullmann also inaugurated movement choirs and courses for teachers and children. Her close collaboration with Laban started in 1938 when he found refuge at Dartington Hall. Since that time she continued to be the mediator and promotor of his ideas and theories. On her initiative, the first Art of Movement Studio was founded in Manchester in 1945 which subsequently incorporated the Laban Centre; she directed both until 1975. Ullmann was also the instigator of the Laban Art of Movement Guild and of the International Council of Kinetography Laban, and also chaired both organizations for a term. Ullmann's particular contribution to the field lies also in translating, editing, and annotating Laban's writings. Until her death, she also curated the Laban Archives, a collection of Laban's manuscripts, drawings and space models.
81. Cf. Prospectus of the "Fachschule für Musik, Tanz und Drama" (Professional School for Music, Dance, and Drama) of the Folkwangschule in Essen (Laban Archives).
82. Cf. Prospectus of the "Jooss-Leeder School of Dance," Dartington Hall, Totnes, Devon, England.
83. Cf. Prospectus in Laban Archives.
84. Cf. Information from a typed manuscript compiled by Martin Gleisner.
85. Cf. Chapter III.

46   *Intents – Actions – Reverberations*

86. Cf. *Schrifttanz*, Heft I, 1929, p. 62; also Lisa Ullmann, "My Apprentice-ship with Laban," *The Laban Art of Movement Magazine*, No. 63, 1979, p. 22.
87. Cf. *Schrifttanz*, Heft II, 1930, p. 42, and Heft III, 1930 p. 57.
88. The course was held in 1932 and Laban was present for approximately five weeks; personal communication from Ana Maletic and Lisa Ullmann.
89. Cf. *The Mary Wigman Book*, p. 33.
90. Ibid., p. 39.
91. Cf. Ibid., pp. 38-40.
92. Cf. Albrecht Knust, "Laban als Erzieher" ("Laban as Educator") *Singhor und Tanz*, December 1929, pp. 304-305.
93. Cf. Lisa Ullmann, "My Apprenticeship with Laban," *The Art of Move-ment Guild Magazine*, No. 63, 1979, pp. 21-30.
94. Schlemmer, an artist conducting stage workshops at the Bauhaus – a progressive teaching institution for the arts, was particularly interested in experiments with moving figures; he created several productions such as "The Triadic Ballet." In *The Letters and Diaries of Oskar Schlemmer* (edited by Tut Schlemmer) one can find a reference to the dance con-gress in a post-card to his wife: "Laban is a good man (the only one of the committee besides me to come). Still the committee will remain in existence for further undertakings, congresses and such" (p. 206).
95. Cf. *Schrifttanz*, Heft I, 1929, p. 17, and Heft IV, 1929, p. 75, and *A Life for Dance*, pp. 43, 171, 185 for Ullmann's notes.
96. Cf. *A Life for Dance*, pp. 165-166.
97. Cf. *Schrifttanz*, Heft II, 1920, p. 42; several scores, such as those for dances from Borodin's *Prince Igor* and Johann Strauss' *Eine Nacht in Venedig* ("Night in Venice") and for dances from Gounod's *Margarete*, are available today. Cf. *Labanotation Scores: An International Biblio-graphy*, Mary Jane Warner and Frederick E. Warner editors, an ICKL publication, 1984.
98. Cf. *A Life for Dance*, p. 174.
99. Both books were published by Gerhardt Stalling Verlag in Oldenburg.
100. Cf. Op. cit., pp. 114-137.
101. Cf. Kurt Jooss, "Rudolf von Laban und das Ballett," *Singhor und Tanz*, Dec. 1929, pp. 296-297.
102. Cf. Fritz Böhme, "Laban's Tänzerischer Nachwuchs" ("Laban's Dance Offsprings"), *Schrifttanz*, Heft IV, 1929, pp. 66-68.
103. Mary Wigman, "Rudolf von Laban," *Singhor und Tanz*, December 1929, p. 295.
104. Mary Wigman, "Rudolf von Labans Lehre vom Tanz," *Die Neue Schaubuhne*, September 1921, p. 100.
105. Source in note (103), Ibid.
106. *The Mary Wigman Book*, p. 32.
107. Cited in Horst Koegler, *In the Shadow of the Swastika: Dance in*

Germany, 1927-1936, Dance Perspectives, 57, Spring 1974, p. 46.

108. *Wir Tanzen* (Berlin: Reichsbund für Gemeinschaftstanz, 1936) p. 34.
109. Rudolf Laban, "A Letter to Guild Members," *The Laban Art of Movement Guild Magazine*, No. 15, 1954, p. 8.
110. Cf. Source in note (107), pp. 45-47.
111. Cf. Lotte Auerbach, "My Memories of Mr. Laban," *The Laban Art of Movement Guild Magazine*, No. 51, 1973, p. 11.
112. Op. cit., p. 47.
113. Rudolf Laban, "The Work of the Art of Movement Studio," *Journal of Physical Education*, Vol. 46, No. 137, 1954, p. 26.
114. Cf. "General Information" the Laban Art of Movement Centre.
115. Personal communication from Lisa Ullmann.
116. Cf. Hans Brandenburg, *Der Moderne Tanz* (München: Georg Müller, 1917), pp. 35-44.
117. Not much has been published on the Loheland school; while Gleisner, 1928, pp. 44-45 refers to feeling as its point of departure, Koegler, 1974, p. 4 describes its admittance of females only and its aim to return to a spontaneous expression of feelings.
118. Cf. Oskar Bie, *Der Tanz* (Berlin: Julius Bard Verlag, 1923), p. 382.
119. John Schikowski, *Geschichte des Tanzes* (Berlin: Büchergilde Gutenberg, 1926), p. 137.
120. Cf. Ibid., pp. 137-147.
121. Cf. Werner Schuftan, *Handbuch des Tanzes* (Mannheim: Deutscher Chorsänger Verband und Tänzerbund, 1928), pp. 24-27, and 84-87; also *Manuel de Danse* (Paris: Éditions Edgar Malfère, 1938) pp. 46-53, and 169-176.
122. Cf. Martin Gleisner, *Tanz für Alle* (Leipzig: Hesse & Becker Verlag, 1929), pp. 79-112; 112-167.
123. Cf. Alfred Schlee, "Wo steht Laban?" *Der Tanz*, Heft 14, 1929, pp. 4-5.
124. This comment may be only partially justified as by 1929 Laban had already published four books in which he discusses, among other things, his theory of harmony of movement.
125. Cf. Joseph Lewitan, "Laban der Tanz-Tribun," *Der Tanz*, Heft. 14, 1929, pp. 6-7.
126. Cf. Herman und Marianne Aubel, *Der künstlerische Tanz unserer Zeit* (Leipzig: Karl Robert Langewiesche Verlag, 1935), pp. 74-75, and *Tänzer unserer Zeit* (München: Piper and Co. Verlag, 1937).
127. Irma Otte-Betz, "The Work of Rudolf von Laban," *Dance Observer*, December 1938, p. 147.
128. Max Terpis, *Tanz und Tänzer* (Zürich: Atlantis Verlag 1946) p. 93.
129. Cf. Ibid., pp. 93-97.
130. Cf. *The Mary Wigman Book*, p. 84.
131. Cf. Ibid., p. 34.
132. Cf. Herta Feist, "Laban unser Wegbereiter" ("Laban our Pioneer"), lecture given in Hannover, November 6, 1954 (2 pp.).

133. Cf. *A Life for Dance*, p. 172, note (11).
134. Cf. Source in note (92) above, p. 304.
135. Cf. Sources in notes (51), p. 296, and (50), p. 298.
136. Cf. Source in note (119), pp. 140-141.
137. Cf. Fritz Böhme, "Vorstellung und Erlebniss in Tanz: 'Gaukelei,' 'Drosselbart," 'Schwingende Landschaft'" ("Representation and Experience in Dance: 'Jugglery,' 'Thrashbird,' 'Swinging Landscape.'"), *Schrifttanz*, Heft II, 1929, pp. 37-39.
138. Cf. Fritz Braur, "Einblick in die Deutsche Tanzkultur" ("Insight into the German Dance Culture"), *Der Tanz*, Heft 14, 1929, p. 5.
139. Rudolf Laban unpublished manuscript from 1957 (Laban Archives).
140. Cf. Hans Brandenburg *Der Moderne Tanz*, pp. 40-41.
141. Cf. *A Life for Dance*, p. 175.
142. Cf. Ibid., pp. 174-175.
143. Cf. Jennifer K. Holbrook, "Laban, Wagner and the Gesamtkunstwerk," *Movement and Dance: Magazine of the Laban Guild*, No. 70, 1983, pp. 17-24.
144. Cf. *Letters and Diaries Oskar Schlemmer*, ed. Tut Schlemmer, Transl. by Winston Krisham (Middletown, Conn: Wesleyan University Press, 1972), p. 206.
145. Cf. Ibid., p. 298.
146. Cf. Elizabeth Mauldon, "Oskar Schlemmer – Rudolf Laban: Similarities and Differences," *The Laban Art of Movement Guild Magazine*, No. 54, 1975, pp. 7-17.
147. *A Life for Dance*, pp. 146-147.
148. Hedwig Müller, "Jooss and Expressionism," *Jooss: Dokumentation von Anna und Hermann Markard*, (Köln: Ballet-Bühnen-Verlag, 1985) p. 13.
149. Cf. A. Schlee, "Wo steht Laban?" *Der Tanz*, Heft 14, 1929, p. 5.
150. Cf. Hans Richter, *Dada: Art and Anti-Art*, p. 70 and 77-79 mentions Suzanne Perrottet, Käthe Wulff, and Sophie Taeuber.
151. Cf. Naima Prevots, "Zürich Dada and Dance: Formative Fermant," *Dance Research Journal*, 17/1 (Spring/Summer 1985), pp. 3-8.
152. Ludmilla Vachtova, [review] *Neue Züricher Zeitung* (vol 24, no. 29/30, Zürich, January 1977), p. 57.
153. This manuscript from the Laban Archives is referred to in Chapter IV.
154. Cf. Richter, 1965, p. 78.
155. Cf. Rudolf Wagner-Regeny, "Neue Grundzüge der Musikalischen Theorie als Ergebnis der Schrifttanzforschung," ("New Foundation of Music Theory resulting from the Scriptdance Research") *Schrifttanz*, Heft I, 1928, pp. 13-15.
156. *Principles of Dance and Movement Notation*, p. 8.
157. Alan Salter, "An Art of Movement," *Laban Centenary Symposium Report*, 1979, p. 13.

PART TWO:

THE EMERGENCE OF CONCEPTS, THEORIES AND CLASSIFICATIONS

Introduction

The main thrust of this section is the investigation of the beginnings of Laban's concept formulation and the gradual forming of his movement classification. Several important areas to which Laban referred only briefly in his English texts or which were completely omitted, are elucidated through the study of his first German writings. It is believed that such a perspective may provide a better insight, and a more comprehensive understanding of Laban's theoretical framework.

In his first book *Die Welt des Tänzers* (published in 1920), Laban presented his artistic creed: "My aim is not to establish norms and dogmas but to awaken dance insights."[1] Six years later in his *Choreographie* he wrote: "Basically one has to start with the description of movement, and occasionally mention single space forms, form transformations, and their laws. Our aim is thus *the mastery of movement through its explanation*."[2] Here Laban attempts to give a dynamic rather than a static description of dance elements, and outlines the first design of his notation which is to serve dance practice and study. Also published in 1926 were *Gymnastik und Tanz* and *Des Kindes Gymnastik und Tanz* in which Laban delineates the function and purpose of dance versus gymnastics. *Choreutics*, Laban's first book written in English in 1939 (published posthumously in 1966, and republished in 1974 in the U.S.A. as *The Language of Movement: A Guidebook to Choreutics*), aims at a multilateral description of movement, integrating the experiential perspective of the mover, the bodily perspective, with emotional and mental movements, as well as with its objective observations.

The common thread in the above texts is Laban's confrontation with the absence of a contemporary dance terminology, description, and theory. This he expresses clearly in the introduction to *Die Welt des Tänzers*: "When I undertook as the first one among dancers of today to speak of a world for which language lacks words, I was fully aware of the difficulty of this undertaking. Only a firm conviction that one has to conquer for dance the field of written and spoken expression, to open it up . . . to widest circles, brought me to tackle this difficult task."[3] Thus it appears that the intent of Laban's initial writing was, on one hand, to restore the validity of the dance experience itself, and on the other, to develop a descriptive vocabulary for the phenomenon of movement for the purpose of mastering its *techne*.

The search for theoretical principles is more apparent in his English texts of the 40's and 50's. The book *Effort*, written in 1947 with the industrial consultant F.C. Lawrence, proposes to study movement rhythms in order to compile a systematic survey of the forms that motivation and movement can take in human action through designing training methods for achieving greater efficiency, enjoyment, and satisfaction in work. The outcome of this investigation, to which Laban refers as "industrial movement research," was new conceptions of the movement components of space, weight, time and flow. These are then applied in *Modern Educational Dance*, published in the following year, 1948. The purpose of the book is to provide an understanding of movement principles through the integration of intellectual knowledge with creative activity. Laban's *The Mastery of Movement on the Stage* (1950), aims to promote the freedom and spontaneity of movement for the actor and dancer by helping them to think in movement terms and offering them guidance in the knowledge and application of common principles of the motivation and function of movement. Laban's last book, *Principles of Dance and Movement Notation* (1956), is a restatement of the foundation of Kinetography or Labanotation, after 26 years of its existence, based on the unchanging conviction of the necessity to think in terms of movement and its structural analysis.

For the purpose of this study a comparative analysis of ideas, concepts, classification, and terminology in both German and English texts has been carried out. In addition a selection from early writings by Laban's students-collaborators in Germany were examined and other significant aspects of the oral tradition of the Laban-based teaching were recollected and scrutinized. The presentation of key concepts is the result of this author's interpretation of the primary source readings and of her exposure to the European legacy of Laban's teaching.

A discussion of Laban's fundamental views of movement as a dynamic process on a continuum between polarities, and that of the unity of all movement components will preface the exposition of Laban's major systems of movement classification. The continuum between movement and stillness is manifest in several phenomena, such as the change from asymmetry to symmetry, from disequilibrium to equilibrium, and from mobility to stability. The principles of *stability* and *mobility* (which Laban refers to in his German writings as "Stabilität" und "Labilität"), run throughout the various levels of considerations of movement and dance. Mobility or lability, the overcoming of inertia, promotes movement, and stability facilitates stillness. Not unlike sound and silence in music, movement and stillness are certainly among the most fundamental aspects of dance. Laban writes in his first book: "Dance challenges the overcoming of inertia . . . [it] brings about liberation . . . in that man has crossed the threshold at which inertia is overcome by the desire for freedom and lightness."[4] While stability has a tendency toward temporary rest and quietude or equilibrium, mobility/lability drives toward the temporary loss of equilibrium or to disequilibrium. Laban discusses the tendency for equilibrium in movement as a manifestation of harmony:

> Relationships of parts, the whole rhythm of life, all its harmony show a unified striving for equilibrium . . . All movement is an alteration of the state of equilibrium, its aim being equilibrium again. [It is] a mutual adjustment of tensile states, a changing play which leads to stillness which is again only a gathering of strength for the movement. One can state that all stillness is gathered movement, and all movement is collected stillness.[5]

Referring to dance Laban writes that "dance is movement, thus its tendency is labile. The harmony of movement is, however, linked with a tendency for stability. The simplest form of harmony is symmetry, balance."[6] Within the symmetry and asymmetry of movement, Laban sees another link between stability, equilibrium, and lability, loss of equilibrium:

> The asymmetrical always arises from the symmetrical through a one-sided emphasis. . . . The return to equilibrium, the symmetry, as well as the temporal persisting in asymmetry, are phenomena of movement and stillness – the great symmetry of all tension. The stabile and labile balance is finally that which differentiates these phenomena.[7]

Thus there is an affinity between symmetry – equilibrium – stability, and asymmetry – disequilibrium – lability.

In his first English text, *Choreutics*, Laban associates stability with knotted movement shapes which have a power of binding; lability is now referred to as mobility and is coupled with the loosening or the untying, untwisting movement shapes.[8] Here stability and mobility are linked with the aspect of the shape and the quality of flow of movement. The text also provides a clear description of both movement phenomena in terms of promoting movement or stillness. Stability has the tendency to facilitate temporary quietude, which is equilirbium, but does not need to be identified with stillness. Mobility, on the other hand, through its tendency for vivid, flowing movement, leads to a temporary loss of equilibrium.[9]

One can see from the above how stability and mobility/lability have been associated with other fundamental aspects of movement and dance, such as motion and stillness, equilibrium, symmetry, shape of movement and its flow. Laban's further correlation of stability and lability with spatial directions will be discussed below. An overview of the interdependence of this concept with other aspects of Laban's classifications can be gained from Table 1. This overview also shows that references to the principles of stability and lability can mostly be found in Laban's German books. The concern with these phenomena has, however, persisted vividly in the oral tradition of Laban-based teaching, as well as in some writings by Laban's collaborators.[10]

In Laban's first writings all the components of movement and dance are considered in close association with one another. Discussing the interrelationship and unity of space-direction, time-duration, and force-energy, he argues that the division of a gesture into space, time, and force is only an apparent one. Fundamentally one cannot imagine any of these three concepts without the other two.[11] Another explicit statement can be found in Laban's comments on movement classification: "As all systematization of a single gesture, its splitting into time, force, space, and flow parts is only arbitrary, one could say an illusory one."[12] He points to the difficulty of thinking of force, time, and space without considering bodily situations and movement forms, as well as the degree of fluidity. These views are corroborated in Laban's first English text, *Choreutics*, where he discusses the correlation of the spatial unfolding of movement and its dynamics which — due to the amazing number of possibilities — must be considered from two distinct angles. In reality Laban sees them as entirely inseparable from each other, such as a light upward gesture of the arm and a strong downward movement of the whole body.[13]

One can recognize the nucleus of the principles of Laban's notation and of his space and Effort concepts in the 1926 outline of the "Elements of Form Theory."[14] As the most important components in movement observation he lists:

- Bodily participation from the point of view of laterality and symmetry;
- Spatial-directional participation determined by the angle of deflection from the vertical;
- The shape of the moving body in space with regard to the three-dimensional distribution of the body mass in relation to verticality, sideways, backwards, and forwards (or its plasticity). It can be predominantly stable, promoting equilibrium, or labile, promoting movement, such as fall, thrust, swing.
- Constituent parts of form seen as a temporal sequence with a beginning, a middle, and end.

The movement form is characterized by:

a) Kinetic content (degree of lability) referring to flux or flow
b) Dynamic content (degree of tension) referring to force
c) Rhythmic content (degree of velocity, speed) referring to time
d) Metric content (degree of extension) referring to space.[15]

The above can be seen as Laban's first explicit attempt to classify movement. Its significance is twofold: it restates his unified concept of movement, and it provides insight into Laban's process in formulating his key concepts.

The synthesis of movement components is also evident from the principles of Laban's notation formulated in 1928. Here one movement symbol, when placed in the notational staff, signifies which part of the body is moving, its spatial placement, and temporal unfolding; aspects of dynamics are either drawn from the context of the description or indicated by additional signs.

For the sake of examining the full complexity of Laban's movement classification we will consider particular key concepts and principles in the following text, remaining aware of their constant simultaneity. The theory of space will be examined first. The rationale for it may be found in Laban's view that movement concerns primarily the body in space. In the 1920's he formulated this view in several complementary ways. He maintained, for instance, that every movement impulse prompts the body to abandon equilibrium and to deviate from the vertical into one or several of the innumerable oblique directions. These directions can be identified in relation to the current notion of the three dimensions (the vertical, and the forward-backward, and side-to-side horizontals). The perpetual striving for equilibrium also guides the mover to select one direction as a position of repose, thus creating a rhythmical juncture in a movement sequence.[16] While the identification of the spatial direction is here coupled with the striving for equilibrium, the following passage states more explicitly the primacy of spatial direction:

> Undoubtedly the most important and significant element of bodily movement affects our experience through the direction of its departure from the vertical. This is true not only for the observer but also for the moving person. Man feels in movement a certain lability. This state is similar to the swing, the flight and the fall. The body is momentarily released from the experience of weight. This is the case in particular oblique directions, and particular bodily carriages. In addition, these bodily carriages arise in a well-ordered fashion, and we arrive thus at a new sequence of exercises . . . which are nearest to equilibrium exercises, although a new element takes place, the element of the fluency of movement . . . [with the] contrast of bound and fluent. For most bound movements we can obviously take a firm, rigid position, in which the whole equilibrium is divided over and around the center of weight. For most free/fluent movement [we can take] the jump which leads away from the floor in an oblique direction.[17]

Beside references to links between spatial directions and the lability-stability continuum, the above passage also indicates movement qualities which are associated with it. The bound and free elements of fluency announce the two polarities of the motion factor of the Flow of the 1940's.[18] The examination of the qualities or of the dynamics of movement and dance will follow the exposition of the theory of space. The last chapters in this section will examine the development of the principles of Laban's notation as an objective analysis of movement, and his views of composition as a synthesis of all the above aspects.

Notes to Introduction

1. Op. cit., p. 9.
2. Op. cit., p. 2.
3. Op. cit., p. 7.
4. *Die Welt des Tänzers*, p. 16.
5. Ibid., p. 233.
6. *Choreographie*, p. 15.
7. *Die Welt des Tänzers*, p. 238.
8. Cf. *Choreutics*, p. 94.
9. Cf. Ibid.
10. Cf. – Lisa Ullmann. *Some Preparatory Stages for the Study of Space Harmony in Art of Movement*, (Republished by The Laban Art of Movement Guild Magazine, 1971);
    – Sylvia Bodmer. *Studies Based on Crystalloid Dance Forms* (London: Laban Centre for Movement and Dance. 1979.);
    – Irmgard Bartenieff with Dori Lewis. *Body Movement: Coping with the Environment* (New York: Gordon & Breach, 1980), pp. 30-33;
    – Gertrud Snell & Lisa Ullmann, "Stabile and Labile Relationships," in Part II of *Choreutics*, pp. 199-210;
    – Valerie Preston-Dunlop. *A Handbook for Modern Educational Dance*, (London: Macdonald & Evans, 1963) p. 88; Second edition, 1980, pp. 118, 134.
11. Cf. *Die Welt des Tänzers*, p. 54.
12. *Gymnastik und Tanz*, p. 72.
13. Cf. Op. cit., p. 36.
14. *Choreographie*, pp. 3-5.
15. Ibid., p. 4.
16. Cf. Rudolf von Laban, "Der Tanz als Eigenkunst," *Zeitschrift für Ästhetik und Allgemeine Kunstwissenschaft* (XIX Band, Stuttgart, 1925), p. 363.
17. *Gymnastik und Tanz*, p. 67.
18. Cf. Chapter II.

CHAPTER I

Theory of Space

Among Laban's German texts *Choreographie*, First Part is the main source for tracing the development of his theory of space. This work presents an outline of the spatial order of the new dance or choreography, as well as of the first concepts of his notation. Key aspects of what is to be later known as Choreutics and Space Harmony are discussed in the following chapters of the book: "Elements of the Theory of Form," "Theory of Directions," "Harmonies of Main Directions" including the A and B scales, "Four-rings," "Three-rings," "Volutes," "Axis and Equator Scales." From these headings one can gather that *Choreographie* was the first outline of *Choreutics*, which can be taken as its second volume.

With regard to the terms "choreutics" and "space harmony," they seem to have emerged after the publication of *Choreographie*, i.e. in the late 1920's. The prospectus of the *Choreographisches Institut Laban* from 1927/28 lists amongst subjects for dancers Choreutics and Eukinetics – the practical dance theory of space and expression. Laban's assistant Gertrud Snell wrote in her 1929 and 1930 articles in *Schrifttanz* that choreutics deals with the principle of form which is built on directional elements or in other words that it considers laws of structuring movement.[1] Choreutics, identified as space theory, is, along with eukinetics (theory of expression), a key subject in Laban's Central School incorporated into the dance department of the Folkwangschule in Essen in 1929 under the direction of Kurt Jooss. The prospectus of "The Jooss-Leeder School of Dance" at Dartington Hall from 1934 brings a description of choreutics in the context of professional dance training. It is "the theoretical knowledge of the harmony of forms and practical training in sequences of dance movements. [It is] the technique of composing from the point of view of form and spatial expression." Hence, the theoretical and practical aspects of choreutics are to assist dance performance and choreographic crafting. Laban's own descriptions of choreutics are multifaceted. On one hand it is seen as "the art, or the science dealing with the analysis and synthesis of movement. . . ."[2] On the other, "choreutics may be explained as the practical study of the various forms of (more or less) harmonised movement."[3] It is also associated with the differentiation of various bodily-emotional-mental movements and their notation.[4] The term "space harmony" is used in Laban's *Choreographie* interchangeably with "spatial order," "harmony of main inclination," "spatial interrelationships," and "simple forms of harmony."[5] Snell refers to space harmony as to a relationship between directions and states that "dance science is founded on space harmony created in dance."[6] Although in *Choreutics* Laban refers to harmony and harmony in space, as well as to harmonic laws of movement, as a relationship between the spatial structure and the dynamic content of movement,[7] it appears that the term "space harmony" replaced the earlier term "choreutics" in most of the dance practices in England during the 1950's, 60's and 70's.[8] On the other hand, the "harmony of movement" — as described in the syllabus of the Laban Art of Movement Centre from the 1970's — deals with "the relationships of dynamic stress and spatial patterns of bodily actions."[9]

The following presentation of major aspects of Laban's theory of space will be guided by the progression of concepts from the elementary principles of directional orientation and the consideration of shape and size, to the more complex elaborations of choreutics or space harmony, as well as harmony of movement. An analogy with the theory of music may be suggested where the initial practice in pitch and basic intervals is followed by the study of the harmony of chords and counterpoint.

Directional Orientation and Levels

Laban views spatial direction as the most significant element of bodily movement.[10] The whole complexity of movement and dance can be deduced to basic directions which derive from our basic orientation in space related to the vertical and the horizontals of the three dimensions (height, width, and depth). When moving, we frequently depart from these dimensions and incline toward space diagonals and diametral directions. Laban's principle of spatial orientation according to these three systems has been stated very clearly in *Choreutics* and also in *Modern Educational Dance*.[11] Our discussion will therefore offer an historical perspective on the elaboration of these systems.

Laban establishes an area of reference for directional orientation in the centre of the body:

> With every movement innumerable single tensions arise in the body, conditioned through anatomic articulation. They appear to our eye and perception of tensions as at least four components which we imagine irradiating from the center of gravity. The simplest way to describe a person is to determine the placement of the ends of the limbs in relation

to the center of gravity of the body. We say: the head is carried upright, right arm tends somewhat toward right-forward, the left arm left-deep, the right leg . . . . The actual directional energy irradiates from the center of the body, approximately the body's center of gravity, toward the corners of a tetrahedron [created through an imaginary linking of the reach points of the limbs].[12]

Besides hinting at some harmonic interrelations of directions (the tetra-hedron) and approximating the centre of the body with the placement of the center of gravity, the above considerations will give rise to the "first fact of space movement" in *Choreutics*. Accordingly "innumerable directions radiate from the centre of our body and its kinesphere into infinite space."[13] Laban distinguishes the space in general, the infinite space, from the reach space immediately around the body — the Kinesphere. (He coined the term from Greek *kinesis* — movement, and *sphaira* — ball, sphere, according to the rotatory nature of the movement of our joints.) Another early passage announces the notion of the reach space, the kinesphere: "The human body is completely oriented toward itself. It stands free in space. Its only resource, if we can call it that, is its environment, the spatial sphere which surrounds it, and into which it can reach with its limbs."[14]

In the process of developing his systems of spatial orientation, Laban drew from the traditional teaching of ballet based on a static theory dealing with states of bodily carriage and positions. In contrast to these, Laban intended to create a dynamic theory of form which will deal with the process of movement and dance. Due to many gaps in this framework, he felt, however, that one has to start with the static theory of ballet. While in *Choreutics* there is only one paragraph addressing this issue, it is preceded by several elaborations in *Choreographie* such as in the following:

"The so-called five positions have been handed down to us as the simplest means of *spatial orientation* in the art of dance. It is generally accepted that these *positions* only refer to the placement of the feet. This is not so. Rather they are *spatial directions* towards which the legs move, and to which the upper body makes an obvious counter-movement."[15] As already mentioned, Laban maintains that "we observe . . . a *spatial directional attitude* which we determine according to its angle of deflection from the vertical."[16] From this point of view, the first and fifth positions lead vertically down-ward, the second is stressed sideways, the third is more oblique, and the two fourth positions are stressed forward and backward. To these six low posi-tions of the legs, Laban projects six upper counter-positions of the arms, so that a total of 12 spatial situations arises.[17]

In his chapter on "The Spatial Order of the New Choreography," Laban includes three diagrams illustrating human figures within three systems of orientation. The first illustrates the dimensions or the *six dimensional*

directions of high, low, left, right, backwards, and forwards, which form the
corners of an *octahedron*, (see Figure 1). The second diagram shows the
eight diagonal directions of high-right-forward, low-left-backward, h-l-f,
l-r-b, h-l-b, l-r-f, h-r-b, and l-r-f, which form the corners of the *cube*, (see
Figure 2). The third diagram illustrates the human figure in each of the
dimensional planes reaching thus into *twelve diametral directions*, (see
Figure 3, p. 62). Laban explains the origin of these directions from the point
of view of three bodily symmetries:

> Spatially considered: high and low is divided through our *body symmetry*
> into two high and two low directions, so that we find high-right (hr) and
> high-left (hl) to be two points which we experience as high directions;
> conversely low-right (lr) and low-left (l l). The direction forward-backward
> is split through the division into *upper and lower body* (bending possi-
> bilities of the spine) into a higher and deeper forward-back line so that we
> find four points forward-high (fh), forward-low (vl) backward-high (bh)
> and backward-low (bl). The third, right-left dimension is deflected through
> the *most natural movement range of our arms and legs* . . . . [or the
> crossing of the limbs, either in front or behind, when reaching over to the
> other side] into right-forward (rf), right-backward (rb), left-forward (lf),
> and left-backward (lb). We have thus a high-low *plane*, a back-forward
> plane, and a right and left plane.[18]

When these planes are intersected and their corners connected they form an
icosahedron (see Figure 4, p. 62). [It is puzzling that in *Choréographie* there
is no explicit verbal reference to this crystalline form although it is presented in
seventeen photographs of the book as a space-grid within which dancers
move.] Laban searched for the ordering principle within the structures of the
various crystalline forms and, based on his findings, he established spatial
scales and so-called rings, i.e., shorter circuits of spatial movements in which
varying numbers of angles, such as three, four, six, etc., created a spatial
rhythm for the sequence. These are discussed in the section on space
harmony below. Laban found the icosahedral scaffolding the most suitable
for practicing harmonious movement sequences as they are nearest to the
sphere designed in space when our limbs reach freely around the three-
dimensional space; it also corresponds to the structure of the body since its
three bodily symmetries are contained within the inner structure of the three
dimensional planes.[19] (See Figures 3 and 4).

> The high-low plane divides the space in front from the space behind the
> body, while the forward-backward plane creates the division between right
> and left, and the right-left plane, which lies horizontally in space, divides
> high from low.[20]

The above considerations have expanded our insight into how Laban
unfolded the spatial orientation of his dynamic form theory by departing
from spatial directions of the static theory of form. Various aspects of his

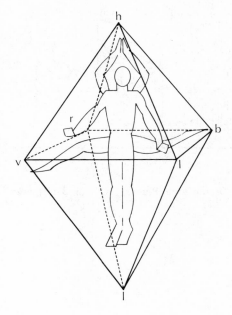

Figure 1. The Octahedron*

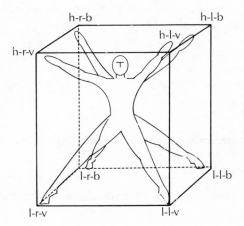

Figure 2. The Cube **

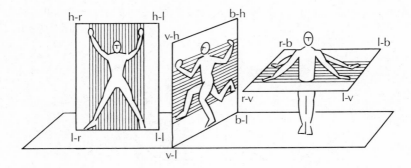

Figure 3. Three Dimensional Planes: Vertical, Sagittal, and Horizontal***

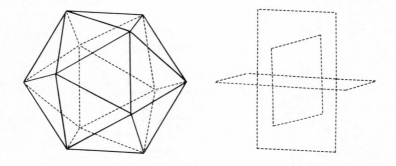

Figure 4. The Icosahedron and its inner structure (three dimensional planes)

*Adapted from *Choreographie* p. 20; **Ibidem p. 21;***Ibidem p. 23.

form theory, later referred to as choreutics and space harmony, will be considered below.

Shape-Form and Extension-Size

A spatial path which links two, three, or more directions creates various shapes or formal elements, such as straight, curved, rounded, and twisted ones. The performance of these shapes is conditioned through the anatomical structure of our joints. While bending and stretching can create straight and angular shapes, its combination with the twisting actions can produce a variety of curved, rounded, and twisted forms.[21] Laban also ascribes various perceptual qualities to the elements of form: "The straight line has a character of stillness, the bent line the character of movement. The curved line is oscillation, thus labile; it can be varied and differentiated. . . . Strongly curved arcs appear to embody the element of speed.[22]

In classifying fundamental elements of form, Laban draws from the theory of movement of the ballet as systematized in Feuillet's *Chorègraphie*. Here he finds four modes of forms in which steps can be performed: straight –*droit*; open outwardly or inwardly – *ouvert*; circular – *rond*; and wavy – *tortillé*.[23] Laban had already referred to these elements of form in his first book when discussing basic elements of symbolic forms: "We can find in the three-dimensionality of signs in the traditional ballet choreography (movement script) proper movement symbols; here the most distinct tension combinations of movement are represented through | (*droit*) – the pull of one tension of the straight movement; ʔ (*tortillé*) – the two directed wavy movement; and ϶ (*rond*) – the three directed spiral."[24] This statement points to the one, two, and three dimensionality of shapes. Laban sees in the form structures of *ouvert, tortillé*, and *rond*, the origins of motility.[25] He also associates them with movement sequencing in that the simple curve (*ouvert*) can be reversed in a pendular way, the wavy, S-formed line (*tortillé*) is formed by a movement wave followed by a counterwave, and the movement can reach its completion in a circle (*rond*). Laban also observed that these form elements can be found in the first three Arabic numerals, as well as in the letters of the Greek alphabet.[26]

Spatial forms and shapes resulting from the linking of several directions are seen as creating space-rhythms. These rhythms can be produced successively as a melodic line in music or through simultaneous actions of different body parts.[27] While the former refers to trace-forms or air and floor patterns, the latter is articulated further as the shapes of body carriage which can be straighter, one-dimensional or *pin-like*; two-dimensionally flat or *wall-like*; three-dimensionally rounded or *ball-like*; and twisted or *screw-like*[28] The classification of shapes into linear (one-dimensional), plane-like (two-dimensional), and plastic (three-dimensional), had already been suggested in the 1920's.[29]

Laban refers to shape or path as one of the most salient structural aspects of movement in dance: "The essential is whether the *directions* are dimensionally or diagonally emphasized, then the *path* into which these directions fuse, such as round, spiral, straight, and perhaps also the way in which the body holds its *equilibrium*, for which the limbs are used."[30] According to Laban, this spatial language is used by the dancer as his or her means of expression.

The aspect of shape is an intrinsic component of composition and performance. The articulation of dance exercises from the point of view of Laban's classification of the four elements of form discussed above have been particularly emphasised in some Laban-based dance techniques, such as those of Mary Wigman and Kurt Jooss.[31]

Shape patterns and the *size* of movement are taken as a joint consideration in Laban's themes concerned with the shape of movement.[32] Large and small patterns are explored under the aspect of *extension* in the elementary themes concerned with the awareness of space as narrow and wide extension in relation to the body centre and the environment.[33] The vertical and the bilateral structural extension of the human body can be articulated through the stretching, bending, and twisting functions of the joints which create the extension and contraction of the kinesphere.[34] The degree of extension (as metric content) is cited as one of the four characteristics of a movement form, and the polarities of near and far are listed among the four regulators of movement intensity in Laban's early classifications.[35]

Table 2 (p. 85) gives an overview of references to orientation, including direction and level of movement, to shape and form, and to the extension and the kinesphere. These references are drawn chronologically from both Laban's German and English books.

Choreutics – Space Harmony

The consideration of movement in relation to the centre of the body may be seen as the transitional stage from a general spatial awareness to the study of choreutics or space harmony. In his German texts Laban refers to *central* and *peripheral* transitions, and describes the nature of the *transversals*: "We have to imagine central spatial directions as always going through the centre of gravity of the body. Besides there are also peripheral inclinations...."[36] The latter are performed mostly with extended limbs moving around the centre, near to or on the periphery of the kinesphere, while central movements engage the bending and stretching functions of the joints by linking the centre and the periphery of the kinesphere. Laban describes the notion of transversal movements from the possibility "to deflect a diagonal through a near dimensional, or the dimensional through the nearly placed diagonal."[37] In other words, the transversals lie between diagonals and dimensionals and do not intersect in the centre of the kinesphere. A transversal movement starts on the periphery of the kinesphere, traverses through it by approaching the centre of the body, and continues towards the opposite side of the periphery.[38] Such an action requires fine shadings of bending between the two stretching functions of the joints.

Although the theory of choreutics is the subject of Laban's first English text, the matter of spatial harmony or of harmonic laws, orders, progressions, and relations is mostly implied. We are confronted with passages such as "Knowing the rules of harmonic relations in space we can control and form the flux of our motility"[39] or "the structure of the body which is bound up . . . with the harmonic laws of space,"[40] without being explicitly told what these are. In this area, the comparative analysis of Laban's German writings is particularly beneficial. That harmony arises out of spatial relationships of movement, and that symmetry and balance are the simplest forms of harmony is clearly stated in his writings of the 1920's;[41] the 1939/66 elucidations of the latter add an interesting dimension in that the wish to establish equilibrium through symmetric movement aims to achieve a unity of form, a completeness.[42] There are several principles or laws of movement which Laban sees as instrumental in creating symmetry, balance, and other forms of harmony. They are to be extrapolated by crossreferencing sections of *Choreographie, Gymnastik und Tanz*, and *Choreutics*.

Laban refers to the law or principle of *counter-movement* or *opposition* which "requires that each movement of the limb into a particular direction be counterbalanced by an approximate counter-direction. . . . For example, when one wants to reach with the right arm towards a distant object without stepping towards it, one has to . . . lift the left leg backward in order to prevent oneself from falling into the reaching direction."[43]

The law or principle of *sequence* deals with the initiation and the follow through of the movement from the center of the body to its periphery, and also back to the center which tends to have the quality of easy fluency. Laban exemplifies it with an arm gesture which is initiated by an impulse from the torso and followed by the movement of the shoulder, upper arm, lower arm, and finally hand.[44]

Both the principle of counter-movement or opposition and of sequence are referred to as fundamental laws and as the basis of all movement harmonies, and can have many variations.[45] A variation of the former occurs when several limbs move into different directions at the same time, thus creating bodily tensions within a kind of *spatial chord*. For example, the left leg can move into the horizontal forward direction at the same time as the right arm reaches upward emphasizing the vertical dimension as a continuum from the supporting leg and the left arm moves horizontally to its side. Such a three-dimensional chord establishes stability through its equal pull toward three directions over the supporting vertical, as well as the relationship of right angles among the directions of the reaching limbs. A more mobile chord is created by moving simultaneously into three different diagonal directions, such as the right leg into right-down-forward, the left arm into left-high-forward, and the right arm into right-high-backward. The relationship of these three directions divides space into uneven sections, i.e., the angles between the directions of the arm and that of the leg are sharp and obtuse, creating a certain lability, or the possibility for the continuation of the movement.[46]

Another aspect of simple harmonies of counter-movement or opposition can be seen in the leading of movements one against the other in a canon-like way which consists of one body part abandoning the main direction when another body part starts moving in the counter-direction. Laban also refers to that as *contrapunctal* movement and exemplifies it with counter-movements of the upper and lower limbs within the up-down and right-left symmetries of the body, such as the left leg moving across to the right side and the right arm following with a crossing movement to the left, while the left arm reaches to the right.[47]

The principle of sequence can also differ from the unfolding of a limb into the direction as described earlier. Laban elaborates on it by describing the dancer's transpositions of *scattering and gathering gestures*. In the performance, the sequential flow of scattering from the centre of the body outwards into the surrounding space alternates with the action of gathering from the periphery of the kinesphere inward towards the centre. When performing both actions, "the whole body participates. The movement is initiated from the center of gravity and follows like a wave through the spine of the torso and neck, and sideways into the arms through to the fingertips. This movement wave (also) spreads downwards into the muscles of the pelvis and further into the upper and lower legs, feet, and toes."[48]

Laban maintains that through our bodily structure we are normally able to reach towards all points of an imaginary sphere-like environment — the kinesphere. He sees *directional exercises* as a means of gaining awareness of the relationship of body movement to spatial dimensions. Thus "directional exercises can serve the aim of harmonizing our sense of space . . . As a matter of fact harmonious movements in many cases are also the most efficient and functional movements in achieving an aim."[49] For the purpose of gaining proficiency and skill in producing harmonious responses in life and dance,

Laban encouraged the practicing of *spatial* sequences or *scales* which link a particular set of directions in a certain harmonic or logical order.[50]

The first of Laban's spatial scales is the so-called *swing-scale*, also referred to as *defence-scale* or the *dimensional scale*. It is based on movements which link the six dimensional directions in a particular order. (While the term "dimensional" is an objective qualifier, referring to the six dimensional directions, the term "defence" scale shows Laban's attempt to draw universal movement principles from natural or behavioral movement. The term "swing" scale derives from the whole body participation in the performance of the scale, as different from ballet sequences executed with a greater isolation of arms and legs, as well as from the swing-like shape and quality of its performance.) Laban found that the order of the scale was also used in combat as the basis for systematic defence exercises, e.g., in sword fencing, the parrying for the purpose of protecting the six vulnerable areas of the body: the *high* swing deflects the blow from the face, *low* swing from the flank, the two sideways swings, i.e., *left* and *right*, ward off the attack to both jugular veins, the *backward* swing from the other flank, and the *foward* swing from the abdomen.[51] Laban maintains that regardless of the combat exercises "the constant pendular swinging into these directions will slowly educate the body to a more exact spatial feeling, i.e., the swing scale will give a foundation from which knowledge of the complications and combinations of spatial directions can be built up."[52] In addition to gaining spatial awareness, Laban sees the value in the practice of the dimensional scale (as well as other scales) also in terms of muscular development: "Muscles which are to move particular parts of the skeleton degenerate when these spatial directions are not exercised. There is a form building force in spatial directions themselves, similar to the building of form which lies in crystallization."[53]

These considerations reveal a deeper reason for Laban's usage of crystalline forms, particularly the octahedron, cube, and the icosahedron, in the context of spatial exercises. The five polyhedra or Platonic solids (the cube, octahedron, tetrahedron, icosahedron, and dodecahedron), serve not only as visualizations or schematizations of the environmental space directions, but also as metaphors for the dynamic shaping of expressive movement forms. This is succinctly expressed in Laban's words: "The skeleton delineates in its functional as well as expressive movements, the edges and inclinations of an invisible spatial crystal. This spatial crystal is the medium in which the structural tension of man is built. The building power of space induces the drawing together of the skeletal parts to which muscles are attached, the swinging out and executing of the full range of movement for which there is potential."[54] The relationship between the structure of the body and the performance of spatial patterns is here again clearly stated. Laban found the crystalline form of the icosahedron to closely correspond with the movement potentials of the human body; he even drew analogies between the proportions of the body and those of the inner structure of the icosahedron — both following the laws of the Golden Section.[55]

The crystalline form of the dimensional orientation is the *octahedron* incorporating the vertical height of the body with the arms stretched upwards, its width in unfolding the limbs to the side, and depth through the swinging of the extremities forward and backward in locomotion. The *center* of the octahedron coincides with the center of the moving body (see Figure 1).

The harmonic aspects of the dimensional scale can be seen from several points of view. There is a relatedness to the center brought about through central and peripheral movements. The order of the scale is designed according to the principle of counter-movement or opposition in that each movement into one pole of a dimension is followed by the movement into its opposite pole. The alternation of the vertical and two horizontal dimensions creates a balancing out of any one-sided stress, thus following the principle of equilibrium. The whole scale can also be performed with gathering and scattering gestures, which are — as discussed above — a variation of the principle of sequence. The aspect of a unified mind-body participation in the performance of the scale can be seen in the emphasis on spatial intents of the movements, i.e., on rising, sinking, crossing, opening, retreating, and advancing.

While Laban describes the performance of dimensional directions as promoting stability and having a tendency to stillness, the oblique, diagonal directions promote lability and movement: "Stillness is a dimensional balancing of the body mass around the centre of weight. Movement is a diagonal overcoming of this state of equilibrium . . . Dimensional directions are namely carriers of stability whereas the obliques promote labile flux."[56] Laban describes the pull of oblique or diagonal directions as leading towards the periphery of our moving space and through this lability tear the body centre away from the support.[57] Thus "the diagonal movement is more active, positive, motile, (while) the dimensional has a tendency to rest."[58] In a juxtaposition of the ballet and new dance notation, Laban ascribes the predominant use of the stable-dimensional orientation to ballet and the labile-diagonal one to the new dance.[59] (See Table 4, p. 90, for survey of links between stability and lability and directional orientation and space harmony.)

The movement scale based on diagonal directions or the *diagonal scale* is referred to only implicitly in Laban's German texts. Diagonal or oblique movements are discussed in the context of their predominantly mobile or labile tendencies; the eight diagonal directions are presented within its crystalline form of the *cube* discussed in *Choreographie*.[60] (See Figure 2). The practice of this movement scale remained, however, a significant aspect of training within the oral tradition of Laban-based teaching, particularly in

England via Ullmann and Bodmer, France via Bereska, and Yugoslavia via Maletic.[61]

The *A* and *B scales*, or as later referred to as the transversal standard scales, are introduced in *Choreographie*. For the elaboration of these scales Laban refers to tradition: "Already in the old ballet a division of space is anticipated which offers approximately the following picture: the upward swing leads to side-high-forward, the downward swing to low-back-side, the inward swing to forward-side-high, the outward swing to side-deep-back, the backward swing to high-back-side, and the forward swing to forward-side-low . . . . There is, of course, a reverse performance of the directions of these swings which amounts to 12 basic directions."[62] The placement of the 12 directions is specified by the differentiation of spatial emphases: the first of the three directional descriptions is dominant, the second has a lesser stress, and the third the least. For example, in the upward swing the most important spatial emphasis is sideways, secondarily upwards, and thirdly forwards. Discussing the harmony of these 12 directions, the so-called inclinations, Laban maintains that "this harmony is manifested in the fact that to every swing ("Aufschwung") belongs a preparation, and that the preparatory swing ("Anschwung") lies in a determinable direction which is not exactly opposite to the directions of the main swing."[63] The inclinations of the A and B scales and the order of the right A-scale are illustrated in Figures 5, 6 and 7 (pp. 71f.).

It is interesting to note that Laban numbered the movements of the inclination rather than the points in space; this expresses his dynamic view of dance in contrast to the traditional thinking in terms of positions. In Laban's oral tradition, however, there was a phase in England when he numbered from 1-12 the corner points of the icosahedron according to the order of one of the Primary or Peripheral standard scales.[64] This allowed him to elaborate further on the structure of scales and rings in terms of numerical relationships of intervals, i.e., distances between directions.[65]

There are two A-scales according to the right-left symmetry of the body. The two B-scales are formed through the forward-backward symmetry in relation to the A-scales, i.e., the inclination of the right-A-scale which leads from left-back to high-right corresponds to the inclination of the left B-scale right-forward to high left, etc. Each of the two scales moves in relation to three different diagonals, the fourth diagonal becoming the structural axis of the entire sequence. This relationship will be referred to as the principle of *complementarity*. The character of the A-scales is influenced by their backwards tilted axes, giving them a softer, more defensive mode to which Laban refers as feminine or compares with the minor scales in music. In contrast the B-scales, influenced by their forward tilted axes, gain a harder, more attacking character which is referred to as masculine and compared with the major scales in music.[66] (Those patriarchal paradigms obviously belong to a turn-of-the-century society.) Figure 7 (p. 72) illustrates the B-scale.

The harmonic structure of the A and B scales is further elucidated through the principle of *parallelism*, according to which each inclination of the first half of the scale has its parallel counter-inclination in the second half of the scale. These spatial relationships can be traced in the drawing in Figure 5: inclination 1 is parallel to inclination 7, 2 to 8, 3 to 9, etc. When isolating two parallel inclinations and linking them with peripheral inclinations over the edge of the icosahedron, a so-called *four-ring*, later referred to as *two-ring* sequence, arises[67] (Figure 9, p. 72). (We have clarified the term ring on p. 60) The inner harmonic structure of the A and B scales is further revealed in terms of *volutes*, or volute-like, coiling movements which are created through the transition between the inclinations which form an obtuse angle, such as high-right to back-low inclination and back-low to left-forward inclination. According to the "feminine" or "masculine" characteristics, the volutes of the A-scales appear more passive and softer, having an emphasis on the first of the two inclinations, while the volutes of the B-scales have a harder character, finishing with an emphasis.[68] When a volute is closed with a third inclination which returns to its starting situation, the so-called *three-ring* is created (Figure 8, p. 72). Laban considers that the formation of three-rings as the principle of *triad* or *trialism* differs from parallelism.[69] (Each three-ring, later referred to as transversal three-ring, has one parallel to it as well as two smaller ones on the periphery of the icosahedron: thus there are four three-rings around each space diagonal.) While there is no explicit reference in *Choreographie* to the so-called *steeples* or the transitions between two inclinations of the A or B scales which occur with a narrow, sharp angle, they are clearly articulated three years later in the oral tradition of Laban's teaching by his assistant Gertrud Snell.[70]

Two further scales are designed within the structure of the icosahedron: the *Axis-scales* (See Figure 10, p. 72) which cluster six inclinations around each of the four spatial diagonals at a time, and the *Equator-scales* which enclose peripherally one of the chosen diagonal axes. In the context of the description of the Axis-scales, Laban differentiates three types of inclinations by calling them *steep* (those gravitating toward the vertical), *flat* (influenced by the side-to-side dimension), and *flowing* (by the forward-backward dimension).[71] This differentiation allows us to refer back to the A and B scales and point to the characteristic rhythm of the alternation of the inclinations constantly keeping the same order, i.e., flat-steep-flowing executed four times. The same rhythm is also kept in the Axis-scales with the difference being that the sequence of the inclinations is repeated only twice and that it does not change diagonals. The logic of this structural rhythm is part of what is later referred to as *sequential laws*; in the case of the A and B scales (or the Trans-

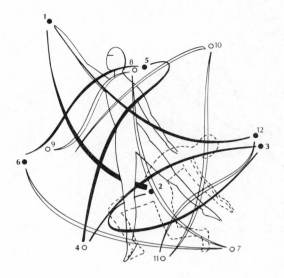

Figure 5. Inclinations of the A-scale*

[From] Point 1(left)	b(ack) to h(igh)	r(ight) is inclination 1 (rhf)
'' hr	'' bl (low)	'' 2 (lbl)
'' bl	'' lf (forward)	'' 3 (flh)
'' lf	'' lr	'' 4 (rlb)
'' lr	'' bh	'' 5 (hbl)
'' bh	'' rf	'' 6 (frl)
'' rf	'' ll (low left)	'' 7 (llb)
'' ll	'' vh	'' 8 (hfr)
'' fh	'' rb	'' 9 (brl)
'' rb	'' hl	'' 10 (lhf)
'' hl	'' fl	'' 11 (lfr)
'' fl	'' lb	'' 12 (blh)

Figure 6. Order of the A-scale from *Choreographie* p. 29

*Adapted from *Choreographie*, pp. 30-31.

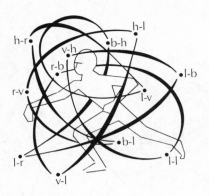

Figure 7. Inclinations of the B-scale*

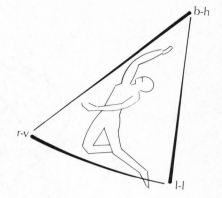

Figure 8. A Three-Ring**

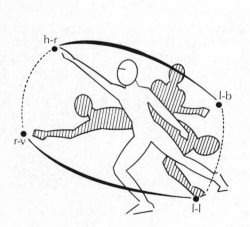

Figure 9. A Four-Ring***

Figure 10. The Axis-Scale****

*Adapted from *Choreographie* p. 33; **Ibidem p. 70;
***Ibidem p. 43; ****Ibidem p. 47

versal standard scales), these rhythms are carried through 12 inclinations, and in the case of the Axis-scales through 6 inclinations.[72] The principle of *complementarity* governs the relationship of the space diagonals to all of the above scales.

One can trace some analogies between Laban's principles or laws of harmony and Delsarte's laws and orders of movement. Laban's principle of *counter-movement* or *opposition* can be compared with Delsarte's *great order of opposition*, according to which two parts of the body are moving simultaneously into opposite directions as an expression of physical and emotional power.[73] For both Laban and Delsarte, opposition and counter-movement are connected with the principle or law of equilibrium. We have discussed Laban's view of equilibrium as one aspect of harmony; Delsarte who sees balance, poise, and equilibrium as vital skills for the dancer describes them in terms of counter movements within body parts when moving away from the vertical.[74]

Laban's law of *sequence*, dealing with the initiation and the follow-through of the movement from the centre of the body to its periphery, can be compared with Delsarte's *great order of succession*, according to which a movement begins at the centre of the body and works outward ("true succession") or begins at an extremity and works inward towards the centre ("reversed succession"). It is the greatest order for the expression of emotion; its quality is fluid, wave-like.[75] It is interesting to find that Laban did not make any explicit reference to principles of counter-tension and succession in his English books. In *Choreutics* there is mention of *"sequential laws"* referred to above in the context of the Transversal standard scales (A and B-scales) and the Axis-scales. On the other hand, harmonizing aspects of equilibrium are articulated further in terms of it being established with symmetric or asymmetric movements.[76]

There is also reference to *parallelism* which exists in the structure of A and B scales, in that the inclinations of the first half of the scale are parallel to those in the second half. When performing the scales, the parallel inclinations executed are starting from different directions, such as from left-backwards to high-right, and from right-forwards to down-left. Thus Laban's notion of parallelism differs from Delsarte's second great order of motion, according to which two parts of the body move simultaneously in the same direction, and which denotes weakness.[77]

Survey of Laban's Theory of Space

The close interrelationship of bodily structure and the structure of movement in space is the foundation of all aspects of Laban's theory of movement in space and spatial harmonies. Like the relationship of the theory of music to harmony and counterpoint, the prerequisites for Space Harmony or Choreutics are the awareness and mastery of directional orientation (with its inherent stabilizing and mobilizing tendencies) and the appreciation of the extension and shape of movement.

(a) The notion of *extension* and *size* of movement is associated with the structure of the human body, such as the vertical and bilateral extension, and with the notion of the sphere of movement which can grow and shrink by means of the stretching and bending of joints. Laban distinguished space in general from the reach space immediately around the body and named it *kinesphere*.

(b) *Directional orientation* is approached from several points of view. The directions are related both to the vertical and to the centre of the body; they are judged from the front of the mover when upright. The kinesphere is divided into twenty-six space directions which radiate from the space-centre which is the twenty-seventh point of orientation. These main directions are classified within three systems of orientation: (i) *6 dimensionals* based on three dimensions — height, width, and depth — with directions and counter-directions high-low, left-right, forward-backward; when linked they form the *octahedron*, the inner structure of which is the three-dimensional cross; (ii) *8 diagonals* based on four space diagonals with directions and counter-directions high/right/forward-low/left/backward, high/left/forward-low/right/backward, high/left/backward-low/right/forward, and high/right/backward-low/left/forward; when linked these directions form the corners of the *cube*, the inner structure of which is the four-diagonal cross; (iii) *12 diametrals*[78] based on six diameters of the three dimensional planes — vertical, horizontal, and sagittal — with directions and counter-directions high/right-low/left, high/left-low/right, left/forward-right/backward, right/forward-left/backward, forward/high-backward/low, forward/low-backward/high; when intersected the three planes form the *icosahedron*. This regular solid most closely resemble the sphere when our limbs reach freely around the three-dimensional space; it also corresponds to the right-left, up-down, and forward-backward symmetries of the body contained within the three dimensional planes, the icosahedron's inner structure. The planes are also referred to as "door" (the vertical), "table" (the horizontal), and "wheel" (the sagittal) (See Figure 3).

Directions are associated with two states of equilibrium: stable and mobile. Dimensionals are predominantly stable due the balancing of the body mass around the centre of weight and its perpendicular relationship to the support. Diagonal directions move the body centre out of the vertical alignment over the support and are thus promote lability or mobility. (Laban used the term lability in his German texts and mobility in the English writings.)

Diametral directions can emphasize either the stabilizing or mobilizing tendencies according to their particular configurations.

(c) Linking of directions results in shapes. The classification of *shape* or *formal elements* into straight, curved, twisted, and rounded is based on movement possibilities of the joints. Laban also drew from Feuillet's reference to four modes of form in which steps can be performed: *droit* – straight; *ouvert* – open outwardly or inwardly; *rond* – circular, rounded; and *tortillé* – wavy or twisted.

Survey of Space Harmony – Choreutics

Spatial relationships investigated in Space Harmony or Choreutics are established by means of harmonic principles. "There is a logical order underlying the evolution of the various shapes in space which can be realized in scales. Scales are graduated series of movement which pass through space in a particular order of balancing tensions according to a specific scheme of relations . . . ."[79] In Laban's spatial scales directions are linked in three possible ways: (i) *centrally* – originating from the centre or moving from the periphery towards or through the centre of the body, engaging contraction and extension of the joints; (ii) *peripherally* – by moving around the centre and keeping the joints at the same degree of extension, and (iii) *transversally* – when starting the movement on the periphery of the body, approaching but bypassing the centre and continuing towards the opposite end point of the periphery; in this kind of transition finer shadings of contraction between two extensions are performed.

(a) Laban's *spatial scales* evolved within the scaffoldings of regular polyhedra and are based on various harmonic principles. The crystalline form of the *Dimensional scale* is the octahedron. Its center coincides with the centre of the moving body to which movement is related by central and peripheral links. The order of the scale is designed according to principles of countertension (or opposition) and of equilibrium. Each movement into one pole of the dimensions is followed by a movement into its opposite pole. The alternation of the vertical and two horizontals creates a balancing effect. As discussed above the vertical and horizontal structure of the scale also promotes the principle of stability. Six movements of the scale link the dimensional directions in the order of high-low, sideways across-sideways open, and backward-forward.

The crystalline structure for the *Diagonal scale* is the cube which incorporates the four space diagonals and their 8 directions. The order of the scale is also arranged according to the principles of counter-movement and equilibrium: high/right/forward-deep/left/backward, high/left/forward-deep/

right/backward, high/left/backward-deep/right forward, high/right/backward-deep/left/forward. (This order can also be performed with the left side leading.) The spatial intent of diagonal directions is more complex since each direction includes three dimensional intents such as rising/opening/advancing-sinking/crossing/retreating. The eight directions are linked centrally and peripherally. In contrast to the predominant stability of the dimensional scale, the diagonal scale is the prototype for mobility or lability, thus its movements lead to locomotion, elevation, and falling.

(b) *Scales* and *rings* within the crystalline scaffolding of the *icosahedron* differ in structure from the dimensional and diagonal scales. They are formed by linking diametral directions peripherally and/or transversally. Each scale and ring creates a closed circuit around an axis which is predominantly a space diagonal. Similar to the principle of counter-movement, oppositional parallelism is established between the first and second parts of the scales and most of the rings.

The prototypes for peripheral circuits are the four *peripheral standard scales* around the four diagonals which link all 12 diametral directions within one interval distance. They are also referred to as *"Primary scales,"* being among the first scales Laban designed. At one time he numbered the corner points from 1 to 12 according to the order of the scale around the high/righ/forward-deep/left/backward diagonal axis.[80] This allowed Laban to elaborate further scales and rings in terms of numerical relationships of intervals or distances between directions. While the series of one interval among odd numbers creates the structure of the *Axis-scale* or "cluster," the sequence linking even numbers creates *Equator scales* or "girdles." The three dimensional *planes* are created by linking each third number; peripheral *three-rings* are created by linking each fourth odd number, and transversal three-rings by connecting each fourth even number. Transversal standard scales arise from the linking of each fifth number.

The prototype for the transversal scales which link all the 12 diametral directions are four *transversal standard scales* − two *A-scales* (according to the right-left symmetry) and two *B-scales* (formed through the forward-backward symmetry in relation to the A-scales). Each of the four scales consists of 12 transversals which are inclined towards three different diagonals, the fourth one becoming the structural axis of the scale. The 12 transversals or *inclinations* alternate in the order of *flat* (inclined toward the right-left horizontal), *steep* inclination (gravitating toward the vertical), and *flowing* inclination (moving toward the forward-backward horizontal); this spatial rhythm is repeated four times to accomplish the circuit of the scale. The inner harmonic structure of the scale is further manifest in terms of *volutes*, coiling movements formed by the obtuse angle of juncture of two inclinations, and *steeples*, angular movements formed by two inclinations linked under a sharp angle. The principle of *parallelism* (mentioned above) is manifest in each inclination of the first half of the scale having its parallel counter-inclination in the second half of the scale (See Figure 5). Besides spatial configurations which use only transversal or only peripheral links, there are also mixed forms consisting of transversals and peripheral movements such as *mixed four-rings* and *mixed seven-rings*. Several of these choreutic forms, such as five- and seven-rings, and mixed seven-rings, are not included in the historical considerations above because they were published later in *Choreutics* (1939/66). A choronological survey can be traced in Table 3 (p. 87), which presents concepts and forms as they appeared in Laban's writings.

Harmony of Movement

While space harmony deals with spatial relationships of movement which implies a harmonic relationship of bodily structure and its movement patterns in space, the harmony of movement considers the relationship of the dynamics of bodily actions and their spatial patterns. Before discussing Laban's theory of affinities between the quality of movement and its spatial placement it is appropriate to address briefly his observations about dynamic characteristics of deep, medium and high movers/dancers (which may be seen as analogous to the predominant pitch and quality of a singer's voice.)

In fact in an account of Laban's theories in 1921, Mary Wigman refers to his differentiation of "soprano dancers" whose main movement expression consisted in light, upward streaming jumping, the "bariton mover" who predominantly enjoyed the dark softness of the deep swing; the "mezzo-soprano" whose lilting float is held between upward and downward; and the masculine "bass" whose harsh wildness of deepest gestures borders on mime.[81] In Laban's first discussion from 1926, he describes the tendencies for moving predominantly in one of the three spatial levels as being the result of both bodily proportions and some innate movement qualities: "The difference [amongst three types of movers] is mainly in the various bodily predispositions, a heavy or delicate build, and in the dynamic capacities connected with it."[82] Laban elaborates on these qualities in the 1950's associating the rhythmic stamping and crouching bodily actions with deep movers; in contrast to these the high movers show more tension in order to act against gravity and produce an erect carriage and light gestures and leaps. The medium movers prefer freely flowing, swinging and turning actions on the horizontal level of space. Laban sees these predilections as being influenced by mental and emotional qualities, as well as bodily structure.[83]

The discussion of Laban's theory of affinities is of particular interest from two points of view. The correspondence between the mover's spatiality and his/her intensity or dynamic range clearly displays Laban's holistic view of movement, on the one hand. On the other, this particular concept has pervaded the Laban-based work in the U.S.A. through the so-called "Effort-Shape" methodology of movement observation and assessment, initially developed by Warren Lamb.[84]

The first theoretical presentation of the affinities between the spatial placement of movement and its quality can be found in the descriptions of "Main and Secondary Tendencies" in *Choreographie*. The main tendencies of movement are described as basic directions or basic forms, whereas secondary tendencies are associated with the movement nuance or intensity as well as with the degrees of lability. Laban formulates the four regulators of intensity as being force, time, space, and flux (or lability), and their respective polarities are described as weak-strong, fast-slow, extended-narrow, and mobile-rigid. These have a particular tendency towards the six dimensional directions as will be shown below. Both the spatial and the dynamic aspects of movement are also defined by means of attempted notation symbols.[85]

Affinities are further elaborated in *Choreutics*. Intensity is here referred to as "dynamic qualities" and "dynamic traits," as well as "secondary tendencies" of movement into the six fundamental directions in space.[86] (The correlation of both sources is presented in Table 5 (p. 91) and will be discussed further in the next chapter.) In "Exploration of the Dynamosphere" and "Natural Sequences of the Dynamosphere" (Chapters III and VI of *Choreutics*), Laban refers to the "dynamosphere" as the space in which our dynamic actions take place. Thus the six dimensional directions in the kinesphere may each have a specific dynamic nuance; for example, the direction high may be associated with the quality of lightness, the direction sideways across with the quality of directness, and the direction forward with the quality of slowness. Elaborating compounds of these, Laban arrives at eight diagonal directions of the kinesphere each of which may be associated with a "fundamental dynamic action" in the kinesphere. Discussing ways of notating such dynamic actions, Laban suggests that special "dynamospheric symbols" (later the Effort-graph of the 40's) may be preferred to the spatial notation symbols since particular movement qualities are not always derivative of the placement of movement in space.[87] Also "movement of any dynamic shade can, of course be made into any desired direction."[88] These statements appear to delineate the boundaries of the concept of affinities which may not always occur either in everyday movement or in dance. On the other hand, Laban suggests that it may be beneficial to develop an awareness of the connections between the kinespheric and dynamospheric sequences. In this context he points to the *law of proximity* according to which a bodily feeling for harmonious movement does not permit immediate transitions between distant dynamic actions in the dynamosphere.[89] The notion of movement harmony is hinted at earlier in its derivation from the correlations of dynamic nuances with spatial directions.[90] Laban's concept of affinities thus branches into the area of *general movement harmony* which had been distinguished in the oral tradition of Laban's teaching.[91] (See also Table 4, p. 90, for survey of links between stability and lability and aspects of harmony.)

In summarizing both chapters III and VI of *Choreutics*, Laban strongly restates his view of the inseparability of spatial form and dynamic stress: "It is only the amazing number of possible combinations which, in order to comprehend them, makes it necessary for us to look at them from two distinct angles, namely that of form and that of dynamic stress."[92] He further argues that "the conventional idea of space as a phenomenon which can be separated from time and force and from expression is completely erroneous."[93] These points of view have guided our presentation of Laban's concepts which for the purposes of the study so far have been considered from the kinetic aspect of stability and mobility/lability and from the aspect of spatiality. The consideration of affinities creates a bridge to the next chapter on the dynamic qualities of movement in which some of its aspects will be reconsidered.

Notes to Chapter I

1. Cf. Gertrud Snell, "Grundlagen einer Allgemeiner Tanzlehre" ("Fundamentals of a General Dance Theory"), *Schrifttanz*, Heft, I, 1929, pp. 8-11; Heft II, 1929, pp. 21-24, Heft II, 1930, pp. 48-50.
2. *Choreutics*, p. 8; the term was coined from Greek *Choros*=circle/dance, and *Eu*=good, harmonious.
3. Ibid., p. viii.
4. Cf. Ibid., p. 8.
5. Cf. *Choreographie*, p. 86, and the Table of Contents.
6. Cf. Gertrud Snell, "Tanzwissenschaft," *Die Schönheit*, II, 1926, pp. 62-67.
7. Cf. *Choreutics*, Chapters III and VI.
8. Cf. Lisa Ullmann, *Some Preparatory Stages for the Study of Space Harmony in Art of Movement*; the booklet is a reprint of articles first published by *The Laban Art of Movement Guild Magazine* between 1952 and 1955. In the Preface Ullmann refers the reader to more detailed elaborations of the subject in Laban's *Choreutics*.
9. From "General Information 1973/74, The Laban Art of Movement Centre."
10. Cf. *Choreographie*, pp. 3-4.
11. Cf. "Principles of Orientation in Space," in *Choreutics*, pp. 10-17, and "The Conception of the Sphere of Movement," in *Modern Educational Dance*, pp. 83-94.

12. *Die Welt des Tänzers*, pp. 24-25.
13. *Choreutics*, p. 17.
14. *Gymnastic und Tanz*, p. 7.
15. *Choreographie*, p. 16.
16. Ibid., p. 3.
17. Cf. Ibid., pp. 13-14.
18. Ibid., p. 22.
19. Cf. Ibid., pp. 20-23; The three dimensional planes are referred to in Laban-based teaching as the vertical or "door" plane, the horizontal or "table" plane, and the sagittal or "wheel plane."
20. *Choreographie*, p. 22
21. Cf. *Choreutics*, p. 84.
22. *Gymnastik und Tanz*, pp. 16-17.
23. Cf. *Choreographie*, p. 54.
24. *Die Welt des Tänzers*, pp. 40-41.
25. Cf. *Gymnastik und Tanz*, p. 165.
26. Cf. "Der Tanz als Eigenkunst," *Zeitschrift für Ästhetik und Allgemeine Kunstwissenschaft*, XIX Band, Stuttgart, 1925, p. 363, and *Choreutics*, p. 83.
27. Cf. *The Mastery of Movement*, 1960 ed., p. 128.
28. Cf. Ibid., pp. 69-70.
29. Cf. *Gymnastik und Tanz*, p. 16.
30. *Choreographie*, p. 84.
31. Personal communication with Isa Partsch-Bergsohn in March 1983. Chair of the Dance Program, University of Arizona in Tucson, Ms. Bergsohn studied with Wigman from 1943-45, and from 1949-1952 with Kurt Jooss at the Dance Department of the Folkwangschule in Essen; she was subsequently on the Faculty of the department as the assistant to Jooss until 1957.
32. Cf. *Modern Educational Dance*, pp. 32-22.
33. Cf. Ibid., p. 29.
34. Cf. *Choreutics*, pp. 29, 41.
35. Cf. *Choreographie*, pp. 4, 74.
36. *Choreographie*, p. 27.
37. Ibid., p. 28.
38. Cf. *Choreutics*, p. 68.
39. *Choreutics*, p. 25.
40. Ibid., p. 44.
41. Cf. *Choreographie*, p. 15; and *Die Welt des Tänzers* p. 37.
42. Cf. *Choreutics*, pp. 89-90.
43. *Choreographie*, p. 18; Cf. also *Gymnastik und Tanz*, p. 69.
44. Cf. *Choreographie*, p. 18; Cf. also *Gymnastik und Tanz*, 69.
45. Cf. *Choreographie*, p. 18.
46. Cf. *Choreographie*, pp. 17-18; Cf. also *Gymnastik und Tanz* pp. 73-74, 86.
47. Cf. *Choreographie*, pp. 86-88.

48. *Gymnastik und Tanz*, p. 70; Cf. also pp. 69-72 with further descriptions of the performance and accompaning imagery. Cf. also *Choreutics* pp. 49-50, and *The Mastery of Movement* (1960 ed.) pp. 87-90. In the tradition of Laban-based teaching the sequences of gathering and scattering are a significant part of the body-mind training. When linked they form a kind of three-dimensional figure of eight. In the teaching of the Art of Movement Studio of the 1940's, '50's and '60's the performance of such sequences served also as a metaphor for the linking of the outer and inner worlds: the gathering of outside impressions, experiences, knowledge, and the scattering of personally assimilated insights. The bodily performance requires a complex coordination of bending, stretching and twisting of the joints of limbs and torso, as well as a clarity of shaping.

49. *Gymnastik und Tanz*, pp. 75, 21.

50. At the outset of designing scales Laban intended to juxtapose to spatial sequences of the old ballet (divided into directions for arms and legs) sequences of the new dance (which should be performed in various directions with the whole body as a more natural way of moving). Cf. *Choreographie*, p. 12.

51. Cf. *Choreographie*, pp. 24-26; *Gymnastik und Tanz*, pp. 85-87; and *Choreutics*, pp. 37-42.

52. *Gymnastik und Tanz*, pp. 75-76.

53. Ibid., p. 76.

54. *Gymnastik und Tanz*, p. 114.

55. Mathematical laws associated with the aesthetic sense of harmony; Cf. *Choreutics*, pp. 107-108.

56. *Choreographie*, p. 75.

57. Cf. Ibid., p. 21.

58. Ibid., p. 14.

59. Cf. *Choreographie*, p. 64.

60. Cf. Op. cit., p. 21.

61. For Bereska and Bodmer see Part One, notes 16 and 26; Ana Maletic — the author's mother — studied with Laban, Bereska and Jooss, and founded the first Laban-based school in Yugoslavia in 1931.

62. *Choreographie*, pp. 25-26.

63. *Choreographie*, p. 29.

64. Primary or Peripheral standard scales are sequences which link the twelve corner points of the icosahedron peripherally; each of the four scales has a diagonal axis. As they were amongst the first harmonic sequences Laban established, he gave them the name of "primary" scales. Cf. *Choreutics*, pp. 179-180, and footnote on p. 180.

65. Personal communication with Laban in 1956 at the Art of Movement Studio/Laban Centre, Addlestone, England.

66. Cf. *Choreographie*, p. 34.

67. Cf. Ibid., pp. 36-39.

68. Cf. Ibid., p. 49.
69. Cf. Ibid., pp. 40, 49-50.
70. Cf. "Grundlagen Einer Allgemeiner Tanzlehre; II. Choreologie," *Schrift-tanz*, Heft II, 1929, pp. 21-24.
71. *Choreographie*, pp. 43-48.
72. Cf. *Choreutics*, p. 153.
73. Cf. Ted Shawn. *Every Little Movement: A Book about Francois Delsarte* (Pittsfield, Mass: Eagle Printing Co., 1954), p. 35.
74. Cf. Ibid., pp. 70-71.
75. Cf. Ibid., p. 35.
76. Cf. Op. cit., p. 153.
77. Cf. Shawn. *Every Little Movement*, p. 35.
78. Although a diameter or a diametral line is defined in geometry as a straight line passing from side to side and through the centre of any two or three dimensional geometrical figure, in Laban's space theory the 12 diametral directions (or 6 diametrals) refer to the lines which link opposite angles of the three dimensional planes. (Cf. *Choreutics*, pp. 11, 15.)
79. *Modern Educational Dance*, 3rd ed., 1975, p. 27.
80. Cf. *Choreutics*, p. 180.
81. Cf. Mary Wigman, "Rudolf von Labans Lehre vom Tanz," *Die Neue Schaubühne*, September, 1921, p. 103.
82. *Gymnastik und Tanz*, p. 148.
83. Cf. *The Mastery of Movement*, p. 134-137 (1960 ed.): Gleisner (1928, p. 102) and Knust (1929, p. 305) also mention the strong, impulsive quality of the deep dancer.
84. Warren Lamb trained in the Manchester Art of Movement Studio in the 40's, and assisted Laban and Lawrence in probing their Effort assessment tests. Since the 50's he has headed a management consulting firm in London, concerned with individual counseling, action profiles, and top management team building. In *Posture and Gesture* (London: Duckworth Co., 1965) Lamb presents his "Scheme for Detailed Observation and Analysis of Physical Behavior" which "has been adapted from the codification of movement made by Rudolf Laban" (p. 51). The emphasis of this observation is placed on degrees of affinity between "Shape" and "Effort" variations, including Lamb's elaborations of "shape flow" versus "effort flow," as well as observation of "Posture/Gesture mergings" (Cf. pp. 51-68). The observation of affinities between shaping in the three-dimensional planes and the components of space, weight, and time is based on Laban's concept of affinities presented in this chapter. In the 60's Lamb's Effort/Shape construct contributed to the forming of Laban-Lamb-based methodologies in the U.S.A. developed by Irmgard Bartenieff and Dr. Judith Kestenberg.
85. Cf. *Choreographie*, pp. 74-79.
86. Cf. *Choreutics*, pp. 31-32.

87. Cf. Ibid., p. 35.
88. Ibid., p. 31.
89. Cf. Ibid., pp. 66, 67.
90. Cf. Ibid., p. 31.
91. Lisa Ullmann, in her teaching at the Art of Movement Studio/Laban Centre, emphasized the distinction between space harmony dealing with spatial relationships and general movement harmony dealing with the balance between the movement's energy and its placement in space.
92. *Choreutics*, p. 36.
93. Ibid., p. 67.
94. Cf. *Choreographie*, pp. 74-76, and *Choreutics*, pp. 31-32.

Table 1

STABILITY AND LABILITY/MOBILITY

Chronological Survey of Concept Formulation and
Links with other Concepts

1920:
Die Welt des Tänzers

p. 16   (Lability as) overcoming inertia
p. 233   (Stability as) equilibrium – harmony
p. 238   Stabile balance – equilibrium –
         symmetry
         Labile balance – (disequilibrium) –
         asymmetry

1926:
Choreographie

p. 3   Stable——stillness   aspects of plas-
         (equilibrium)   ticity or 3-
         Labile——movement   dimensionality
         (fall, thrust, swing)   of body in space
         Kinetic content of form: degree of lability

p. 14   Stable – dimensional directions; tendency
         of leg movements; associated w/h
         harmony – symmetry, balance
         Labile – oblique (diagonal) directions;
         arm and torso movements associated
         w/h dance

p. 17   Stable – (chordal) streaming into
         three dimensions
         Labile – one or two dimensional

p. 21   Stable associated w/h deflection from
         obliques (diagonals)
         Lability of obliques (diag.) tears the body
         centre away from the support

p. 64   Stable – dimensional orientation
         associated w/h Ballet notation
         Labile – diagonal orientation assoc.
         w/h New Dance

p. 74   Lability synonymous with flux & fluency
         as one of the four regulators of Intensity

p. 75   (Stability) stillness – dimensional balancing
         of body mass around centre of weight
         (Lability) Movement – diagonal overcoming
         of this equilibrium

p. 77   Stable + attempts of
         Labile notation

p. 85   Stability and Lability linked w/h temporal
         nuances and large and small motility

1926:
Gymnastik und Tanz

p. 67   Lability – movement: swing, flight,
         fall; weightless into obliques
         (diagonals), fluent, flowing
         (Stability) – equilibrium, bound

1939/66:
Choreutics

p. 92   Stabilizing and Mobilizing Trace –
         Forms, Chapter X.

p. 94   Stable – binding – knotting; movement
         w/h axial counter-tension

p. 100   Mobile – loosening – untwisting; surface
         movement affecting the whole body

BODY

DYNAMICS

Table 2   85

Table 2

THEORY OF SPACE

Chronology of Concept Formulation and Sources
and
Links with other Concepts

ORIENTATION: DIRECTIONS & LEVELS

1920: *Die Welt Des Tänzers*	pp. 24-25	Directions of spatial tensions as related to the centre of gravity approximately coinciding with the centre of the body
1962: *Choreographie*	pp. 6-14	Directional orientation derived from the five positions of classical ballet.
	pp. 20-23	Six Dimensional directions Eight Diagonal directions diagrams & descriptions Twelve Diametral directions
1926: *Gymnastik und Tanz*	p. 77	Spatial sphere around the body as resource for orientation
1939/66: *Choreutics*	pp. 10-17	27 main directions (26 + centre) three-dimensional cross four-diagonal cross six-diametral cross
	pp. 141-142	three dimensional planes
	pp. 101-110	Polyhedral-scaffoldings
1948: *Modern Educational Dance*	p. 35	Themes concerned with space orientation
	pp. 84-86	Twenty-six space-directions radiate from the space-centre, which is the twenty-seventh point of orientation

SHAPE – FORM

1920: *Die Welt des Tänzers*	pp. 31, 38	Form elements correspond to psychological components
	pp. 149-150	The shape of movement transpires from the shape of appliances
	p. 209	The perception of vertical, horizontal and inclined lines
	pp. 40-41	Spatial pulls of *droit, torillé* & *rond*
1926: *Choreographie*	p. 54	*Ouvert, tortillé, rond* & *droit* as fundamental forms of step patterns first cited in Feuillet
	p. 16	Three kinds of form: linear, plane-like, and plastic (3-dim.)

Table 2   (Cont'd.)

SHAPE – FORM

1926: *Gymnastik und Tanz*	p.p. 16-17 p. 165	Perception of straight and curved lines Primary forms of motion found in Arabic numerals & letters of Greek alphabet, as well as in the ballet's *ouvert, tortillé,* and *rond,* and the use of modern Eurhythmy
1939/66: *Choreutics*	pp. 83-85	Four basic formal elements or shapes: *droit*-straight, *ouvert*-curved, *rond*-round, *tortillé*-twisted
1948: *Modern Educational Dance*	pp. 32-33	Themes concerned with shapes of movement including size
1960: *The Mastery of Movement*	p. 42 p. 70 p. 128	Path: straight – angular – curved Four shapes of body carriage: pin-like, wall-like, ball-like, screw-like Space-rhythm created by spatial forms/shapes: a) successive, b) simultaneous

EXTENSION – SIZE – KINESPHERE

1926: *Choreographie*	pp. 4-5 p. 75	Metric Content of Form: degrees of extension Polarities of space: near and far
1939/66: Choreutics	p. 41 p. 29	Degrees of spatial extension: narrow and wide Kinesphere and general space
1948: *Modern Educational Dance*	p. 29 p. 32-33 p. 83	Themes concerned with the awareness of space including extension: narrow – wide Themes concerned with shapes of movement including size: small and large Sphere of movement [Kinesphere]
1960: *The Mastery of Movement*	p. 38	Kinesphere

Table 3   87

Table 3

CHOREUTICS – SPACE HARMONY

A. Concepts

1920: *Die Welt des Tänzers*	p. 24	Placement/directions of limbs in relation to centre of gravity
	p. 37	Simple form of harmony: symmetry Golden Section governing the proportionality of body, positions, and sequences of movement
1926: *Choreographie*	p. 14	Simple forms of harmony: symmetry & balance
	pp. 17-18	Chord of spatial directions
	p. 18	The laws of balance [counter-movement] and sequence as basis of all movement harmony
	p. 27	Central and peripheral in relation to the centre of gravity; [transversals] deflected diagonals through dimensions
	p. 34	The axis of A and B scales influencing their character [complementarity]
	p. 36	Parallelism between the first and second half of the A scale
	p. 40	Trialism [triad] vs. parallelism
	p. 29	Harmony of main directions [preparation and exertion]
	p. 86	Harmony arises from spatial relationships of mvt; Harmonic laws permit simplification; Simple form of harmony: canon-like or contrapuntal movement of upper & lower limbs
1926: *Gymnastik und Tanz*	p. 9	Harmonious & disharmonious (grotesque) links of swings
	p. 16	Simplest and most limited form of harmony: symmetry as balanced opposition; Triad [trialism] vs. Dyad
	pp. 73-74	Spatial chord
	p. 74	Law of sequence and of counter-movement
	p. 86	Law of sequence and of counter-movement & the chord of spatial directions
1926: *Des Kindes Gymnastik und Tanz*	p. 56	Harmony as equilibrium of flowing spatial directions.

Table 3   (Cont'd.)

A. Concepts

1927/28: Prospectus of *Choreographisches Institut Laban*		Choreutics as the practical dance theory of space
1929: Prospectus of *Laban Central School* Essen		Choreutics as space theory
1939/66: *Choreutics*	p. viii.	Choreutics as practical study of various forms of harmonised movement.
	p. 8	Choreutics as the art and science dealing with analysis and synthesis of movement
	pp. 25-26	Harmonious patterns, harmonious relations as harmonious movement following the circles most appropriate to the bodily structure; Choreutic laws: the laws of interdependent circles
	p. 44	Bodily structure linked with harmonic laws of space
	p. 68	Transversals traversing the kinesphere but not intersecting at its centre
	p. 74	Steep, flat, flowing
	p. 81	Parallelism of first and second half of standard scales as a kind of symmetry moving in opposite directions.
	p. 82	Harmony in space as the order ruling the unfolding of trace forms
	pp. 89-90	Simple manifestations of harmony: establishing equilibrium through symmetry of movement
	p. 108	Laws of Golden Section and the proportionality of structures of body and icosahedron
	p. 122	Spatial harmony as the basic experience in dance
	p. 153	Sequential laws

B. Choreutic Forms – Scales, Rings

1920: *Die Welt des Tänzers*	p. 25	Edges of tetrahedron formed by linking directions of four stretched limbs into two spatial tensions which lie across one another.
	p. 23	Dimensional planes (3)

Table 3 89

Table 3   (Cont'd.)

B. Choreutic Forms — Scales, Rings

1926: *Choreographie*	pp. 24-25	Swing scales [Dimensional scale]
	pp. 29-34	A & B scales
	pp. 36-39	Four-rings [Two rings]
	pp. 40-41	Three-rings
	pp. 43-46	Axis & Equator scales
	pp. 49-53	Volutes
1939/66: *Choreutics*	pp. 37-42	Defence-sequence [Dimensional scale]
	p. 71	Peripheral standard scale
	p. 74	Steep, flowing, flat inclinations
	p. 76	Peripheral & transversal triangles [three-rings]
	pp. 78-82	Transversal standard scale
	p. 141	Planes in three dimensions
	pp. 182-184	Five-rings
	pp. 185-187	Seven-rings (pheripheral)
	pp. 193-4	Seven-rings (mixed)
1948: *Modern*	p. 27	Scales & shapes of the path of movement
Educational Dance	pp. 87-89	Structuring of closed circuits: scales and rings

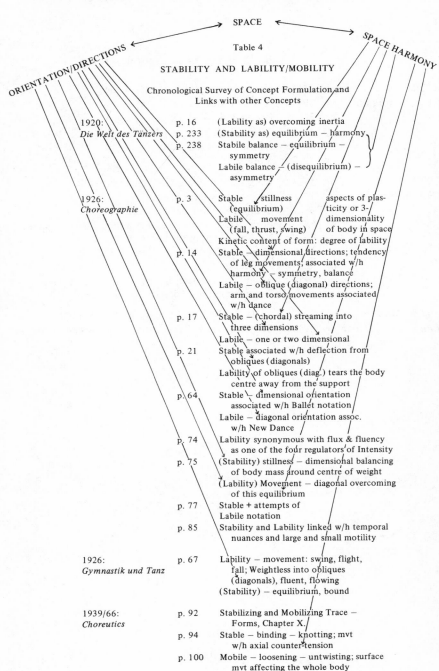

SPACE

Table 4

STABILITY AND LABILITY/MOBILITY

Chronological Survey of Concept Formulation and
Links with other Concepts

ORIENTATION/DIRECTIONS

SPACE HARMONY

1920: *Die Welt des Tänzers*	p. 16	(Lability as) overcoming inertia
	p. 233	(Stability as) equilibrium — harmony
	p. 238	Stabile balance — equilibrium — symmetry
		Labile balance — (disequilibrium) — asymmetry
1926: *Choreographie*	p. 3	Stable stillness (equilibrium) aspects of plasticity or 3-dimensionality of body in space
		Labile movement (fall, thrust, swing)
		Kinetic content of form: degree of lability
	p. 14	Stable — dimensional directions; tendency of leg movements, associated w/h harmony — symmetry, balance
		Labile — oblique (diagonal) directions; arm and torso movements associated w/h dance
	p. 17	Stable — (chordal) streaming into three dimensions
		Labile — one or two dimensional
	p. 21	Stable associated w/h deflection from obliques (diagonals)
		Lability of obliques (diag.) tears the body centre away from the support
	p. 64	Stable — dimensional orientation associated w/h Ballet notation
		Labile — diagonal orientation assoc. w/h New Dance
	p. 74	Lability synonymous with flux & fluency as one of the four regulators of Intensity
	p. 75	(Stability) stillness — dimensional balancing of body mass around centre of weight
		(Lability) Movement — diagonal overcoming of this equilibrium
	p. 77	Stable + attempts of Labile notation
	p. 85	Stability and Lability linked w/h temporal nuances and large and small motility
1926: *Gymnastik und Tanz*	p. 67	Lability — movement: swing, flight, fall; Weightless into obliques (diagonals), fluent, flowing
		(Stability) — equilibrium, bound
1939/66: *Choreutics*	p. 92	Stabilizing and Mobilizing Trace — Forms, Chapter X.
	p. 94	Stable — binding — knotting; mvt w/h axial counter-tension
	p. 100	Mobile — loosening — untwisting; surface mvt affecting the whole body

Table 5   91

Table 5

CORRELATION OF DYNAMICS OF MOVEMENT ITS SPATIAL PLACEMENT AS PRESENTED
IN CHOREOGRAPHIE AND CHOREUTIC[94]

	Choreographie (1926)		*Choreutics* (1939/66)
Four regulators of Intensity		Three basic Dynamic Traits	
FORCE	The gathering of *force* leads *downwards*	FORCE	*Strength*, firmness is correlated with the tendency *downwards*
	If the body stretches *high*, there is a state of *weakness*		*Lightness*, losing strength is correlated with a tendency *upward*
SPACE	A *narrow* movement turns towards the *opposite* side of the body.	SPACE	A *straight*, *direct* movement is correlated with one leading to the lateral direction opposite to the moving part of the body
	A *far reaching extension* can be achieved with the body turning towards the *open* side		*Flexibility*, a roundabout movement is correlated with an opening outwards
TIME	Each *fast* movement is marked through the jerk of the middle of the body *backwards*	TIME	*Quick, sudden* movements are correlated with moving into a *backward* direction
	Slow movements are linked with arching and turning the body *fowards*		*Slowness* and *sustainment* are correlated with reaching into *forward* direction
FLUX	*Rigid* or *Stable* and *Static* movements are associated with *dimensional* directions		
	Mobile, *Labile* movements of fluency and flight are associated with *diagonal*, oblique directions		

Table 6

HARMONY OF MOVEMENT

Chronology of Concept Formulation and Sources

1920: *Die Welt des Tänzers*	p. 26	Harmony of gesture: correspondence between spatial direction and bodily tension
1926: *Choreographie*	pp. 74-76	Primary (direction & shape) and secondary (intensity) tendencies; Four regulators of intensity
1926: *Gymnastik und Tanz*	p. 17	Spatial directions are performed with differing temporal rhythm and muscular force
1939/66: *Choreutics*	pp. 27-36	Ch. III: Exploration of the Dynamosphere: the connnection between outer movement – path, and the mover's inner attitude – dynamic stress [Affinities]
	pp. 55-67	Ch. VI: Natural Sequences of the Dynamosphere: connection between motion – trace-forms, and emotion – shadow form; [Effort cube] Harmony between shape and dynamic sequences [Affinities]
1948: *Modern Educational Dance*	pp. 37-39	Themes concerned with the performance of Shapes and Efforts . . . . [Affinities]
1960: *The Mastery of Movement*	pp.134-137	Dynamic characteristics of high-medium-deep dancers
1973: General Information The Laban Art of Movement Centre	p. 5	Harmony of movement: the relationship of dynamic stress and spatial pattern

CHAPTER II

Development of Concepts of Dynamics, Eukinetics and Effort

A comparative analysis of Laban's German and English writings in the area of dynamic qualities of movement and dance reveals several interesting dimensions. The continuum of approaches to some components is juxtaposed to a change in points of view in others. Problems with terminology are emerging even before the attempts to translate or transpose the technical terminology from one language to another; some terms selected from the English language require additional interpretation. Furthermore written accounts of the oral tradition of Laban's concepts are examined to complete the missing links in his writings.

The following aspects are included in the discussion below: The Beginnings, Rhythm and Phrasing, Emergence of Eukinetics, The Concept of Effort and The Effort Theory, and A Summary in terms of the Correlation of Early Concepts to Concepts formulated in the 40's, 50's and 60's.

The Beginnings

The origins of what Laban later developed as a theory of Eukinetics and Effort can be found in all his German texts. Early references to tension or tensility (Spannung) and agglomeration or nucleation (Ballung) — in which "nucleation arises, lasts, vanishes and generates through this play of tension, the feel of time-space-force"[1] — show a general indication of movement dynamics with some specific movement components.

First attempts at classification are found in *Choreographie* and *Gymnastik und Tanz*. We have referred to Laban's analysis of characteristics of movement forms which he describes as their kinetic, dynamic, rhythmic, and metric content.[2] A further articulation of this area can be seen in the classification of the four regulators of intensity which govern the range of force, time, space, and flux or lability. The extreme polarities of:

force: weak — strong;
time: fast — slow:
space: near — far;
flux: rigid — mobile (flowing, centrifugal).[3]

In a further discussion of movement components, Laban writes:

> There are mainly three properties of movement which bring a certain relationship of proportionality to it. We name these three as basic properties of force, time, and space proportionality. Now we can also see a fourth property — fluency, which we are briefly going to call flux. While we saw in force, time, and space the contrasts of strong and light, slow and fast, wide and narrow we have in fluency the contrasts of bound and loosened or released.[4]

It appears that Laban assumed that the notion of movement properties in terms of space, time, and force are general knowledge, while the notion of fluency, flux, flow — with its contrasts of bound and released — seems to be his own observation arising from the concepts of the kinetic content of movement in terms of stability and lability.

The matter of qualitative and quantitative aspects of movement dynamics, as well as their coexistence, are suggested or implied. In his first book, Laban refers to the time duration of a gesture and describes the lively mood of a short bodily tension, and the heavier, weighty mood of a longer one.[5] The qualitative dimensions of time are further discussed in *Gymnastik und Tanz*:

> In our perception time is completely relative. Torturing tension feels endless, of long duration, and joyous tension, however, quickly vanishes. Half an hour feels three times as long in fearful anticipation than a whole hour in pleasant company.[6]

Spatial, temporal, and dynamic nuances of movement are also referred to as "quantitative phenomena" in which stability and lability play an important role.[7] Thus the holistic view of movement in terms of acknowledging the significance of its qualitative and quantitative dimensions is already announced in Laban's first writings.

Rhythm and Phrasing

The rhythm of alternating tension and release or relaxation (Anspannung — Abspannung) in movement was a significant aspect of body training in Laban's time. Ullmann reports that early on Laban developed exercises which were designed to train the body as an instrument of expression. These were built on "the principles of tension and relaxation (principles of strength and gravity)," and on other organic movements of the body.[8] Laban discusses these aspects of human movement in *Gymnastik und Tanz*:

> When we observe human movement we can notice first of all its regular change. It is a change between waxing and waning of the manifestations of force between tension and release which extends and contracts, lifts and sinks the body, which subjects all movement to a kind of pulsation, to breathing.[9]

The moving body is further seen as spatially contracting, gathering the movement energy toward the center in preparation (Anschwung) before it lashes, swings, thrusts out or gently glides into centrifugal exertion (Ausschwung) which is followed by a release of tension. Relaxation and tension are determined by various proportions of space, time, and force, as well as lability and stability: "Rhythm . . . unfolds at times more fluently, at others less so. Through that a tension and relaxation arises in the body which creates nuances of force."[10] Thus rhythm for the dancer is not only time duration divided through strong emphasis but equally a spatial and dynamic event of nuances and tensions. Max Terpis writes that Laban recognized the great expressive value of the whole range of nuances between extreme tension and total relaxation. "One could call it a dramatic area because tension and its release are actually dramatic events."[11]

In an overview of practical exercises following the table of contents in *Gymnastik und Tanz*, Laban incorporates tension and relaxation as well as rhythm within the following scheme:

I.   Body:
    A. Breath regulation
    B. Tension of force (tension-release/relaxation)
    C. Fluency
II. Space:
    D. Equilibrium
    E. Spatial Orientation
    F. Metrics (wide-narrow)
III. Expression:
    G. Rhythmics
    H. Dynamics
    I. Gesture[12]

This guideline for exercises shows Laban's comprehensive approach to movement and dance training as well as his view of a close link between considerations of energy (I. B, II. D, III. H) and bodily, spatial, and expressive dimensions.

A further articulation of Laban's view of rhythm as a temporal, spatial, and dynamic experience can be found in his later work. While *space-rhythm* consists in the alternative use of various directions resulting in various forms and shapes, *time-rhythm* is manifest in the division of the continuous flux of movement into parts of duration in time which can be either metrically regular or free, irregular. In associating time-rhythm with the *weight-rhythm* of accented and unaccented parts of movement sequences, Laban refers to six fundamental rhythms which have already been found in Greek metrics.[13]

Related to the area of rhythm is the consideration of phrasing of movement and dance. An implicit reference to this aspect of rhythm can be found in the following considerations:

Every movement has a *beginning* in *stillness*, a path which leads to a new *stillness* which is its *termination*. The path can be performed:
a) with an increase or decrease of force
b) with an increase or decrease of speed
c) with an increase or decrease of extension in space
d) with an increase or decrease of stability

This initial intensity (in force, speed, extension in space, and flight) can also be related to previous or consecutive movements in terms of increase or decrease. Movements which are performed without increase or decrease are thus always led at the same distance from the body, and with the same emphasis retaining the same muscular tension and speed, they appear mechanical, lifeless. The harmonious liveliness of movement requires a constantly fluent change of shades of intensity.[14]

Besides Laban's preference for the rhythm of change, one can discern from the above a classification of phrasing into movement sequences with even intensity, with increasing intensity, and decreasing intensity. The latter can be related to the "impulse" which is described as "a movement starting from the middle of the body, the centre of movement, and has mostly a thrust-like character."[15]

More information about this area can be gleaned from Martin Gleisner, in addition to Terpis and Ullmann. Gleisner refers to Laban's classification of three basic ways in which movement can be performed: with flowing swing, an impulsive outburst, and with tension.[16] This is corroborated by Terpis and Ullmann, the former referring to tensions-swings-impulses as Laban's most important dance concepts and Ullmann describing swing-tension-impulse as three typical kinds of movement underlying the mastery of a broad range of the flow of movement.[17] *Tension* is, according to Gleisner and Ullmann, a movement which is consciously guided and controlled, evolving mostly on a straight line, thus aiming at great precision of form. Terpis associates tensions with a central or peripheral guidance of the movement. Because tensions which lead into particular directions start from the diaphragm they are described as "centrifugal" or "centripetal" guidances, while movements which bypass the centre — leaving the dancer more objective or less involved — are called "peripheral" guidances. The flow of the *swing* is a curve which leads the body to and from various directions, Terpis continues. Its characteristic sequence is a rhythmic chain of a preparatory swing (Anschwung) followed by a main swing (Aufschwung) and its expiration which can coincide with its re-initiation. "Laban applies in his pedagogy pendular, circular, and figure-eight swings . . . . As an amusing aid he found the relationship of swings to arabic numerals (number swings) and sought among human characteristics (pride, hatred, joy, etc.) a corresponding formal expression in the swing directions."[18] Ullmann supports the fact of rhythmical repetition of swings which are fluent movements toward an aim on a curved or double curved pathway. Gleisner adds that the swing-like way of moving is most comfortable to the body when moving in spatial directions. The rhythm of the *impuse* is described by Gleisner and Ullmann as a movement with sudden ejection which fades away into relaxation; owing to its explosive nature it is the least formed movement of the three. Terpis cautions that impulses should be used economically to avoid a ridiculous or awkward effect; if brought into the flow of movement as initation or emphasis, the impulse can, however, be particularly expressive. These three types of movement occur in movement and dance intermixed in various ways; they can be classified and separated for the purpose of their mastery, maintains Gleisner.

Emergence of Eukinetics

Between the references from the 20's and Laban's 1947 publication of *Effort* (with Lawrence), there is an apparent gap of documentation about further developments of his concept of dynamics, particularly with regard to *Eukinetics*, a term Laban coined from the Greek words *Eu* — meaning good, and *Kinesis* — movement. One may speculate that he devised the term to differentiate his work from various Eurhythmic methods (discussed in Chapter V). In his *Choreutics*, he describes Eukinetics as a part of the study of choreutics in which the dynamic structure of movement can be determined.[19] He exemplifies traditional ways of describing basic forms of dynamic movement with the *battu*, *fouetté* and *glissé* of French ballet terminology which corresponds to thrusting, slashing, and gliding — descriptive terms which Laban used within the framework both of Eukinetics and Effort. In annotating *Choreutics* Ullmann writes that "Laban introduced this term many years ago when exploring the laws of harmony within kinetic energy."[20] Elsewhere she writes that Eukinetics as the theory of expression considers "the laws of harmony of movement from the point of view of the relationships between the various expressive qualities springing from an inner source."[21] She also differentiates Eukinetics as the theory of the expressive qualities of dance as distinct from Effort which deals with the theory of expressive qualities in human exertion that are visible in the rhythm of bodily movement.[22]

The absence of the term Eukinetics from Laban's 1926 publications is puzzling since in the information about his Choreographic Institute from the same year he refers to the "recorded eukinetic experience of all races and periods." In a subsequent prospectus of the Institute, Eukinetics is referred to as the practical theory of expression.[23] Laban defines Eukinetics as "good movement in terms of harmonious rules of dance" in the glossary of the

1928 publication of his system of notation.[24] Two of his student-collaborators, Dussia Bereska and Kurt Jooss, were particularly instrumental in discussing and elaborating Eukinetics with the master and frequently taught the subject.

It appears that further information about this significant area has to be gleaned from a few sources, such as four articles by Laban's assistant Gertrud Snell in 1929 and 1930, as well as from some school prospectuses and the oral tradition of Laban's teaching as it has been preserved and developed by his foremost pupil of that period, Kurt Jooss.

In her second article on "Fundamentals of a General Dance Theory," Snell writes that Choreology, the science of movement laws, consists of Choreutics and Eukinetics.[25] While Choreutics considers laws of structuring movement within the rhythm of forms, Eukinetics deals with the temporal and dynamic occurrences within the rendering of expression. Although time rhythm gains its clarity and meaning through weight emphasis, it is only the fusion of the three factors of movement — the sequentiality of time, strength of force, and extension in space, which gives movement the intended expression. The elements of the Time factor are *slow* and *fast*; of Force are *little* or *much* strength; of extension in Space are *central*, more narrow, and *peripheral* more wide movements. These elements underlie the "four most primitive modes of expression" which are conveyed in action verbs such as press, pull, slash and thrust, and can be transformed into light press, light pull, light slash and light thrust, thus giving the basis for the "eight basic effort actions" of the 1940's. The relationship of the centre of weight to the active limb is crucial in determining the spatial extension, i.e., in central, narrow movements the centre of weight moves with the gesture, whereas in peripheral, wide movements it pulls against the gesture. In another article on "The Science of Dance," Snell also describes Eukinetics as a choreographic theory which includes the spatial theory and a theory of the psychology of the dance content.[26] While summarizing Laban's classifications from the 1926 publications (referred to above), Snell's considerations also offer some information about the developments of Eukinetics as the theory of expressive qualities in dance.

Kurt Jooss incorporated the theory of Eukinetics as well as the theory of Choreutics into the syllabus of the dance department of the Folkwangschule in Essen (also affiliated with the Central School Laban). The prospectus from 1930 redefines Eukinetics and Choreutics as "the awakening and fostering of movement phantasy and expression; the study of harmonious movement sequences and their spatial and expressive relationship."[27] A further integration of Eukinetics (and Choreutics) into the dancer's training can be seen from the earlier mentioned prospectus of The Jooss-Leeder School of Dance in Dartington Hall, England: "[Eukinetics comprises] practical studies covering the entire sphere of dance expression: enriching and clarifying the expression-content of movement; cultivation of perfect presentation." While awaiting the appearance of some posthumous publications of writings by Jooss and Leeder, or interpretative works from some of their collaborators, we have to refer to selected parts of Jane Winearls' *Modern Dance: The Jooss-Leeder Method* (London: A.C. Black, 1958).

In her chapter on "Dynamics," Winearls refers to three basic elements of movement: energy, design, and speed. They are articulated into energy components: strong-light (tension), and heavy-soft (relaxation); design components: central (undulating), peripheral (undeviating); components of speed: quick (sudden), slow (sustained). The eight basic combinations or fundamental qualities resulting from combining three elements are: strong-central-slow, strong-central-quick, strong-peripheral-slow, strong-peripheral-quick, light-central-slow, light-central-quick, light-peripheral-slow, and light-peripheral-quick. Winearls further refers to transitions from one quality to another as a one, two, and three degree change.[28]

It appears that Winearls made some modifications of her source materials, such as adding some Effort terms to the original Eukinetic ones for elements of speed (sudden and sustained). She also omitted the terms for the eight qualities which were used in the Laban-Jooss-Bereska tradition of the 20's and 30's: *Gleiten*=gliding, *Schweben*=floating, *Druck*=press, *Zug*=wring, *Stoss*=thrust, *Schlag*=slash, *Schlottern*=dabbing and *Flattern*=flicking.[29]

The information gleaned from Snell and Winearls on matters of Eukinetics shows considerable concordance and provides a basic orientation within this theoretical framework which Laban further developed in the 40's and 50's. (See Table 7, p. 109, for overview of sources on concepts of Dynamics and Eukinetics.)

The Concept of Effort

Contrary to other key terms which Laban initially coined or selected from the German language, the term "Effort" was created and/or selected from the English.[30] The complexity of its intentional and unintentional connotations, however, requires some interpretative assistance.

Laban and Lawrence refer to Effort as mental and manual processes of individual people building up collective actions such as "cultural effort" and "industrial effort."[31] The term thus appears to be derived from the notion of human striving for values and human efforts for survival. As Efforts are visibly expressed in the rhythms of bodily movement, the authors propose to study movement rhythms in order to extract from them those elements which will help in forming a systematic survey of Effort manifestations in human action. The most significant carriers of rhythmic movement are phenomena such as children's play, mime, dance, and work. While *Effort* focusses on movement rhythms in work and industry, *Modern Educational Dance* proposes a new dance education or a "free dance technique" based on the study of Effort rhythms. *The Mastery of Movement on the Stage* and subsequent editions of *The Mastery of Movement* elaborate on Effort expression in mime, acting, and dance. Hence the presentation of the concept of Effort in the above books shows some variations in approaches, descriptions, and classifications.

Examining Laban's presentation of the concept from the point of view of its holistic dimensions, including the qualitative and quantitative aspects as well as mental and physical components of Effort, one finds that they differ from one book to the other. In *Effort* the distinction between qualitative and quantitative aspects of movement rhythms is predominantly implicit. Its Chapter VI, however, considers "Psychological Components of Effort Control," where the two polar attitudes of "indulgence in" and "fighting against" all four motion factors of space, time, weight, and flow are highlighted and associated with the ease or struggle of various activities. Furthermore, the phases of attention, intention, decision, and precision in the context of an action are discussed, thus accounting for the link between mental and physical components of movement.[32] In *Modern Educational Dance* Laban explicitly points out that "Effort is the common denominator for the various strivings of body and mind."[33] Referring to Effort training, Laban states that it involves the bodily performance connected with mental assimilation of the underlying rules of Effort – coordination, which aims at a proportioned use of a number of different Efforts.[34]

In the first edition of *The Mastery of Movement on the Stage*, Laban refers to Effort as the inner impulse from which movement originates.[35] The second edition, titled *The Mastery of Movement*, includes several elaborations on the mental and physical strands of Effort. A further analysis of Effort elements distinguishes their two components – the one which is operative and objectively measurable and the other which is subjective and *classifiable*. The combinations of the latter are referred to as movement sensations giving psychosomatic experiences both to the performer and the observer.[36] Most significant is Laban's correlation of the attitudes towards motion factors and the various levels of consciousness. Attitudes towards *space* are associated with attention and man's power to *thinking*, attitudes towards *weight* with intention and with *sensing*, attitudes towards *time* with decision and *intuiting*, and attitudes toward *flow* with progression and *felling*.[37] Here the link between Effort and the human faculties of perceiving reality are clearly stated.[38]

Drawing from Laban's presentations in the books discussed, one may conclude that the concept of Effort unifies the actual, physical, quantitative, and measurable properties of movement with the virtual, perceivable, qualitative, and classifiable qualities of movement and dance. Implicit in the concept is the human faculty of perceiving reality which leads to various modes of experience and to externalized activities. This is expressed in the fundamental concept of mental or inner attitudes of resisting or accepting the physical conditions influencing movement or fighting against or contending with the motion factors of *space, weight, time,* and *flow* in both a qualitative and quantitative manner. These choices create a polarity of opposing Effort elements of *direct* versus *flexible/indirect, strong* versus *light, sudden* versus *sustained,* and *bound* versus *free.* It is interesting to note that when Laban refers to the polarity of resisting and accepting in the context of mime, he presents it as deriving from the psychological attitudes of hate and love.[39] Polarity is also visually expressed in the design of the Effort graph which facilitates the descriptive or prescriptive application of Effort observation and training (see Figures 11-13, p. 108).[40] The attitudes of accepting or resisting may not always be consciously and voluntarily exercised but can also be applied unconsciously and automatically.[41] Thus the potential variety of dynamic qualities of movement arises from the innumerable variety of the moving person's situations and/or actions, and therefore varies the choices among attitudes of accepting or resisting which may be deliberate or not. Taking an example from classical ballet, the dancer's *grand jeté* (leap covering a great distance) could described as direct, sudden and free (space, time, flow), while an adagio *port des bras* (arm gestures or carriage) could be described as light and bound (weight and flow).

The Effort Theory

In its performance, every human movement engages all four factors of motion — space, weight, time, and flow — in a more or less active or clear fashion. There is no movement which does not evolve in space as well as time, bringing the weight of the body into flow.[42] The particular emphases or selections of attitudes from the four factors of motion either make up what Laban calls the characteristic effort patterns of a person or are required by the sequence of particular activities. Thus the patterning or sequencing of Effort can be seen as macrostructures resulting from idiosyncratic microstructures of Effort combinations. In summarizing the Effort theory we will have to keep in mind their interdependence: in other words, while studying the following microstructures of the various Effort emphases or of Effort combinations, we have to remember that their full significance and/or meaning emerges only when they are related to what precedes and what follows within the composition or the structure of the whole movement event.

1. One movement quality seldom appears in isolation. A predominance of variation within *one factor of motion*, however, may be observed indicating a particular preference:

— The emphasis on attitudes towards *space* in its qualitative sense of directing the focus of movement or giving it a multi-focussed, flexible quality can be associated with the cognitive capacities of orienting, *attending*, and organizing. Its mastery can give clarity to a dance execution, both in the dancer's alignment and his/her relation to the environment.

— The predominance of *weight* qualities (strong and light, including the variables of weak, heavy, weighty, resilient) may indicate a *sensing* or sensibility for assuming light or firm *intentions* for action. The control of various muscular tensions creates an appearance of the bodily consciousness of the dancer in the intent of his/her movement performance.

— A great frequency of *time* qualities may indicate an *intuitive* readiness for *decision* making, either suddenly or with sustainment. Its mastery gives an alert, nervy effect to dance performance.

— The emphasis on *flow* can be associated with the emergence of *feelings* which according to the interaction with self and/or others binds or frees the continuity of movement and gives a dance either a controlled and careful or exuberant and outgoing progression.[43]

2. Further specifications of movement qualities depend on their association with other qualities. *Combinations of two qualities* denoting inner attitudes, moods, or states are observable in transitions between actions and are frequently elaborated in dance:

— While the combination of *weight and time* elements (of sensing and intuiting) create a rhythmical, earthy, *near* mood or attitude, its opposite associations of *space and flow* elements (of thinking and feeling) give a more abstract, *remote* mood or attitude.

— Whereas the associations of *space and time* elements (of thinking and intuiting) create an alert, *awake* attitude, its opposite combinations of *weight and flow* (of feeling and sensing) are more *dreamlike*, unaware.

— While the combination of *flow and time* (feeling and intuiting) can create a *mobile*, adaptable attitude, its opposite associations of *space and weight* (thinking and sensing) are likely to produce a *stable*, steadfast attitude. Each of the six combinations has a potential for four variations: the combinations of weight and time include, for example, light & free, strong & bound, strong & free, and light & bound variations. There are thus twenty-four distinct qualities within this range to which Laban refers as "incomplete efforts" or inner attitudes.[44]

3. The combinations or associations of *three movement qualities* bring about more intense and pronounced movement expressions which are referred to as *drives*:

— The *action drive* combines *space, weight,* and *time* elements (thinking, sensing, and intuiting), while flow (feeling) remains latent. The eight possible combinations of the above elements are also described as "basic effort actions" of thrusting-floating, pressing-flicking, gliding-slashing, and dabbing-wringing. As referred to above, several terms denoting the vocabulary of classical ballet derive from the description of the quality of performance. *Battu* or thrusting is a direct, strong, and sudden gesture, while *glissé* has a direct, light, and more sustained quality.

— When the flow factor replaces qualities of space, the action may transform into a more emotionally stressed drive also referred to as a *passion drive*. It includes the eight possible combinations of *weight, time,* and *flow* (sensing, intuiting, and feeling) which override the clarity of spatial placement and shaping (thinking).

— When the flow factor is substituted for the weight factor the movement may change into a more weightless *vision-like drive*; its eight possible combinations of *space, time,* and *flow* (thinking, intuiting, and feeling) override the bodily import (sensing).

— When the flow factor replaces time qualities, the movement transforms into a timeless *spell-like drive*; its eight possible combinations of *space, weight,* and *flow* (thinking, sensing, and feeling) override the sense for timing (intuiting).

As shown above, each of the four drives has a potential for eight variations, which provide for thirty-two more qualities.[45]

4. The maximum of intensity is achieved in some exceptional performances when all *four factors* are clearly present in a so-called *complete effort action*. The combination of *space, weight, time,* and *flow* allows for an additional sixteen distinct variations.[46]

All the seventy-two qualities listed can be further articulated in several ways. They may be performed with a greater concentration or clarity on one of the components; this differentiation is referred to as *ranking*.[47] On the other hand, the effort combinations may be varied through *grading* of the intensity of the performance which can be diminished or exaggerated to provide for a vast number of variations. The ranking and the grading can also occur together.[48]

The significance of particular qualities emerges within the macrostructure, the context of a movement sequence, and these qualities gain meaning when they are related to what precedes and what follows. Thus the sequencing, phrasing, or the rhythm of effort sequences is identifiable from several points of view:

a) how particular qualities build up with regard to the optimal sequence of attention (space), intention (weight), decision (time), and precision or progression (flow).[49]

b) how effort qualities change into another quality; these mutations can occur either gradually with the change of one element, more surprisingly with the change of two, or they can be contrasted with the change of all elements.[50]

c) what the compositional pattern of the sequence is, such as repetition, rebounding, contrasts, variations, development.

d) whether the effort sequence is performed with the whole body being attuned to it or whether different qualities are performed at the same time by different body parts.

As indicated above, Effort observation and training can be geared either towards its descriptive or its prescriptive application according to its purpose.

Summary in Terms of Correlation of the Early Concepts to Concepts Formulated in the 40's and 50's

The early classification of the characteristics of movement forms can be seen as the precursor of the four motion factors formulated in the 40's: the early kinetic components correspond to the later motion factor of flow, the dynamic component corresponds to the factor of weight, rhythmic to time, and metric to space.[51] This kinship is even more manifest in elaborations of the four regulators of the intensity of force, time, space, and flux, and their polarities.[52] The search for terminology or its disregard can be seen in the fact that Laban names the above phenomena as movement properties in another book published at the same time.[53] Thus what would become *motion factors* is called interchangeably the *characteristics of movement forms*, the *four movement properties*, and the *four regulators of intensity*. The motion factor of Flow is referred to as the kinetic component and further *flow/flux* and *fluency*; *Weight* as the *dynamic component* and *force*; Time as the *rhythmic component* and *time*; Space as the *metric component* and *space*. Terminology indicating polarities of the motion factors also show some variation: what in the 40's was labeled as the *effort elements* was referred to in the 20's as the *extreme polarities* and the *contrasts*.

This comparison shows, on one hand, that terms used in the 20's are more descriptive of Laban's process of classification, whereas the later English words constitute a more hermetic technical terminology. On the other hand, the comparison displays the continuum of Laban's views of weight and time, his change of approach to space, and his special treatment of flow. The initial quantitative approach to *space* as a metric component changed in the 40's to a qualitative focus on attention. This can best be seen from the correlation of the polarities of Effort elements. While the measurable aspect of *narrow, near* movement, which is directed towards the opposite side of the body, gains its qualitative aspect of a *direct* focus, the *wide*, far reaching extension achieved through the body turning towards the open side gains a qualitative aspect of "everywhereness" or *flexible* approach. The English term *flexible* does not fully capture the three-dimensionality of the movement which is better expressed in the descriptive word "every-whereness." (The placement of the movement on the closed and open side of the body is referred to in Laban's presentation of affinities discussed on pages 77-78, and 91 of this text.) Another transformation of the spatial elements can be found within the framework of Eukinetics where the earlier near/narrow-far/wide polarity became *central* or *peripheral*.[54]

The conceptualization of the *flow* factor is of particular interest. Laban appears to have formulated the notion of fluency, flux, or flow from the kinetic content of movement where stability tends to be associated with rigid or bound flow and lability with mobile, flowing, or released flow.[55] The polarities of *rigid, bound*, and *mobile, flowing, dissolved* are, however, congruous with the elements of *bound* and *free* in the 40's. The factor of flow disappeared from the framework of Eukinetics where time, strength or force, and space elements constitute the "four most primitive modes of expression."[56] It is also interesting that in the 20's the aspect of flow or flux was included in the correlations of the dynamic and spatial aspects of movement; its polarities are associated with the dimensional and diagonal orientation, i.e., the rigid or static aspect of flow is associated with dimensional directions, and the mobile aspect is associated with diagonal directions. The flow factor as a separate consideration is left out in the 30's.[57] In Laban's English books, flow surfaces again with a seemingly ambiguous status. It is at times referred to as the control of weight, space, time and exertion, and at others as one of the four motion factors.[58] It is also discussed with regard to the initiation of movement and its articulation through the body.[59]

While Laban's formulation of his concepts and theory of the dynamic qualities of movement gained a greater clarity as well as complexity in the 40's and particularly the 50's, some of his early formulations are, not unlike his early terminology, more indicative of his process of observation. This can be exemplified by comparing his first formulation of the correlation of the movement dynamics and its placement in space referred to earlier.[60] While in *Choreutics* the description of strength connected with the stance and correlated with the downward tendency is merely a statement of fact,[61] the earlier description in *Choreographie* about the gathering of force which leads to bodily contraction and draws downwards to the support provides for greater kinesthetic participation.[62] On the other hand, descriptions of other elements in both sources are complementary. A quick movement, for instance, which in the 20's is associated with narrowness and marked by a jerk of the body moving backwards, is later elucidated through references to retracting bodily contractions as in a jerk of fright[63] (See also Table 5).

Notes to Chapter II

1. *Die Welt des Tänzers*, p. 12.
2. See Introduction to Part Two.
3. Cf. *Choregraphie*, p. 74.
4. *Gymnastik und Tanz*, pp. 67-68.
5. Cf. *Die Welt des Tänzers*, p. 56.
6. *Gymnastik und Tanz*, p. 72.
7. Cf. *Choreographie*, p. 75.
8. Lisa Ullmann, "My Apprenticeship with Laban," *The Laban Art of Movement Guild Magazine*, No. 63, 1979, p. 27.
9. *Gymnastik und Tanz* , p. 48.
10. Ibid., p. 73.
11. Max Terpis, *Tanz und Tänzer*, p. 95.
12. Op. cit., after p. 176.
13. Cf. *The Mastery of Movement on the Stage*, pp. 130-135.
14. *Choreographie*, pp. 75-76.
15. Ibid., p. 39.
16. Cf. Martin Gleisner, *Tanz für Alle*, pp. 100-101.
17. Cf. Ullmann, "My Apprenticeship with Laban," *The Laban Art of Movement Guild Magazine*, No. 63, 1979, p. 27, and Terpis, *Tanz und Tänzer*, pp. 94-97.
18. Terpis, p. 97.
19. Cf. Op. cit., p. 30.
20. Ibid., footnote.
21. Lisa Ullmann, "My Apprenticeship with Laban," p. 28.
22. Cf. Letter from Lisa Ullmann to Kurt Jooss, March 1977 (Laban Archives).
23. Cf. Prospectus of the Choreographic Institute Laban from 1927/28.
24. "Erläuterungen" *Schrifttanz*, 1928, p. 19.
25. Cf. *Schrifttanz*, Heft II., 1929, pp. 21-24.
26. *Die Schönheit*, II, 1926, pp. 64-67.
27. Prospectus of "The Dance School Jooss – Central School Laban."
28. Cf. Op. cit., pp. 85-87, 1978 publication.
29. Personal communication with Ana Maletic who studied with Jooss in Dartington Hall, summer 1934. It is also interesting to find that Laban's musical collaborator Rudolf Wagner-Regeny in his article "Neue Grundzüge der Musikalischen Theorie als Ergebnis der Schrifttanzforschung" (*Schrifttanz*, Heft I, 1928, pp. 13-15) describes gestures of *Zug, Stoss* and *Schlag* (p. 13).
30. Responding to A. Maletic's enquiry about translating the term Effort into Croato-Serbian Laban wrote: "The translation of the word 'effort' is enormously difficult, and I always advise people, whatever language

they speak, to use simply 'effort' and to explain its meaning as best as they can. The Germans have tried to say 'Antrieb' but I don't think this is a good rendering of the idea." (Letter from 12-3-1951).

31. Cf. *Effort*, Preface, x.
32. Cf. Op. cit., pp. 54-67.
33. Op. cit., p. 18.
34. Cf. Ibid., p. 51.
35. Cf. Op. cit., p. 23.
36. Cf. Op. cit., pp. 78-80.
37. Cf. Op. cit., pp. 85, 120-121.
38. As will be referred to in Chapter V, Laban's reference to thinking, sensing, intuiting, and feeling, coincides with Jung's dvision of consciousness.
39. Cf. *The Mastery of Movement* (1960 ed.), p. 116.
40. Cf. *Effort*, p. 58.
41. Cf. *The Mastery of Movement* (1960 ed.), p. 24; see Figures 11-13.
42. Cf. *Effort*, p. 58, and *The Mastery of Movement* (1960), pp. 22-24.
43. Cf. *The Mastery of Movement* (1960), pp. 120-212.
44. Cf. Ibid., pp. 82-84.
45. Cf. Ibid., pp. 84-85.
46. Cf. *The Mastery of Movement* (1980 ed.), p. 182.
47. Cf. *Effort*, pp. 26-42, *The Mastery of Movement* (1980 ed.), pp. 170-172.
48. Cf. *The Mastery of Movement* (1980 ed.), pp. 173-175.
49. Cf. *The Mastery of Movement* (1960 ed.), pp. 121-122.
50. A helpful visual aid for devising transitions among basic effort actions is the scaffolding of the cube. According to Laban's theory of affinities between the dynamic and spatial components of movement, each of the eight corners of the cube corresponds to the spatial placement of one of the eight basic effort actions; the over the edge transitions thus create sequences with changes of one element, across the planes of the cube produces sequences with changes of two elements, and the diagonal transitions through the cube embody opposites. Cf. *Effort*, pp. 18-26, and *Modern Educational Dance*, pp. 33-34.
51. Cf. *Choreographie*, pp. 3-5, and *Effort*, p. 5.
52. Cf. *Choreographie*, p. 74.
53. Cf. *Gymnastik und Tanz*, p. 68.
54. Cf. p. 98 of this Chapter.
55. Cf. p. 55 of this Chapter.
56. Cf. p. 98 of this Chapter.
57. Cf. Table 5.
58. Cf. *The Mastery of Movement* (1960 ed.), p. 81, and *Effort* pp. 8-12.
59. Cf. *The Mastery of Movement*, pp. 21-22.
60. Cf. Table 5.
61. Cf. *Choreutics*, p. 31.
62. Cf. *Choreographie*, p. 74.
63. Cf. *Choreographie*, p. 75, and *Choreutics*, p. 31.

The Effort Graph

representing the four
Motion Factors
W = Weight,
T = Time,
S = Space,
F = Flow
each with their two Elements:

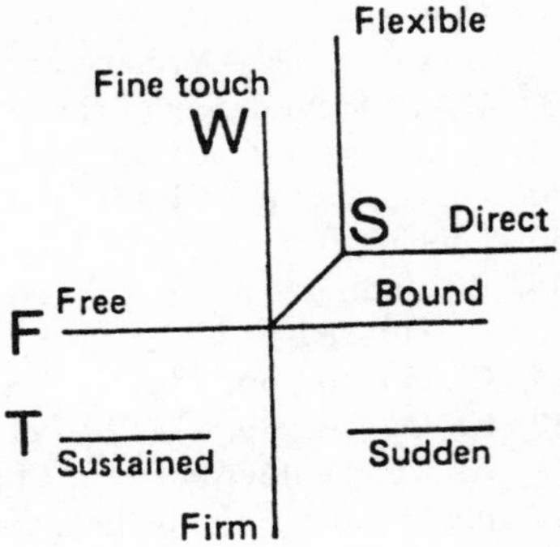

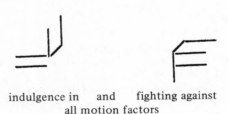

Figure 11 *

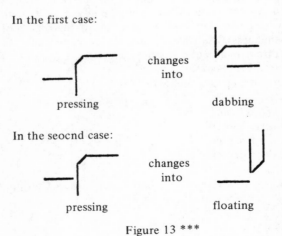

indulgence in   and   fighting against
all motion factors

Figure 12 **

In the first case:

pressing   changes
into   dabbing

In the seocnd case:

pressing   changes
into   floating

Figure 13 ***

*From *The Mastery of Movement* (1960 ed) p. 81; **From *Effort* p. 58;
***Ibid. p. 22

Table 7   109

Table 7

THEORY
of
DYNAMICS – EUKINETICS

Chronology of Concept Formulation & Sources

1920: *Die Welt des Tänzers*	p. 12	Spannung & Ballung – tensility & nucleation of space-time-force
	p. 56	Time perception
1926: *Choreographie*	pp. 3-5	Kinetic (degree of lability), dynamic (degree of force), rhythmic (degree of speed), & metric (degree of extension) content of movement forms
	p. 74	Intensity range of force, time, space, flux (lability) Polarities: weak-strong (force) fast-slow (time) near-far (space) rigid-mobile (flux, lability)
	p. 75	Spatial-temporal-dynamic nuances of movement and stability-lability as quantitative phenomena
1926: *Gymnastik und Tanz*	pp. 48-49	Tension & relaxation determined by proportions of space-time-force-lability/stability
	pp. 67-68	Three basic properties of movement + one: force, time, space + fluency/flux proportionalities; strong-light, narrow-wide, slow-fast, bound-released
	p. 70	Rhythm
	p. 72	Time perception
	Appendix	I. B. Tension of force (tension-relase/relaxation) C. Fluency II. F. Metrics (wide-narrow) III. G. Rhythmics H. Dynamics
1926: *Prospectus of Choreographic Institute Laban*		Recorded Eukinetic experience
1927/28: *Prospectus of Choreographisches Institut Laban*		Eukinetics as practical theory of expression
1930: *Prospectus of Laban Central School/Dance School Jooss,* Folkwangschule, Essen		Eukinetics & Choreutics as the awakening and fostering of the movement imagination and expression; the study of harmonious movement sequences and their spatial and expressive relationships.
1939/66: *Choreutics* p. 30		Eukinetics as part of Choreutics dealing with dynamic structure of movement.

Table 8

EFFORT

I. Description of the Term

1947: *Effort*	p. x	Effort – cultural . . . industrial
	p. xi	Efforts – visibly expressed in the rhythm of a person's bodily motion
1948: *Modern Educational Dance*	p. 18	Effort – common denominator for the various strivings of body & mind
1950: *The Mastery of Movement of the Stage*	p. 23	Effort: inner impulse from which movement originates
1960: *The Mastery of Movement*	p. 24	Effort: origin and inner aspect of movement

II. Motion Factors

1947: *Effort*	p. 4	Motion factors (3): weight, space, time & the control of flow
	p. 5	Factors of motion (3): weight, space & time, and their controlled flow
	pp. 8-4	Exertion: weight, space, time Control: flow
	p. 57	Four motion factors
1948: *Modern Educational Dance*	p. 34	Table: weight, space, time
1950: *The Mastery of Movement of the Stage*	p. 22 p. 117	Natural accidents: weight, space, time (flow) Motion factors (4): weight, space, time, flow
1960: *The Mastery of Movement*	p. 23 pp. 74-75	Motion factors/natural accidents: weight, space, time (flow) Motion factors: weight, space, time, flow

III. Attitudes

1947: *Effort*	p. 54	Easy effort – indulging & stressed effort-struggling/fighting against
	p. 58	Indulgence in & fighting against motion factors

Table 8   111

Table 8   (Cont'd.)

III. Attitudes

1950: *The Mastery* *of Movement* *of the Stage*	p. 13 p. 22 p. 177	Effort attitudes Fighting against & indulgence in Attitudes toward motion factors of weight, space, time, flow resulting in 8 effort elements
1960: *The Mastery* *of Movement*	p. 23	Attitudes of ↗resisting, constricting, with- holding, fighting ↘yielding, enduring, accepting, indulging
	pp. 75-81	Mental attitudes

IV. Effort elements

1947: *Effort*	pp. 20-22 pp. 8-12	reference to effort elements light-strong; fluent-bound; flexible-direct; sustained-quick
1948: *Modern* *Educational Dance*	p. 8 p. 45	Effort elements are attitudes of the moving person towards the motion factors weight, space, time & flow Strong or light; direct or flexible; quick or sustained; bound or fluent
1950: *The Mastery* *of Movement* *of the Stage*	p. 117	8 Elements of movement: light-strong; flexible-direct; sustained-quick; fluent-bound
1960: *The Mastery* *of Movement*	p. 82	Effort elements (table) firm-gentle; sudden-sustained; direct-flexible; bound-free

V. Ranking and Grading

1947: *Effort*	pp. 26-31	One of the three elements can be stressed — derivatives of basic efforts
1980: *The Mastery* *of Movement*	pp. 170-172 pp. 173-175	Ranks: concentration on one of the effort elements Grades: of intensity — more or less than normal

Table 8   (Cont'd.)

VI. Combinations of Motion Factors/Effort Elements

1947: *Effort*	p. 15	Eight basic combinations of W S T exertions: slashing-gliding, pressing-flicking, wringing-dabbing, punching-floating
1948: *Modern Education Dance*	pp. 51-74	Eight basic actions
1960: *The Mastery of Movement*	pp. 82-84	Incomplete Efforts/Inner Attitudes
	p. 121	S & T awake W & F remote W & T near S & W stable T & F mobile
	pp. 84-85	Drives/Movement Drives
	p. 121	S & T & W Action F & T & W Passion S & F & W Spell S & T & F Vision
	pp. 75-77	Basic Effort Actions: thrusting, dabbing, pressing, slashing, floating, wringing, flicking, gliding.
	p. 121	Table VII. Space-Attention-Thinking Weight-Intention-Sensing Time-Decision-Intuiting Flow-Progression-Feeling

VII. Transitions & Mutations

1947: *Effort*	pp. 20-23	Changes with one, two or three elements
1948: *Modern Educational Dance*	pp. 33-35	Themes concerned with combinations of the eight basic actions
1950: *The Mastery of Movement of the Stage*	pp. 128-29	Transitions
1960: *The Mastery of Movement*	pp. 119-20	Transitions

CHAPTER III

Formation of Laban's Movement and Dance Notation Principles

Introduction

The development of movement and dance notation had a central place among Laban's endeavors to find common denominators to all human movement and to place dance on an equal footing with other art forms. In an early article titled "Symbole des Tanzes und Tanz als Symbol" ("Symbols of Dance and Dance as Symbol"), he argues that no temporal art can achieve a full development without a notation which can capture, preserve, and examine its ephemeral creations. Therefore a dance notation has to develop from the knowledge of the dance, and its symbols will derive from the symbology of dance forms and spatial rhythms, rather than from any extraneous sources.[1] Drawing an analogy with the development of poetry and music, inconceivable if based only on oral tradition, Laban writes: "it is necessary to determine the symbols of dance in writing because a tradition which will make possible a deeper evaluation of artistic achievements in dance, can only arise from comparison and examination, repetition and recreation."[2] Laban further emphatically states that "the entire history of the art of movement is also the history of striving for a dance notation in which the dancer sees much more than a useful tool for his professional education. If this art [notation] would have been practiced in previous centuries we would have today an insight into the earlier movement forms and endeavors in our field."[3] In another analogy with poetry and music Laban exclaims: "Only when dance becomes a language of choreographic will, only when it finds its own notation . . . can it offer, as an equal among the arts, . . . what its sister arts music and poetry offer. . . joy, exhilaration, meaning, strength, and culture."[4]

A brief critical survey of the development of movement and dance notation prefaced Laban's lecture demonstration of his own method at the 1928 second German Dance Congress in Essen.[5] Without naming individual systems he presented three basic approaches to notation. The first one consisted of the description of movement by signs, such as words, letters or numbers.

Such a notation indeed presupposes knowledge of the movement vocabulary on the part of its users. "I went through this phase too," Laban said referring to the numbering of his spatial scales.[6] In the discussion of the second approach, namely that of a pictorial notation, Laban accounts for his studies of old music manuscripts in the library of St. Gallen (Switzerland) in which wave-like coloring over the notation indicated the rise and fall of the melody as a representation of the conductor's movement. The limitation of a pictorial notation which included designs of parts or of the entire body and stick figures lies in the fact that "it was necessary to penetrate into the author's way of thinking in order to unite the psychic happening with outside events."[7] The third approach, which Laban fostered, consists in the articulation of movement into basic elements which can be indicated with symbols and their combinations graphically represented. "This appears . . . the most fruitful [approach] because everybody is in the position to draw the necessary material [of symbols] for any purpose which he can think of in the art of dance and in movement research . . . ."[8]

But before Laban formed his system of notation, "years of struggle were filled with the study of ancient movement symbols, with experiments and with controversial discussions."[9] He considered musical notation an important model because it gives the image of musical movement by means of its symbols for the harmonic relations of sounds, for rhythmic-dynamic sequences, and for expressive execution.[10] The most significant influence, however, was that of the seventeenth and eighteenth century French system invented by Beauchamps and published by Feuillet as *Chorégraphie ou L'art de décrire la Danse*. Laban honors his debt to the system by calling his book of the spatial analysis and first attempts of its notation *Choreographie*.

While Laban first refers to his notation, as well as to other systems as choreography (*Choreographie*), for its final form he coined in 1928 the term Kinetography (*Kinetographie*) from the Greek words *kinesis* — movement, and *graphein* — to write.[11] Two subterms were also used in the 1920's: dance-script (*Tanzschrift*) and script-dance (*Schrifttanz*). Both terms are pointed out by Laban and his collaborators. While dance-script is seen as a means for documentation and preservation of dance, script-dance should facilitate the act of dance composition itself. Laban thus maintains that "the ultimate artistic aim of kinetography is not dance-script but script-dance."[12] This is also announced in another statement about the purpose of notation in which Laban maintains that "a dance notation shall not only record and preserve man's spiritual or physical store of movement. The scope of dance notation must also include the representation of the immanent laws of movement in such a way that dance composition and the universal order of movement gain through it both a basis and a guide."[13]

This discussion indicates both the rationale behind Laban's system of notation and its nomenclature. Kinetography — movement notation — included dance-script and script-dance. (It is also significant that both the society and the quarterly magazine for the development of dance scores founded in 1928 took-up the name *Schrifttanz*.)[14] The later term "Labanotation" was proposed by the Dance Notation Bureau in New York and accepted by Laban. While Laban's notation is identified in Europe as Kinetography Laban, Ann Hutchinson's textbook *Labanotation* spread both the name and the system in America.[15]

The Emergence of the Principles of the System

In tracing the formation of the principles of Laban's notation, primary sources consist chiefly of his 1926 book *Choreographie* in general and the chapter "Schriftanleitungen" ("Directions for Writing") in particular. Further sources include Laban's booklet *Schrifttanz: Methodik, Orthographie, Erläuterungen* (*Script Dancing: Methodics, Orthography, Explanations*) published in 1928, and his two articles which appeared in the first two consecutive issues of *Schrifttanz*: "Grundprincipien der Bewegungsschrift" ("Fundamental Principles of Movement Notation"), and "Die Entwicklung der Bewegungsschrift Laban" ("The Development of Movement Notation Laban"). For comparative purposes an important reference book is Laban's 1956 *Principles of Dance and Movement Notation*.

In the introduction to *Choreographie*, Laban announces his intent to overcome the static description of bodily carriage and positions of classical ballet (as captured in the Beauchamps-Feuillet notation) with a dynamic approach emphasizing movement processes: "The intended result of conquering a notational possibility of dance movement in its contemporary freer and richer form is achieved. This notation should serve as a handy basis for practice and research."[16] The dual purpose of practice and research is illuminated from another view point in Laban's article on "Fundamental Principles of Movement Notation" (1928).[17] Here two distinct tasks of Kinetography Laban are specified. The one which deals with the preservation of movement sequences has for centuries already been recognized as important and is constantly aimed at with varying degrees of success. Laban, however, maintains that the other task "lying in the realm of the spiritual is far more important. It deals with making the movement event precise through analysis and freeing it from being blurred, which makes the language of dance appear on one hand unclear, and on the other monotonous."[18] Here the purpose of analysis is to enhance the art of dance composition.

In order to outline the first design of his notation in 1926, Laban determined the most important components of movement observation. As

referred to in the introduction to Part Two, they include the consideration of
the laterality and symmetry of the body, directions in relation to the vertical
constant, the plastic or three-dimensional shape of the moving body with
predominant stable or labile tendencies, and the consideration of movement
as a temporal sequence with a beginning, middle and end.

In the explanation of his fully formulated "fundamental" or "general"
principles of the system in 1928, Laban refers to the observation of the
flow of duration of movement which is associated with its spatial unfolding:

> The first clear distinction which we perceive in a movement event presents
> itself in the distinct observation of the flow of movement (time rhythm),
> on one hand, and of the plasticity of movement (spatial rhythm), on
> the other.[19]

The flow of movement is identified in this context with time rhythm and its
plasticity (three-dimensionality) with varying spatial directions which form
the spatial rhythm.[20]

Further significant differentiations in Laban's movement notation concern
the bilateral structure of the body and two different types of movement
sequencing. He maintains that in a *monolinear* movement sequence one body
part enters into action or moves after another; it is successive and can be
compared with the musical concept of melody. A *polylinear* movement
sequence, on the other hand, activates the movement of several limbs at the
same time with equal emphasis, not unlike a synchrony of several musical
parts in polyphonic music.

(a)

(b)

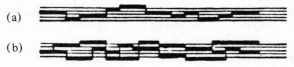

Figure 14. Mono- and Polylinear Sequences

Referring to the illustration of these two types (see Figure 14) Laban
comments on the ease of discerning "the Harmony of structural laws of
movement by means of this notation."[21] While example (a) shows one part
of the body (represented by the placement of the symbol in one of the
columns of the notational staff) moving after another in a monolinear fashion
or style, (b) indicates a polylinear sequence in which the movement of
different body parts either overlaps or is performed at the same time. Laban
refers to the latter as a chord. "The theory of movement harmony knows
about chords as in music."[22] (The matter of spatial chords of polylinear
nature and the predominantly monolinear principle of sequence have been
discussed in Chapter I.) Laban also sees polylinear movements as having
"different expressive possibilities such as an absolute synchrony or an over-
lapping duration of the movement of particular limbs."[23]

The observation of these two types of sequencing of bodily movement implies several other principles underlying the notation. In Laban's own words and examples:

Time rhythm is represented through longer and shorter lines, which correspond to the proportional duration of movement. For example:

By grouping [symbols] around a middle line one can clearly specify each particular movement of the right and left half of the body, as well as of particular limbs . . . .

. . . .

If we endow the symbol — which represents the reciprocal duration of the movement flow as performed by particular body parts — with a directional element, then the *spatial division* [articulation], or more exactly the picture of the spatial rhythm and directional harmony which holds the balance during the movement, is formed.

For this only three symbols or three variations of the duration are necessary, which indicate the various rules of all spatial directions as well as deviations, arches, and loops leading into particular directions.[24]

The three variations of the rectangular symbol indicating center or place are forward, sideways, and diagonal which by their reversals into the three symmetries (left-right, backward-forward, up-down) and additional shadings signifying three levels denote 27 main directions including place or the center.

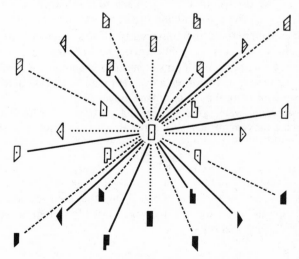

Figure 15. Symbols for 27 Main Directions

The directional orientation is taken from the front of the moving person and the line of gravity or the three dimensions (height, width and depth).[25] Related to the area of directional orientation is another of Laban's distinctions of movement styles (in addition to the mono- and polylinear discussed above) brought about by the predominant use of stabile — dimensional and labile — diagonal combinations of directions.[26] As discussed in previous chapters, the dimensional and diagonal spatial orientations play a significant role in Laban's considerations of the dynamics of movement in space, which is associated with stability and lability/mobility, as well as with particular Effort elements.

The above discussion of the emergence of the principles of Laban's notation show an oscillation between his initial intents. On the one hand, he aimed at a universal notation which would not be rooted in any style and period. On the other hand, Laban's initial considerations in inventing the dance notation are based on his theories of space harmony and to a certain extent on Eukinetics or the harmonics within the kinetic energy. This duality is commented on by Gertrud Snell, Laban's assistant during the 20's:

> Together with his movement and harmony theories, Laban continuously was thinking of a notation for writing dances. The ideal he sought was a kind of notation which should be independent from the laws of movement harmony, so that it could be useful for all kinds of movement. However, we did not get these for a long time.[27]

In the 30's Laban expressed yet another view of his notation as instrumental in a multilateral description of movement, viewing it from many angles. Such descriptions are a part of choreutics which is seen as comprehending all kinds of movements including those motivated by thought and emotion, as well as their notation.[28] Laban's comprehensive view of movement in terms of engaging the mind and the body is here apparent.

In the 50's, Laban took the universality of his sytem of notation for granted, arguing that a generally acknowledged and readable notation of movement, based on the combination of motion characters, is needed for all forms of dance, as well as for other movement studies.[29] He refers to motor elements which constitute the main bulk of movement:

> Just as poetry, in every language, can be written down phonetically, so every stylized movement can be written down "motorically." The motor movement notation is the equivalent of the alphabet.
>
> . . . .
>
> Our movement notation is based on the elementary motor principles of the human body and can be applied to a larger range of activities . . . .[30]

Laban refers to *our* notation, acknowledging the contribution of other persons in the development of the final version of his system, as will be discussed in the following section.

History of the System

A brief account of the development of symbols and of writing conventions may enhance the understanding of the process of Laban's theoretical thinking behind it. The crucial turning point appears to have arisen from the separation of Laban's notation from its initial integration with space harmony concepts. However, even before his elaborations in *Choreographie*, Laban went through various phases of searching.

Several statements by his student-collaborators point to the fact that Laban started his investigations very early, possibly around 1900 in Paris. Mary Wigman refers in the 20's to Laban's thirty years of struggle for dance notation as a rendering of "harmonic and organic movement relationships and processes."[31] Describing his collaboration with Laban in 1913 and 1914, writer Hans Brandenburg mentions the common preparation of a promotional brochure including the first attempts of Laban's movement notation; these were explained through a series of figures drawn by Brandenburg's wife.[32] Referring to the second and third edition of his book *Der Moderne Tanz* (The Modern Dance), Brandenburg writes: "Those knowledgeable in notation can find here the only presentation of Laban's first attempts in choreography [notation], and can thus follow his completed work from its beginnings."[33] In his description, Brandenburg refers more to principles than to writing conventions. He prefaces this with a brief historical perspective: "Laban's choreography [notation] arises not only from his rich personal experience, but also historically from old ballet choreographers, dance music, military tactics, from Delsarte and from modern dance. It originated from the . . . phenomenon of movement."[34] Accordingly the primary elements of movement consist of force, time and space effectuating in a network of directions. These can be seen as a sphere-like structure of varying size; Laban thus differentiates expansive, medium size and concentrated movements. As an indication of its various levels, he uses five vowels to denote forward, backward, right, left, etc. If a particular point, such as forward, is to be performed with the arm, it will result in the movement of the whole body. Following the laws of equilibrium, every movement requires a simultaneous countermovement from the body centre successively into its opposite point, as well as an unfolding into its main direction (i.e., torso, upper arm, lower arm, and hand moving forward). "Such a central concept of movement makes it the expression of an intent."[35] Although Brandenburg's interpretations have to be viewed critically, some basic concepts emerge here even before Laban's own first publications. Indicated are the notion of movement components such as force, space, time resulting in various directions, the concept of the sphere of movement and degrees of extension, and finally the body flow from the centre outward, as well as the principle of opposition. Brandenburg's reference to the five vowels indicating spatial direction, however, as well as his statement that "each movement evolves . . . in a staff within which one can determine its most important features" are vague.[36]

In Gertrud Snell's article "The Beginnings of Kinetography Laban," she accounts for the phase of Laban's explorations in the early 20's and refers to the search for symbols which would capture the three-dimensional icosahedral movements onto two-dimensional paper. Signs such as "swallow-tail writing" were used to denote particular movement characteristics of the space harmony scales, such as steep, flat, and flowing inclinations.[37]

Figure 16. Swallow-tail Writing

In the period of the publication of *Choreographie* (1924-26), the so-called "bodycross" (*Körperkreuz*) was used: the vertical line separates the right and left sides of the body, whereas the horizontal divides the upper from the lower body. However, instead of symbols, numbers pertaining to icosahedral directions can be found in most examples of this book.

Figure 17. Bodycross Writing

In the chapter "Directions for Writing," Laban states:

> In order to write movement we have to clarify three components of the movement picture:
> 1. The division of the limbs
> 2. The spatial placement
> 3. The progression in space[38]

The division of the limbs is organized according to the "bodycross" described above. Laban's elaboration of the spatial placement of movement into various spatial orientations is indicative of his elaborations on the spatial theory discussed in Chapter I. He gives the option of determining directions either according to the dimensional or diagonal orientation (which Laban sees as generally known) or according to the five positions of classical ballet, or according to his harmonic scales such as the A and B scales. The description of each of the three systems used either letter abbreviations or numbers for the scales. Progression in space can be given in drawings of floor patterns but can mostly be deduced from the symbols.[39]

Of particular interest were additional signs for qualitative interpretation, such as slow, fast, strong, weak, wide, narrow, stable, labile, as well as signs for intensity borrowed from musical notation. Another interesting writing possibility is indicated in relation to oblique directions for their performance with tension or with naturalness or with an impulse, as well as with width or narrowness.[40] The notation of several of these qualitative aspects already became integrated within the structure of the system in 1928, such as the slow-fast timing in the length of the symbols and wide-narrow extension by means of pre-signs.[41] The insertion of bar lines also implies a certain accentuation of the first movement in a regular meter and lesser emphasis on the other parts.[42]

The break-through towards solutions to problems such as how to write the flow of bodily movement in space and time came in the summer of 1927. Reports from three Laban student-assistants at that time: Gertrud Snell, Fritz Klingenbeck, and Albrecht Knust, give us insight into this crucial period leading up to Laban's publication of the system in 1928.[43] According to Snell and Klingenbeck, changes happened after the first German Dance Congress in Magdeburg at the Laban summer workshop in Bad Mergentheim. Kingenbeck reports that while discussing how dance notation was not yet efficient in relation to the theory of harmony, Laban mentioned for the first time the new notation: "I have a complete script already in my pocket."[44] The new script essentially differed from his early attempts in that he abandoned the idea of the theory of harmony which dominated his first explorations and thus the script became understandable to everybody. "A short time afterwards, the fundamental principles of the new script, which was ready in half a year, were taught to Laban's pupils . . . . The climax of the first stage of development came as Laban wrote a movement motif of a waltz, a polka, and a syncopated one."[45]

While Klingenbeck gives a more general description of those beginnings, also depicting heated discussions in notation classes, and Laban's extremely intensive way of working, probing and bringing changes to the new script/notation, Snell gives some specific information about the system itself:

> The signs in the upper half of the bodycross were set *beside* those in the lower half. Thus, now, movements to be made at the same time were *beside each other*. Movements of the lower body were divided into two parts; those affecting transfer of weight, steps, and those without weight transfer gestures. This decision made it logical to write the signs for direction within five note lines. Laban wanted the notation completely separated from all visual references to his theories of movement. . . . The missing third dimension was indicated by colouring (black, diagonally striped, or white). Thus I started to indicate duration of movements, the rhythm, by prolongating or shortening.[46]

Knust reports that while at the first German Dancer's Congress Laban referred to notation only in relation to his movement scales, the following winter he used notation scores written in the new system to stage his choral work *The Titan* in Hamburg. "Laban seems to have worked out the final version of Kinetography during the winter of 1927-28, at his Choreographic Institute in Berlin."[47] Several other reports corroborate this information. The foundation of the Deutsche Gesellschaft für Schrifttanz (German Society for Script-dance) was prompted by Laban's demonstration of his new dance notation at that time. His subsequent lecture-demonstrations in Vienna and notation courses (co-taught with Snell), rousing enthusiasm from audiences and the press, may have prompted the Austrian Universal Edition to publish the society's quarterly publication *Schrifttanz* (*Script-dance*) and Laban's system of notation.[48] Also in 1928 the second German Dancer's Congress acknowledged the excellence of Laban's system, recommending it for practical application in notating dances.[49] Martin Gleisner (one of the key leaders of Laban movement choirs) argues in the same year that leaders of movement choirs, not unlike conductors of song choirs, cannot rely only on their own compositions: "The notated dance piece for choirs . . . is the prerequisite for a general dance culture."[50]

With regard to Laban's capacity to assimilate suggestions from his contemporaries, Knust maintains that several years before the finalization of the system Laban had already declared that its final version could not be the creation of just one mind. "The combined experience of many different persons would result in the final solution of the problem."[51] Laban also furnished himself specific information with regard to the contributions of his collaborators, such as Dussia Bereska who had "a deciding influence on the rhythmical partitioning of Feuillet's metrical bar-line intervals. Her suggestions that the symbols might be written in different lengths to indicate the relative duration of each movement was an innovation which is still an outstanding feature of our notation today."[52] Laban also credited Kurt Jooss with the proposal "to duplicate Feuillet's right-left division of the movement sequences . . . . This again has become, with some adaptations, a specific feature of our notation,"[53] Laban's debt to the principles of the Beauchamps-Feuillet notation announced in *Choreographie* is explicitly summarized in his *Principles of Dance and Movement Notation* in terms of the central line of the staff dividing the right and left sides of the body, the metrical division of time through bar lines, the use of directional signs and shape symbols, and the indication of qualitative actions by special signs.[54]

All this indicates that besides Laban's sound foundations, creative team work contributed to the possibility of making the enormous jump from Laban's announcement in 1920 of his next publication "The Dancer's Script" and the 1926 exploratory statements in *Choreographie* to the almost complete publication of Laban's system in 1928.[55] In Laban's booklet on

Kinetography, aspects of notation included in the part on methodology (or classification) are levels, directions, duration including stillness, columns for body parts, step, gesture, turning, jumping, dynamic signs, position pins, pre-signs for body parts, relationship signs, starting positions in space, beginning and ending indications.[56] The section on orthography (or on correct writing conventions) shows all the material of methodology in the context of short sequences also including sitting and lying situations.[57] The last part on clarifications is a short glossary of technical dance terms.[58]

Further major steps in the development of the system have been marked chiefly by two authors: first Albrecht Knust who continued to work on the comprehensive and finely differentiated structures of the system and elaborated on the fundamental categorization of group formation; Ann Hutchinson contributed widely, particularly in terms of idiosyncratic choreographic details outside the range of European Modern Dance.[59]

Bodily Articulation

The bilateral structure of the human body is reflected in the organization of the symbols on the right and left side of the central line corresponding to the two body sides; this has been indicated in the above deliberations.[60] Summarizing the essential features of his notation, Laban accounts for the following equally important aspects of movement:

> First it considers movement possibilities of the upper and lower body and of particular limbs, as well as functions of joints which are important for the control of the anatomical and rhythmical flow of movement. In the second place the notation shows the directions of the changing relationships of the body to the environment, and third it represents clearly the rhythm of the body in its directional symbols.[61]

Thus, the articulation of the body in terms of bilaterality, body parts as well as the function of the joints — such as contraction, extension, and rotation — is clearly defined in Laban's notation. The concern with bodily articulation permeated the early "bodycross script" as well as the considerations of mono- and polylinear sequencing. An account from Laban's *Principles of Dance and Movement Notation* (1956) summarizes the classification of bodily movement in different terms. In addition to fundamental movements of the body, the notation considers the effect of an initial impulse which can result in a "tactile effect" of a gesture touching an object or in a "prehensile effect" of grasping. Further, the "support effect" arises when different body parts carry weight; it can be developed into an "ambulatory effect" or locomotion, and a "saltatory effect" or jumping.[62]

The analysis of simple and complex bodily actions is the topic of two chapters in *The Mastery of Movement on the Stage* (1950) (Laban's initial idea of having all examples in the book illustrated with notation has, however, been realized only in the fourth edition.). Here Laban's approach to the classification of body movement is in complete accordance with the analysis underlying his notation: "Bodily actions produce alterations of the positions of the body, or of parts of it, in the space surrounding the body. Each of these alterations takes a certain time, and requires a certain amount of muscular energy."[63] The following questions are included to assist in determining and describing any bodily action:

1) Which part of the body moves?
2) How much time does the movement require?
3) What degree of muscular energy is spent on the movement?
4) In which direction or directions of space is the movement exerted?[64]

It is interesting to compare these questions with statements formulated in the previously mentioned article on "The Development of Movement Notation Laban" from the 20's:

Who   performs the movement, i.e., which limb or upper or lower body part is indicated by the placement of symbols in the *staff*

How   the movement is performed, either slowly or faster, is seen in the *length* of the symbol

Where the movement leads the body in space is seen from the directional symbols.[65]

All but the question concerning the muscular energy or dynamics are accounted for in this presentation; for its description some additional signs are required.

A table showing "Fundamental Subdivisions of the Body Needed for the Description of Bodily Action" is included in *The Mastery of Movement on the Stage*, articulating the head, upper and lower parts of the trunk, and right and left extremities.[66] (It can also be compared with Laban's presentation of "Presigns for Body Symbols" in the section "Methodics" from *Schrifttanz* no. 1. 1928, mentioned previously.) A comprehensive survey of bodily actions is prefaced by a more global view:

Body movement can be roughly divided into steps, gestures of the arms and hands and facial expressions. Steps comprehend leaps, turns, and runs. Gestures of the extremities of the upper part of the body comprise scooping, gathering, and scattering movements. Facial expressions are connected with movements of the head, which serve to direct eyes, ears, mouth, and nostrils toward objects from which sense impressions are expected. Spine, arms and legs are articulated, i.e. subdivided by joints. The articulation of the spine is more complex than that of the arms and legs.[67]

The analysis of particular bodily actions is exemplified through short exercise-like sequences. It considers positions of the feet, transference of weight in steps and supporting weight on various parts of the body: successive and simultaneous gestures of arms, legs, and torso including contraction, extension, and twisting. Further, movement of the center of gravity, turns, jumps, and various forms of locomotion are analysed, as well as movement related to people and objects. (A similar progression is presented in the section on orthography in the above mentioned issue of *Schrifttanz*.)

Within his recommendations for how to observe bodily actions, Laban suggests looking at:

ways of using the body, whether
 upper or lower part
 right or left side
 of or on the floor
 symmetric or asymmetric
 simultaneous or successive movements in one or both limbs.
. . . .

Several parts of the body can perform similar or different acts of movement simultaneously . . . . Movement can result in touch or grip. Feet, hands, or other parts of the body can touch either objects or persons. Hands can grip.[68]

Of particular interest is Laban's claim that "no special method or style of dancing is at the basis of the logical order of movement observation. Dancers in every age and in all countries have thought, and still think, in terms of movement — essentially space, time and energy — indications."[69] He also emphasizes that the analysis of bodily actions in sport, play, acting, work, and everyday behavior is based on the same movement thinking as the analysis of dance movement. These concerns clearly indicate that the endeavor to find common denominators to all human movement underlies all Laban's classification and notation of movement.

Relationship Aspects

Symbols for aspects of relationships between body parts, the body and the environment, between partners and a group, were included in Laban's first publication of the system; this can be seen in Table 7. Further, one of the concerns of Laban's notation is the rendering of prehensile, tactile, and support effects of the movement.[70] This shows how much the aspect of relationships is implicit in Laban's view of movement, in its intentionality of the action relating to self, another person, objects, and environment. An explicit statement can be found in the section on "Movement Related to People and Objects" in *The Mastery of Movement*:

When moving we create changing relationships with something. This something can be an object, a person or even a part of our own body,

and physical contact can be established with any of these.[71]
Laban distinguishes three main phases of such actions: preparation, actual contact, and release. In the preparatory phase, addressing occurs and is brought about through looking. The next phase can be realized through approaching, meeting, surrounding, and penetrating.

Laban's concern with relationships or interactions is evident throughout his activities. It is particularly emphasized in his organization of "movement choirs" discussed in Part One, to which he attributed great social and moral value.[72] Albrecht Knust, who also conducted movement choirs at the Laban School in Hamburg, wrote down complete scores for group compositions; they were distributed to other choir leaders throughout Germany, not unlike musical scores to conductors of choral music.[73] As mentioned previously, Knust developed a detailed notation for recording group formations and group movement.

Laban's Notation in Relation to his Other Theories

Although Laban intended to make his notation independent from his other theories, it is, however, linked with them through a common basis of universal principles. In summarizing the above elaborations these principles can be identified. A primary principle is seen in Laban's analysis of movement in terms of *bodily, temporal, spatial* and *rhythmic-dynamic* components.

The movement of the whole body or its parts is determined both in Laban's classification of bodily aspects of movement and in his notation from the point of view of its anatomical structure (torso & extremities), as well as its bilateral symmetry (right-left) and the forward-backward, upper-lower body articulation. Laban's classification of bodily action includes the consideration of the body in movement — gesture and locomotion — and stillness — position. Arm, leg, and torso gestures are articulated within their contracting, extending, rotating, tilting, and shifting variations; transference of weight is described in steps, jumps, and changes of support on various body parts. Movement related to people and objects is equally described as an important aspect of bodily action. Thus, instead of sweepingly referring to dance movement as "dance steps" — a convention inherited from the tradition of classical ballet and still permeating contemporary dance practices — Laban's classification and notation offer a precise vocabulary and means of identifying and recording fundamental actions and their combinations. This allows for the application of the system to describe any type of movement or dance style.

The temporal aspect of movement in Laban's classification and notation is related to various time units, such as meter and tempi of Western classical music or clock time. Free rhythms with the timing relative to the perception of the performer, as well as *ad libitum* timing can also be notated both in Kinetography/Labanotation and by means of the Effort-graph. The temporal sequencing of movement in Laban's notation through the length of symbols and their simultaneous or sequential placement into the notation staff strongly shows Laban's concept of the unity of all movement components. "The conventional idea of space as a phenomenon which can be separated from time and force and from expression, is completely erroneous," writes Laban in the context of his *Choreutics*.[74]

The description of spatial direction in Laban's classification, notation and theory on harmony of space is determined in relation to both the vertical as a gravity-determined-constant on this planet, and/or the Cartesian coordinates of the vertical and two horizontal dimensions. Laban places the dividing point between the three dimensions in the center of gravity of the upright body which greatly facilitates directional orientation for the mover/dancer. The various systems of spatial directional orientation, such as the dimensional, diagonal, and diametral, are geometrical givens which Laban relates both to the structure of the body and its moving potentials. While these systems are frames of reference in choreutics, they may or may not be used in Laban's notation as an introduction to directions and levels or as a means of viewing the overall spatial structure of a piece. The perceptual experience of moving into various dimensions in space and/or of looking at it is related to verticality: "Each body movement affects our experience through the direction of its departure from the vertical. This is true not only for the observer but also for the moving person."[75] Verticality and the placement of the centre of gravity over the support are also references for creating or determining a predominantly stable or mobile/labile equilibrium in movement and stillness. While this can be indicated in Laban's notation with an additional movement for the centre of gravity, within the framework of choreutics there is an implied association between dimensional movement and stability and diagonal movements and mobility/lability.[76] Finally the consideration of shaping in movement or of form elements is also based on the fundamental motor possibilities of the joints (contracting, extending, and rotating), as well as on the notion of fundamental shapes – straight, rounded, and twisted.[77]

Laban considers the rhythmic-dynamic aspect of movement from several angles. The quantitative, measurable aspect of time rhythm is incorporated in the notational system in terms of the relative length of symbols. Speed, tempo, and time units are also considered as elementary aspects needed for the observation of bodily actions.[78] Elementary aspects of weight, such as accents and degrees of tension are also part of Laban's movement classification but have to be indicated with additional symbols in Laban's notation.[79] While the flow of a sequence can be distinguished in notation in terms of a continuous versus an interrupted, jerky motion, its elementary aspects for observation of actions are flux and control of various types of action.[80]

In order to provide a means for describing the qualitative rhythmic-dynamic aspects of movement and dance in general, Laban, within his Effort theory, classified the qualitative polarities of time (sustained & sudden), of weight (light/fine touch & strong/firm), and of flow (free & bound); to quantitative aspects of space, such as direction, level, and extension, he added the qualitative polarity of direct and flexible/indirect focus or path of action. These components can be combined in a variety of ways, and the resulting combinations of Efforts follow each other more or less gradually or in contrast. Such rhythmic-dynamic sequences can be observed and recorded by means of the Effort-graph.[81] Effort descriptions can also be added to notation scores when a special indication of dynamics is required.

Notes to Chapter III

1. Cf. *Die Tat*, 1922 (?), p. 675.
2. *Die Welt des Tänzers*, p. 65.
3. *Des Kindes Gymnastik und Tanz*, p. 35.
4. *Gymnastik und Tanz*, p. 159.
5. The presentation was illustrated with slides and live performance; its text and illustrations were reprinted in an article titled "Die Entwicklung der Bewegungsschrift Laban," *Schrifttanz*, Heft II, 1928, pp. 27-32.
6. Ibid., p. 27.
7. Ibid., p. 28.
8. Ibid.
9. "Foreword by Rudolf Laban," *Labanotation*, by Ann Hutchinson (New York: A Theatre Arts Book, 1954), p. XV.
10. Cf. *Choreutics*, p. 8.
11. In the preface to his *Methodik, Orthographie, Erläuterungen* (*Methodics, Orthography, Explanations*) published as a special issue of *Schrifttanz* in 1928, Laban refers to his notation for the first time as Kinetographie Laban: the closing section is titled "Erläuterungen zu den in der Methodik und Orthographie der Kinetographie Laban vorkommenden tänzerischen Fachausdrücken" ("Explanations of the dancing technical terms used in the Laban Kinetography, Methodics and Orthography").
12. "Grundprinzipien der Bewegungsschrift," *Schrifttanz*, Heft I, 1928, p. 5.
13. Quoted in Rudolf Sonner, *Musik und Tanz* (1930, p. 111) as cited by Lisa Ullmann, "What Notated Movement Can Tell," *Dance Studies*, Vol. 1., 1976, p. 19 (Roderyk Lange, Editor).
14. In the first communication of the newly formed society for Script-dance, Dr. Edward Moll writes that the new dance-script is a script for notating

all dance creations, such as Pavlova's, Fokine's, Laban's and Wigman's, a script for the preservation of old dance reconstruction as well as of significant directing of operas and plays. Moll concludes that the dance-script is, however, only a means in the same way as dance education and research; the dance-script is only a means to an end. The aim is script-dance which in the process of dance composition creates the spiritualization of dance. (Cf. "Mitteilungen der Deutschen Gesellschaft für Schrifttanz." *Schrifttanz*, Heft I, 1928, p. 16.) These lines of thought are corroborated by Laban's assistant Fritz Klingenbeck in "Schreiben und Lesen" ("Writing and Reading") *Schrifttanz*, Heft IV, 1929, p. 76. He refers to Laban's idea of the script-dance which includes the application of notational symbols to free composition.

15. See note (9) above for reference.
16. *Choreographie*, p. 8.
17. Cf. *Schrifttanz*, Heft I, 1928, pp. 4-5.
18. Ibid., p. 4.
19. Ibid.
20. In Laban's writings from the 50's it can be seen that flow in the context of notation was not interchangeable with time but is perceived as a minor or major motion of one or several parts of the body resulting in a large or slight displacement. Cf. *Principles of Dance and Movement Notation*, p. 22.
21. *Schrifttanz*, Heft II, 1928, p. 30.
22. Ibid.
23. *Schrifttanz*, Heft I, 1928, p. 4: See also pp. 13 and 14 of *Principles of Dance and Movement Notation*, where a specific example of a particular movement (nodding) is considered in different shades of significance depending on the movement of other parts of the body.
24. *Schrifttanz*, Heft I, 1928, pp. 4-5.
25. Other ways of orientation, such as according to the directions of the performing space and the bodily structure, were developed later and indicated by a "clef" or "key." Cf. Ann Hutchinson. *Labanotation*, 1970 edition, pp. 415-16, and Albrech Knust *A Dictionary of Kinetography Laban (Labanotation)*, Volumes 1 and 2 (London: Macdonald & Evans, 1979) Vol. 1, pp. 351-58, Vol. 2, pp. 148-49.
26. Cf. *Schrifttanz*, Heft I, 1928, p. 5.
27. "The Beginnings of Kinetography Laban," *The Laban Art of Movement Guild Magazine*, no. 63, 1979, p. 11.
28. Cf. *Choreutics*, p. 8.
29. Cf. *Principles of Dance and Movement Notation*, p. 14.
30. Ibid., pp. 15, 18.
31. Mary Wigman, "To Rudolf von Laban for his Birthsday," *Schrifttanz*, Heft IV, 1929, p. 65.
32. Cf. Hans Brandenberg, "Reminiscences on Laban's Beginning," *Schrifttanz*, Heft IV, 1929, p. 71.

33. Ibid. It is also interesting to note that Hans Richter (1965) wrote that dancers for the Dada performance of *Die Kaufleute* in 1917 were "drilled and directed according to a choreography written down by Käthe Wulff and Sophie Taeuber in Laban's system of notation," p. 70.
34. *Der Moderne Tanz*, 2nd edition, 1917, p. 39.
35. Ibid., p. 37.
36. Ibid., p. 36.
37. Cf. Op. cit., *The Laban Art of Movement Guild Magazine*, No. 63, 1979, p. 11.
38. *Choreographie*, p. 100.
39. Cf. Ibid., pp. 100-101.
40. Cf. Ibid., pp. 102-103.
41. Cf. *Schrifttanz: Methodik, Orthographie, Erläuterungen*, 1928, pp. 9, 14 (ex. 21), 15 (ex. 28).
42. Cf. *Principles of Dance and Movement Notation*, p. 23.
43. For information on Gertrud Snell cf. note (34), Part One. *Fritz Klingenbeck* who later became a theatre director and playwright in Austria, was Laban's assistant and notated his movement choir *The Titan* in 1928; an excerpt was printed in the playbill which may have been the first printed example of Kinetography (Cf. Knust 1958, p. 8.). Klingenbeck also assisted Laban in staging the pageant in Vienna in 1929. From several of his articles (Cf. annotated bibliography) one can gather that Klingenbeck was steeped in various problems of notation between 1928 and 1931. In the 1929 article "Brief Retrospective," referred to in Part One, Klingenbeck describes his beginnings with Laban in 1927: "Laban appeared personally to introduce us to the new notation in which one had to distinguish clearly . . . the rhythm, and besides directions one could further determine the performing body part. Already then the new solution of the writing problem seemed to us as an egg of Columbus . . ." (p. 306). It is puzzling to find that in the '80's Klingenbeck ascribes the "Egg of Columbus" – the solution of fundamental principles of kinetography – to himself. While organizing the retrospective exhibition on "Rudolf Laban 1989-1958: The Most Significant Dance Reformer," for the Austrian theatre museums in 1980/81, Klingenbeck edited the catalogue furnishing information and illustrations. "'An egg of Columbus' the fundamental principle by Fritz Klingenbeck for Laban's Kinetography" is the subtitle for a drawing on p. 7 which Laban published in the second issue of *Schrifttanz*. Elaborating further on the system Klingenbeck writes on p. 8.: "When I submitted my expose to Laban he said: "'See, these are the five lines of the music notation staff,' which I did not notice. What happened afterwards was Laban's ingenious work." In the information on Laban's curriculum vitae, Klingenbeck writes on p. 4: "Laban made various attempts to realize the 400-year-old dream about a valid dance notation, until in 1927 his then student, Fritz Klingenbeck succeeded with the simple fundamental principle on which

his master could build the longed for dance notation . . . ." He further informs us that in 1928 he became Laban's personal collaborator and that in Berlin he wrote the first choreographic score for the full-length choral work "Titan" which served as the basis for the rehearsals at the circus Busch in Hamburg. While the latter statement seems credible, it will be seen that his claim that he invented the system is contradicted by Laban and Knust. Laban acknowledged his debt to the basic principles of Feuillet's notation in several instances and described it as "the egg of Columbus" in the foreword to Hutchinson's *Labanotation*. Further it was Kurt Jooss who "surprised us one day with the proposal to duplicate Feuillet's right-left division of movement sequences. We proceeded then to record the movements of the trunk and arms in separate columns . . . " (*Principles of Dance and Movement Notation*, p. 8). Knust corroborates this in his article "The Roots of Laban Notation" in the *Dance Notation Record"* Vol. IX, 1958: "Jooss one day began writing the symbols in the four sections of the vertical staff . . . . The two inner columns held the indications for the legs and adjacent torso, and the outer ones described the arms and adjacent torso . . ." (op. cit. p. 9). For information on *Albrecht Knust* cf. note (24), Part One. An excerpt from his festive march for approximately 24 women and eight man was published as a supplement in *Schrifttanz*, Heft II, 1928.

44. "Brief Retrospective," *Singhor und Tanz*, December 1929, p. 306.
45. Ibid.
46. Gertrud Snell-Friedburg, "The Beginnings of Kinetography Laban," *The Laban Art of Movement Guild Magazine*, No. 63, 1979, p. 12.
47. Cf. Albrecht Knust, "The Roots of Laban Notation," *Dance Notation Record*, Vol. IX, Nos. 3 and 4, 1958, p. 8.
48. Cf. The report about the foundation of the society in *Schrifttanz*, Heft II, 1928, pp. 32-33. The list of members in Germany, Austria, Switzerland, U.S.A., France, Holland, Czechoslovakia, Hungary, Yugoslavia and Litwania shows a predominance of Laban trained persons.
49. Cf. *Schrifttanz*, Heft IV, 1929, p. 75.
50. Martin Gleisner, "Schrifttanz und Laientanz" ("Script-dance and Lay-dance"), *Schrifttanz*, Heft II, 1928, p. 22.
51. Albrecht Knust, "The Roots of Laban Notation," *Dance Notation Record*, Vol. IX, 1958, p. 8.
52. *Principles of Dance and Movement Notation*, pp. 7-8.
53. Ibid., p. 8.
54. Cf. Ibid., p. 7.
55. In his first book *Die Welt des Tänzers*, 1920, p. 8., Laban announced his second publication on notation: "One cannot send into the world what I have to say in my second book 'The Dancer's Script' about movement concepts and the perfection of choreography [notation] for the purpose of a useful contemporary dance notation, without a preliminary extensive reference to the nature of the dance and the dancer."

56. Cf. *Schrifttanz: Methodik, Orthographie, Erläuterungen* 1928, pp. 6-11.
57. Cf. Ibid., pp. 12-18.
58. Cf. Ibid., pp. 19-20.
59. Further developments of the system are also due to the activities of the International Council of Kinetography Laban, founded in 1959.
60. Cf. pp. 117, 122, above, and *Schrifttanz*, Heft I, 1928, p. 4.
61. *Schrifttanz*, Heft II, 1928, p. 28.
62. Cf. Op. cit., p. 23.
63. Op. cit., p. 25.
64. Ibid.
65. *Schrifttanz*, Heft II, 1928, p. 29.
66. Cf. *The Mastery of Movement on the Stage*, p. 26.
67. Ibid., p. 20.
68. *The Mastery of Movement*, 1960 ed., p. 54.
69. Ibid., p. 53.
70. Cf. *Principles of Dance and Movement Notation*, p. 23.
71. Op. cit., p. 73.
72. Cf. *Die Welt des Tanzers*, p. 183, and *Gymnastik und Tanz*, pp. 131-143.
73. Roderyk Lange reports in "Albrecht Knust — An Appreciation," *Dance Studies*, Vol. 1, 1976, p. 1, about a movement choir demonstration in 1930 in Munich during the German Dancer's Congress, for which Knust wrote the score.
74. *Choreutics*, p. 67.
75. *Gymnastik und Tanz*, p. 67.
76. Cf. Chapter I.
77. Cf. Chapter I.
78. Cf. *The Mastery of Movement*, pp. 43-45.
79. Cf. Ibid., pp. 46-48, and Table 9d.
80. Cf. *The Mastery of Movement*, p. 54.
81. Cf. Chapter II, Figure 11.

Table 9 a

KINETOGRAPHY LABAN/LABANOTATION

Development of Principles and Chronology
of
Sources and Link with other Concepts

B O D Y

| 1926: *Choreographie* | pp. 4-5 | Observation of: body laterality and symmetry; direction (in relation to the vertical) plastic shape of the body w/h stable and labile tendencies |
| | p. 102 | Intensity of movement: deflating/decrescendo inflating/crescendo use of musical notation |

Observation: Recording:

| 1928: *Schrifttanz,* Heft I. | pp. 4-5 | Time rhythm/flow of movement — length of symbol Spatial rhythm plasticity — directional element Bilateral body structure/ (symmetry) — middle line of stave Monolinear poly-linear sequencing — vertical & horizon-tal writing-reading Stable-dimensional & Labile-diagonal directions — directional symbols |

| 1928: *Schrifttanz,* Heft II. | pp. 28-29 | Movement possi-bilities of upper — placement of the & lower body & symbols in the limbs columns, use of presign for body parts |

Recapitulation of the 1928 aspects

1928: *Schrifttanz: Methodik, Orthographie, Erläuterungen*	pp. 10-11 pp. 7, 12 ex. 7	Body parts Stillness (temporary); transference of weight; steps;
	p. 19	gesture jump kneeling, sitting, lying, etc: turning; inward & upward/rotation;
	pp. 12-18 p. 11	Combinations of the above bodily actions Centre of the Body & centre of levity Contact/relationships:
	pp. 11, 14 ex. 24	amongst body parts
	p. 15 ex. 26-29	" partners
	p. 14 ex. 25	" groups
	p. 11	placement in the performance space Dynamics:
	pp. 9, 12 ex. 8	strong weak

Table 9 b

KINETOGRAPHY LABAN/LABANOTATION

Development of Principles and Chronology
of
Sources and Link with other Concepts

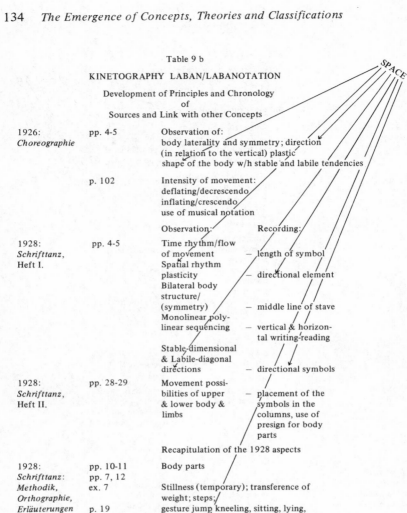

1926:   pp. 4-5   Observation of:
Choreographie   body laterality and symmetry; direction
                                (in relation to the vertical) plastic
                                shape of the body w/h stable and labile tendencies

               p. 102   Intensity of movement:
                                deflating/decrescendo
                                inflating/crescendo
                                use of musical notation

                                Observation: Recording:

1928:   pp. 4-5   Time rhythm/flow
Schrifttanz,   of movement   — length of symbol
Heft I.   Spatial rhythm
                                plasticity   — directional element
                                Bilateral body
                                structure/
                                (symmetry)   — middle line of stave
                                Monolinear poly-
                                linear sequencing   — vertical & horizon-
                                                         tal writing/reading
                                Stable-dimensional
                                & Labile-diagonal
                                directions   — directional symbols

1928:   pp. 28-29   Movement possi-
Schrifttanz,   bilities of upper   — placement of the
Heft II.   & lower body &   symbols in the
                                limbs   columns, use of
                                                         presign for body
                                                         parts

                                Recapitulation of the 1928 aspects

1928:   pp. 10-11   Body parts
Schrifttanz: pp. 7, 12
Methodik,   ex. 7   Stillness (temporary); transference of
Orthographie,   weight; steps;
Erläuterungen p. 19   gesture jump kneeling, sitting, lying,
                                etc: turning; inward & upward rotation;
               pp. 12-18   Combinations of the above bodily actions
               p. 11   Centre of the Body & centre of levity
                                Contact/relationships:
               pp. 11, 14
                  ex. 24   amongst body parts
               p. 15
                  ex. 26-29   "   partners
               p. 14 ex. 25   "   groups
               p. 11   placement in the performance
                                space
                                Dynamics:
               pp. 9, 12
                  ex. 8   strong
                                  weak

Table 9 c

KINETOGRAPHY LABAN/LABANOTATION

Development of Principles and Chronology
of
Sources and Link with other Concepts

MOBILITY/STABILITY/ABILITY/LABILITY

		Observation:	Recording:
1926: *Choreographie*	pp. 4-5	Observation of: body laterality and symmetry; direction (in relation to the vertical) plastic shape of the body w/h stable and labile tendencies	
	p. 102	Intensity of movement: deflating/decrescendo inflating/crescendo use of musical notation	
1928: *Schrifttanz,* Heft I.	pp. 4-5	Time rhythm/flow of movement Spatial rhythm plasticity Bilateral body structure/ (symmetry) Monolinear poly- linear sequencing Stable-dimensional & Labile-diagonal directions	length of symbol directional element middle line of stave vertical & horizon- tal writing-reading directional symbols
1928: *Schrifttanz,* Heft II.	pp. 28-29	Movement possi- bilities of upper & lower body & limbs	placement of the symbols in the columns, use of presign for body parts
		Recapitulation of the 1928 aspects	

1928:
Schrifttanz:
Methodik,
Orthographie,
Erläuterungen
	pp. 10-11
	pp. 7, 12
	ex. 7
	
	p. 19
	
	pp. 12-18
	p. 11
	
	pp. 11, 14
	ex. 24
	p. 15
	ex. 26-29
	p. 14 ex. 25
	p. 11
	
	pp. 9, 12
	ex. 8
		Body parts
		
		Stillness (temporary); transference of
		weight; steps;
		gesture jump kneeling, sitting, lying,
		etc: turning; inward & upward rotation;
		Combinations of the above bodily actions
		Centre of the Body & centre of levity
		Contact/relationships:
		
		   amongst body parts
		
		   '' partners
		   '' groups
		   placement in the performance
		space
		Dynamics:
		
		   strong
		   weak	

Table 9 d

KINETOGRAPHY LABAN/LABANOTATION

DYNAMICS
TIME RHYTHM

Development of Principles and Chronology
of
Sources and Link with other Concepts

| 1926:
Choreographie | pp. 4-5 | Observation of:
body laterality and symmetry; direction
(in relation to the vertical) plastic shape
of the body w/h stable and labile tendencies |
| | p. 102 | Intensity of movement:
deflating/decrescendo
inflating/crescendo
use of musical notation |

		Observation:	Recording:
1928: *Schrifttanz*, Heft I.	pp. 4-5	Time rhythm/flow of movement	— length of symbol
		Spatial rhythm plasticity	— directional element
		Bilateral body structure/ (symmetry)	— middle line of stave
		Monolinear poly- linear sequencing	— vertical & horizon- tal writing-reading
		Stable-dimensional & Labile-diagonal directions	— directional symbols
1928: *Schrifttanz*, Heft II.	pp. 28-29	Movement possi- bilities of upper & lower body & limbs	— placement of the symbols in the columns, use of presign for body parts

Recapitulation of the 1928 aspects

1928: *Schrifttanz*: *Methodik,* *Orthographie,* *Erläuterungen*	pp. 10-11 pp. 7, 12 ex. 7	Body parts Stillness (temporary); transference of weight; steps;
	p. 19	gesture jump kneeling, sitting, lying, etc: turning; inward & upward rotation;
	pp. 12-18	Combinations of the above bodily actions
	p. 11	Centre of the Body & centre of levity Contact/relationships:
	pp. 11, 14 ex. 24	amongst body parts
	p. 15 ex. 26-29	" partners
	p. 14 ex. 25	" groups
	p. 11	placement in the performance space
		Dynamics:
	pp. 9, 12 ex. 8	strong weak

Table 9 e

KINETOGRAPHY LABAN/LABANOTATION

Development of Principles and Chronology
of
Sources and Link with other Concepts

RELATIONSHIPS

| 1926:
Choreographie | pp. 4-5 | Observation of:
body laterality and symmetry; direction
(in relation to the vertical) plastic shape
of the body w/h stable and labile tendencies |
| | p. 102 | Intensity of movement:
deflating/decrescendo
inflating/crescendo
use of musical notation |

		Observation:	Recording:
1928: *Schrifttanz,* Heft I.	pp. 4-5	Time rhythm/flow of movement Spatial rhythm plasticity Bilateral body structure/ (symmetry) Monolinear poly- linear sequencing Stable-dimensional & Labile-diagonal directions	– length of symbol – directional element – middle line of stave – vertical & horizon- tal writing-reading – directional symbols
1928: *Schrifttanz,* Heft II.	pp. 28-29	Movement possi- bilities of upper & lower body & limbs	– placement of the symbols in the columns, use of presign for body parts

Recapitulation of the 1928 aspects

| 1928:
Schrifttanz:
Methodik,
Orthographie,
Erläuterungen | pp. 10-11
pp. 7, 12
ex. 7

p. 19

pp. 12-18
p. 11

pp. 11, 14
ex. 24
p. 15
ex. 26-29
p. 14 ex. 25
p. 11

pp. 9, 12
ex. 8 | Body parts

Stillness (temporary); transference of
weight; steps;
gesture jump kneeling, sitting, lying,
etc: turning; inward & upward rotation;
Combinations of the above bodily actions
Centre of the Body & centre of levity
Contact/relationships:

amongst body parts

!!   partners
!!   groups
placement in the performance
space
Dynamics:

strong
weak |

Table 10

BODILY ASPECTS

Survey of Classification and Sources

1928: *Schrifttanz*, Heft I.	pp. 4-5	Bilateral structure; Mono- and Poly-linear sequencing
1928: *Schrifttanz*, Heft II.	p. 28	Movement possibilities — function of the joints of upper and lower body and of limbs
1928: *Schrifttanz*: *Methodik,*	pp. 10-11	Body parts including centre of the body & centre of levity
Orthographie, Erläuterungen	pp. 7, 12-18 (ex. 1-53)	Bodily actions: stillness; transference of weight/steps; gestures; jumps; kneeling, sitting, lying, etc.; turning; inward & outward rotation; contacts between body parts.
1948: *Modern Educational Dance*	pp. 29-31	Themes concerned with the awareness of the body Themes concerned with the instrumental use of the limbs of the body
1950: *The Mastery of Movement on the Stage*	pp. 20, 26-81	Bodily actions: the stance; transference of weight/steps; leaps, turns, runs; head mvts.: facial expression, articulation of the spine; gestures-scooping/gathering & scattering.
1960: *The Mastery of Movement*	pp. 21-72 p. 53	Ibid.; successive and simultaneous Ways of using the body.

RELATIONSHIP ASPECTS

Survey of Classification and Sources

1928: *Schrifttanz*: *Methodik, Orthographie, Erläuterungen*	pp. 11, 14 p. 11 14, ex. 24 15, ex. 26-29 14, ex. 25	Contact/relationships Starting position in space Body parts touching Contact between partners Group contact
1948: *Modern Educational Dance*	p. 30 p. 41	Themes concerned with the adaptation to partners Themes concerned with the awakening of group feeling Themes concerned with group formations
1960: *The Mastery of Movement*	pp. 73-74	Three phases of relationship actions: preparation, contact and release.

CHAPTER IV

Composition: A Synthesis of Applied Theory

The rationale for including a chapter on composition in the disucssion of Laban's theoretical framework is based on several references found in his publications and manuscripts. It is significant to realize that composition is seen as the common denominator to all main dance areas (dance for layman, the art and science of dance) and that it also describes a link between the laws of the art form and free intuition.[1] Although the title of Laban's *Choreographie* pertains to dance writing — rather than to composition, the book outlines his later developed choreutics and eukinetics defined as the practical dance theory of space and expression.[2] The main issue in clarifying the differences between gymnastics and dance, in his 1926 book of the same title, is composition. We have also seen that one of his concerns in developing the notation was to provide choreographic documentation as well as a means of exploring and developing choreographic ideas. It may also be significant that in the same year when publishing his system of kinetography (1928), Laban also wrote three articles discussing dance composition.[3] Choreographic considerations are, however, frequently implied in Laban's writings, and it is as though one has to draw out of his opus all the wealth of possibilities for compositional studies; this has actually been done by several individuals.[4]

That the art of dance cannot be based on spontaneous improvisation has been stated by Laban on several occasions.[5] "Movement compositions... have to be carefully constructed and built up according to the general rules of artistic composition."[6] In an early article titled "Symbole des Tanzes und Tanz als Symbol," (Symbols of Dance and Dance as Symbol), Laban refers to principles of regularity, symmetry, and proportionality.[7] Because the symmetrical similarity of parts, which promotes stillness, is eliminated in proportionality, it allows for movement, and when combined with symmetry it can create nuances from almost complete stillness to lively movement. The fourth principle of eurhythmy concerns the rhythm of forms as actualized movement. All these principles interact in the creation of solo and group dances. While a solo dance can be seen as a duet between the dancer and his/her environment or the dancer and his/her inner world, being therefore more subjective, group dance can embody a relationship of two or more actual subjects and the interaction of people and may be perceived as more concrete.

Aspects of individual, partner, and group dance were further developed by Laban in the 1940's in the context of his involvement with British education. All of the "sixteen basic movement themes" of his *Modern Educational Dance* (1947) can be seen as compositional material. Themes concerned with adaptation to partners illustrate responses by contrasting, leading-following, and moving together. Themes dealing with the awakening of group feeling suggest common rising-sinking, whirling around a centre, and responses to another group. Themes considering group formation refer to simple formations, such as a row or a circle which can wax and wane, travel, transform its shape, move on various levels, and be grouped symmetrically and asymmetrically.[8]

Laban discusses the particular nature of the dance content and of its polarities in an article titled "Vom Tanzinhalt: Studien über die Pole des Tanzkunstwerkes" ("On Dance Content: Studies of the Polarities of a Dancework").[9] Making a comparison with other temporal arts, such as drama, poetry, mime, and music, Laban maintains that polarities in dance cannot be classified as tragic-comic, major-minor keys, and presto-adagio tempi. Rather they consist of aspects of form and relationships/interactions. In other words dance can be more formally-choreutically emphasized, or it can consist predominantly of relationships, thus being eukinetically stressed. While the formal elements lift the perceiver — so to speak — the relational aspects draw him/her more toward his/her inner vibrations. The body and the space are symbolic mediators of the above. "The body is the subject of motoric energy. The space is its object. Or reversed?"[10] If reversed the space should be seen not as the environment, which is only the extension of body movement, but in terms of its laws and potential configurations. Such statements reiterate Laban's view of spatiality not as an empty receptacle to be filled with movement, but as an area created through movement. Laban further discusses the notion of a synthesized total perception (*Vollsehen*) of dance as different from the understanding of the feeling of a work. The choreological or the interactional-formal logic of the work should mediate the awareness of its energy and power. The representational gesture of mimetic dance or dance drama, for example, loses the power of its own logic in favor of the emphasis on feelings or understanding. Laban, therefore, argues that the art of dance should place the emphasis on strengthening and further clarification of its intrinsic polarities.

"Indulging in feelings and intellectual construction are a great danger to the further development of this art," states Laban in the second article written in 1928, titled "Tanzkomposition und Schrifttanz" ("Dance Composition and Scriptdance").[11] Neither attitude will be possible anymore when both dancers and audiences become aware of the actual language of movement. This can only happen by means of dance notation. After the initial germination and exploration of a dance idea, the notated score will provide an overview of the work: eventual stylistic inconsistencies and lack of clarity, as well as the possibility of combining other elements of dance expression, are discovered. A dancer who does not know the possibilities of dance notation will only cause confusion and undermine the art of dance argues Laban.

Such views are corroborated in "Choreographie und Theater" (Choreography and Theatre),[12] the third article from the same year. Until that time dancers could never objectively confront their work maintains Laban. They would have to work out their improvisations according to their own artistic tastes, and would be able to actually see the dance only if they happened to have the opportunity to teach it to somebody else. The development of contemporary dance theory and notation, however, marks a major change in such practices. Objective criteria are now provided both by the theory of harmony and by dance notation. Every dancer, Laban believes, will soon be able not only to write down his/her own dances but also to evaluate critically the content and form of his/her own works. The publication of dance works both for purposes of repertory building, as well as for the preservation of the dance heritage, is the next significant step. Laban maintains that the composition and notation of a theatre director's movement indications for singers and actors is of the same importance. After all, the first title of his book *The Mastery of Movement* was *The Mastery of Movement on the Stage* (1950).

In clarifying the differences between the composition of movement exercises and of dance pieces, Laban uses the analogy of language.[13] Besides enumerating things by simply classifying them, one can also apply argumentation, definition, and dialectic forms to create concepts. Similarly one can simply string together a series of classified movements (such as gestures, swings, and jumps) as it is done in exercises. On the other hand, one can establish a relationship between movements by crystalizing some to their utmost clarity, tense up and release gestural expression, and therewith embody an interaction between singular movement forms. In that way, one approaches the art of dance which also differs from behavioral, functional, and gymnastic movement in its complexity and precision of spatial configurations. A greater intricacy of movement allows for the personal and trans-personal to emerge, and rather than seeing the sheer mechanics of movement, one can also see the principle behind it in action.

In the context of composition, it is appropriate to discuss Laban's manuscript outlining a "Raumspielpuzzle" ("space-game-puzzle,")[14] and to correlate it to ideas and experiments entertained by Marcel Duchamp and practiced by John Cage and Merce Cunningham. Based on the space-time dimensions of movement, Laban's space-game-puzzle is intended to awaken spatial and spatio-temporal awareness in a game-like fashion. For the artist

Duchamp chance was an expression of the subconscious personality. "Your chance is not the same as my chance just as your throw of the dice will rarely be the same as mine."[15] Duchamp would experiment with his sisters by drawing notes of musical scales out of a hat, setting each their own compositions which he saw as light-hearted expressions of their personal chance ("Musical Erratum," 1913).[16] A similar motivation can be seen in Laban's suggestion that taking up the space-game-puzzle as a pastime could lead to our inner enigmas, to the horoscope which sits, or is ingrained, in our bodies, to the curious game of chess played between our doubts and decisions. Unexpected space-puzzle combinations can offer an insight into the manifold drives of the free power of movement. Because the Dada and Surrealist random associations of unrelated images were also a means of penetrating the dream world of the subconscious, one may find here the only point of approach between Laban's ideas and the Zürich Dada movement referred to in Part One.

Beside the potential personal benefits from using chance methods as a mode of freeing one's imagination from its own clichés, dancer-choreographer Cunningham also espouses a universal vision of chance procedures. These are for him a means to get in touch with the natural resources which rise out of common pools of motor impulses, and is far greater than his own personal inventiveness, much more universally human than the particular habits of his own practice.[17] Laban has similar concerns, arguing that in contrast to mechanical and old-fashioned movement commands which make the dancer into a marionett-like puppet, the puzzle-game can awaken movement forms which emerge out of our natural movement flow. When several people play or attempt to realize the puzzle simultaneously, one may be surprised to find both a multitude of individual characteristics and many common trends which are hidden in the game. It is as though you are giving your personal interpretation of a natural phenomenon. Furthermore Laban maintains that the space-game-puzzle offers a series of directions which, in contrast to their vague usage in everyday life, have a clear spatial placement, spatial boundaires and connections; their harmonic flow has its own natural rhythmic characteristics.

In an attempt to escape from personal idiosyncrasies, to minimize his control over aural resources, and to pursue an art which goes beyond individual self-expression, composer John Cage elaborated complex procedures by means of the Chinese *I Ching* (The Book of Changes). Charts referring to musical tempi, duration, sounds, and dynamics would be manipulated in various ways resulting in compositions by chance.[18] Cunningham would replace music elements with those of movement-stillness-dance such as bodily actions selected from every day movement and dance and use similar procedures for his dance compositions.[19] In Laban's space-game-puzzle various groups of direction (belonging to three systems of orientation: the dimensional, diagonal, and diametral) can be performed in various tempi ranging from very slow to very fast; longer or shorter spans of stillness can also be maintained. The actual execution of the puzzle combination is left to the player's invention, contrary to Cunningham's pre-selected bodily actions. One can engage in the game in two different ways. One can either assemble the cards containing directional symbols according to the rules of spatial games based on Laban's space harmony laws or one can draw them by chance arriving at unpredictable sequences. The game can be played individually and in threes and fours. If the first mode of ordering directions according to spatial laws is chosen, a space model of an icosahedron can assist the visualization of spatial placement and spatial form. In this context, one single direction card has the potential of assuming different functions depending on its placement, such as at the beginning, middle or end of a sequence or circuit. Indeed several cards are required to constitute a spatial form which will also gain its temporal rhythm depending on its angular — interrupted, or rounded — continuous shape. The bodily performance of such spatio-temporal forms, although related to directions and their dynamic rhythm, has the freedom of choices: It can be executed with one or both sides of the body leading in gesture, steps, leaps, runs, and turns. The achievement of the harmonic regularity of a particular combination is, however, suggested. This may be achieved by following one's sense of movement (both natural and learned). When the other mode of the space-game-puzzle is selected — to arrive at sequences by chance — the players are not bound to follow any particular harmonic line, but, on the contrary, they can create the most unpredictable and bizarre combinations. Two attitudes are generally suggested when playing the game: that of inner visualization, of inner movement intent and anticipation which has to precede the transposition of the puzzle structure into movement; the second is that of attempting to suspend one's reasoning, the tendencies of "figuring out" a problem, and yielding to the flow of movement which the puzzle structure generates. The above comparison has shown that the idea of using chance games, as well as compositional procedures by chance, stems from various philosophical, aesthetic and pedagogical attempts to draw from the subconscious mind and establish a link between the personal and trans-personal or subjective and inter-subjective.

At a time when there is an increasing concern about dance on film and television, it is of interest to present a translation of Laban's manuscript *Film ueber die Harmonische Bewegung des Menschlichen Körpers* (Film about the Harmonious Movement of the Human Body). Although it is articulated in five distinct sections and prefaced with an introduction, this manuscript takes the form of a loose scenario. Regardless of whether one shares Laban's aesthetics, the manuscript illustrates his capacity to image movement and dance in cinematic terms rather than theatrical ones. This is a quality which is rare even among contemporary makers of cine-dance and video-dance.[20]

Film about the Harmonious Movement of the Human Body

Introduction: The Dance
    A figure appears in front of a dark background. He/she breathes, walks, bends, and stretches.
    Close-up shot of limbs and torso.
    A second figure joins. Both move against each other and with each other. This formulated movement for the *two* figures is rhythmically accompanied by *two voices*.
    Close-up with increased volume of sound.
The dark background becomes spatially formed. One can see the inside of a crystalline cavity. Movements are adapted to the spatial organisation.
    Following the movement lines the space suddenly starts to be transformed. Lines drawn into space by limbs (arms, torso, legs) become visible as shining circles, clusters of rays and rotating ribbons.
    The figures disappear. The spatial structures shrink and expand. A new musical chord sounds at every turning point.
    Dancing figures suddenly appear again and even new figures stream in until they become a larger group. Together they perform movements in unison. Later they move in opposition.
    Close-up: several of the figures in groups of torsos, and clusters of arms play as clouds or serpents.
    Superimposition of similar phenomena in nature: clouds, water, branches of trees.
    Becoming increasingly wilder, the dance of figures (in free nature) begins. This is accompanied by powerful increasing rhythmical music.
    Sudden break

I. Dance
                (The movement grows)
    Starting with a quiet torso movement, the dance increases in spatial width and leads finally to a flying whirl.
    Close-ups: breathing, tension of anticipation.
    Lap dissolves leading to the unfolding of a bright spot of light which develops into a large rosette of circles.
    Later the rosette enlarges through the arrival of new dancers.
Dances of children, folk dances.

II. Dance

(The space – the movement – circles)

This dance consists of winding-twisting movements of limbs.

An airplane helice and other forms of technical – mechanical origin (ship waves, stream-line forms, turbines, etc.) are shown in motion and stop-frames.

Free space-motifs, twisted bands, lemniscates.[21]

Close-up: wringing arms, force of pressure, and the twisted band-circle (with a light dot passing around it twice).

Tempo, dances of passion, frenzy.

III. Dance

(The movement is transformed)

A simple spatial cross unfolds into a sphere over increasingly complicated breakings and bendings.

A dance at first of one, then two and three figures which follow the same path in space. (In this dance there is a constant interchange of bodily movements and of spatial lines. Individual parts pass over into each other through lap dissolve.

Appearing and disappearing figures create ever new movement motifs (either contrasting or related).

Flying, jumping animals.

IV. Dance

(The movement resounds)

The circle and forms become schematic shapes, structures, and architectures.

The flow of their sections is clearly articulated for the ear by rhythmical means. (Rhythmology).

Dancers with new types of musical instruments.

Social dances.

V. Dance

(The movement is dreaming)

The figures assemble to compose an event (i.e. a dream-like succession of the transformed structures.) A dancer wanders between these as in a temple whose walls and decorations transform meaningfully, e.g. from simple seriousness to gay manifoldness. Figures which appear are partly sketched, partly represented by dancers.

The dance ends in a cultic pantomime.

Cultic dances.

Concluding dance
Ornaments intertwine, the figures interpret their meaning by means of attributes and activities.
Stars dance
Crystals grow
Plants wind
Animals play and fight.

Man builds instruments, buildings, machines.
Man rides, flies, drives.
Everything resounds in music
Everything is interwoven by visible spatial waves.[22]

Notes to Chapter IV

1. Cf. The chart titled "Was tut Not?" (What is Necessary), *Schrifttanz*, Heft I, 1929, p. 19, and reference on pp. 13-14 above.
2. Cf. *Choreographie*, pp. 80-85.
3. Cf. "Tanzkomposition und Schrifttanz," *Schrifttanz*, Heft II, 1928, pp. 19-20.
   "Vom Tanzinhalt: Studien über die Pole des Tanzkunstwerkes," *Der Tanz*, Heft 1, 1928, pp. 2-3.
   "Choreographie und Theater," *Der Scheinwerfer*, Heft 11/12, 1928, p. 22.
4. This author is familiar with choreography courses based on Eukinetics and Choreutics as conducted by Kurt Jooss in Essen-Werden in the 1960's, and Ana Maletic in Yugoslavia (1940's – 60's); Professor Vera Blaine's Foundation of Composition course taught at The Ohio State University draws from Laban's Effort concepts.
5. Cf. "Das Tänzerische Kunstwerk," *Die Tat*, November, 1927 pp. 588-589, and pp. 10-14, 114-115 above.
6. *Principles of Dance and Movement Notation*, p. 15.
7. Cf. *Die Tat*, 1922, pp. 669-675.
8. Cf. Op. cit., pp. 29-50.
9. Cf. *Der Tanz*, Heft 1, 1928, pp. 2-3.
10. Op. cit., p. 3.
11. See note (3) above.
12. See note (3) above.
13. Cf. *Gymnastik und Tanz*, pp. 25-29.
14. Undated manuscript housed in the Laban Archives.
15. *The Bride and the Bachelors* by Calvin Tompkins (Penguin Books, 1977), p. 33.

16. Other important aspects of Duchamp's experimentations with the law of chance and probability, such as the "canned chance" underlying his *Three Standard Stoppages* 1913) and his *Large Glass* (ca 1913-1923), are not discussed in this correlation.

17. Cf. "The Impermanent Art," reprinted in *Esthetics Contempoary*, Edited by Richard Kostelanetz, (Buffalo, New York: Prometheus Books, 1978), pp. 310-314.

18. Cf. *Silence* (Cambridge, Mass: The M.I.T. Press, 1961), pp. 58-59.

19. Cf. *Changes: Notes on Choreography* (New York: Something Else Press, 1968).

20. Unlike the record of an existing dance piece or even its adaptation for filming or videotaping, cine-dance and video-dance is a blending of structural and perceptual elements intrinsic to the media of dance and film or video; it actually exists on film or tape only.

21. Laban refers to spatial forms of twisted band-circles which were defined in the 17th century geometry as "lemniscates." Since the 19th century these are also referred to as the "Moebius Band" or "Moebius Strip" (Cf. *Choreutics*, pp. 85 and 98).

22. Undated manuscript housed in the Laban Archives.

PART THREE:

INTEGRATION OF THE PAST AND PROJECTIONS INTO THE FUTURE

Introduction

Two complementary approaches are proposed in this section: an examination of assumptions which underlie Laban's concepts and a summary of his achievements. It is believed that both approaches can contribute to the multilateral examination of his theories and systems of classification.

The notion of paradigms referred to in Chapter V is derived from Thomas Kuhn's concepts of world views, which are greatly determined by scientific discoveries, and disciplinary matrices influenced by a set of beliefs about values.[1] The chapter investigates the cultural, philosophical, and artistic paradigms which underlie Laban's dance theories and points to his creative assimilations from the heritage of Western and some Eastern dance traditions. Laban's ideas and activities certainly sprang from his particular views of the world. These views may have similarities or affinities with some philosophic or scientific concepts but need not necessarily be the result of a directly or consciously sought influence. It is therefore a dance-historical challenge to unravel those paradigms which Laban inherited as implicit in his cultural milieu from those he acquired through direct exposure or grasped through his intuition.

A brief discussion of Laban's acknowledgements of dance reformers precedes the consideration of his sources for the science of dance — choreology. The extent to which Laban was aware of post-Cartestian and contemporary philosophical stands is further examined and followed by an inquiry into certain models and values in movement and dance education during Laban's early period.

Chapter VI recapitulates the purpose behind the major formulations of Laban's theoretical framework. A discussion of areas which Laban considered in need of further development is included to form a 'bridge' toward Appendix II which shows the interpretation of Laban's concepts and their modifications and elaborations by his students-collaborators.

Notes to Introduction

1. Cf. Thomas S. Kuhn, *The Structure of Scientific* Revolutions (Chicago: University of Chicago Press, 1973), and "Second Thoughts on Paradigms," Frederick Suppe, *The Structure of Scientific Theories* (Chicago: University of Illinois Press, 1974). See also Maxine Sheets-Johnstone, "On

the Nature of Theories of Dance," *Dance Research Collage*, ed. Patricia
A. Rowe and Ernestine Stodelle (New York: Committee on Research in
Dance, 1979), pp. 3-29.

CHAPTER V

Paradigms Underlying Laban's Concepts

The context of Laban's developing ideas will first be considered from the perspective of his references to predominantly Western and some Eastern movement and dance traditions. The purpose of this brief discussion is to gain insight into the assumptions which underlie his views of various topics, such as reflections on the nature of dance, the significance of particular dance reformers, dance books he considered valuable readings, and the historical context of dance notation.

Laban discusses Lucian's dialogue *On Dance* as one of the resources for ancient wisdom about the nature of dance: "It is historically interesting that nearly 2000 years ago there was more knowledge on the nature of the dance and dances than today. Some deeper insights permeate Lucian's writings on dance and gymnastics . . . ."[1] Laban demonstrates a critical approach to the text, stating that one may find among Lucian's predominantly shallow rhetorics, pearls of insight inherited from classical Greek times. "Lucian describes how the language of gesture conveys the invisible, and how the dancer has to master geometry, physics, philosophy, and ethics . . . . He also refers to the power of dance without music, and suggests the unification of intellect, feeling, and will in dance."[2] (In this interpretation of Lucian, Laban applies the concepts of thinking-feeling-willing developed by Wilhelm Wundt in the 1870's.) In an 1925 article Laban also expresses a critical view of Lucian's German translator Wieland who appears not to have taken seriously Lucian's defence of dance but saw the dialogue as biting satire against dance.[3] Laban also comments on a passage from the dialogue in which Lycinus – the dance enthusiast – discusses mind-body dualism. "In thousands of situations only one half of man – either the spirit (mind in the classical sense) or the body – are involved; how different this is in dance! Here the activity of both flow together, each thought being a gesture, and each gesture a thought."[4] From this point of view Laban questions contemporary dance and finds that it does not quite fulfill its purpose due to the absence of this completeness. This overriding concern for the holistic nature of dance is apparent in all Laban's activities and writings.

With regard to the reformers of the art of dance and movement, Laban pays tribute to Noverre and Delsarte: "All one can find today in terms of style tendencies in dance, all the schools of barefoot and rhythmic dancers, arise from Noverre's turning from the medieval art of dancing to naturalness, and from Delsarte's ingenious new concepts of the laws of natural movement."[5] In another reference Laban describes the latter as "having attempted to base the laws of dance expression on the natural everyday movements."[6] In that process, Delsarte, however, also drew from Greek art. He thus inaugurated calisthenics and rhythmic gymnastics spreading from America to Europe and Russia. Laban makes no further evaluations of Delsarte besides mentioning that the Duncan sisters strongly show his influence, and that Delsarte's ideas have been spread by many in the field of dance. The significance of Noverre's views of the *Ballet d'action* is, however, emphasized in several entries. His greatest deed, in Laban's view, was his advice to students to observe and study the movement of people on the streets or at work, rather than to copy the behavior of princes and courtiers.[7] Laban, however, expresses a critical view of Noverre, as well as of Vigano and Angiolini for not being able to abolish the mime form and for attempting to compete with the dramatic theatre.[8] As for the reforms of the Duncans, Laban refers to them as

an American family . . . who tried about 30 years ago to revitalize the dance in our cultural circle . . . . But the Duncans were not the first ones to introduce the art of movement to Europe. This art was always there, and the passionate debates between the Parisian enthusiasts of theatre dance, particularly between Taglioni and Elssler, show us that 100 years ago thought processes had already emerged about a natural dance which was directed towards Greek ideals.[9]

Laban, however, pays tribute to Isadora in that she reawakened the sense of movement poetry in modern man and had the courage to demonstrate the ordering principle within the flow of movement, which cannot, as Laban maintains, be explained in a rationalistic way.[10] It appears that some dimensions of Noverre's and Duncan's activities had been an inspiration to Laban's developing ideas on the expression and flow of movement. (We have referred to some implicit correspondences between Delsarte's and Laban's principles in Chapter I.)

In Laban's first book, several older works as well as more recent writings on dance are included in his list of recommended readings.[11] Among the older ones, besides Noverre's *Lettres sur les Arts Immitateurs en Général et sur la Danse en Particulier*, are Blasis' *Traité Elémentaire, Théorique et Pratique de l'Art de la Danse*, Saint Leon's *La Stenochoréographie ou l'Art d'Écrire Proprement la Danse*, and Zorn's *Grammatik der Tanzkunst*. Laban expands on Blasis' significance in his later 1925 article, describing him as the creator of a number of specific verbal descriptions for dance movements, as well as of a dance notation method leading to a consideration of the whole body.[12] It is also interesting to note that complementary to Blasis' division of dancers into serious, *demi-caractère*, and comic, Laban classified dancers into high, medium, and deep movers.

When considering dance notation in its historical context, it has been seen that Laban repeatedly points to the well known fact of dance research having to rely almost exclusively on pictures and short written reports, in contrast to the well documented tradition of music and poetry. Referring to the development of graphic symbols, Laban saw such signs originally as images of gestures which did not denote a sound, a work or a concept, but rather a thousand unutterable things and emotions; the urge to find symbols for spiritual content is seen as age-old in the culture-forming process of mankind.[13] For instance Laban perceived runes (early Teutonic alphabet) as also being signs for movement and spatial directions.[14] The attempts by Jehan Tabourot, i.e., Thoinot Arbeau, to capture dance with musical notation is mentioned only briefly and described as a bridge to ancient tradition, thus as a basis for all choreographic knowledge.[15] Laban also maintained that continuing to build on Arbeau's *Orchesography*, Feuillet and his colleague Desaix, published a system — *Chorégraphie* — whose inventor was actually Beauchamps. On several occasions Laban acknowledges the Beauchamps-Feuillet notation for its sound principles.[16] It is interesting to find that he ascribes to the reforms of Noverre and Delsarte "a precipitated development of the arts of dance which caused the lack of a suitable movement notation, and left dance nearly without a tradition."[17] Discussing dance composition and notation, Laban points to the significance of script dance for the development of the new dance of our times, differentiating it from the tradition of classical ballet, as well as from the Greek and oriental influences of Duncan and St. Denis: "The new script dance will bring liberation from all these traditions in that it offers a clear application of all possible movement combinations as material for dance expression."[18]

The classical knowledge of dance is referred to in *Die Welt des Tänzers* under two headings: "Choreography" and "Choreosophy." Choreography, a description of dance with either words, technical terms, signs, pictures or musical and rhythmic notation, becomes understandable only when the fundamental views of the creeds behind it are clarified through Choreosophy. To exemplify Choreosophic attitudes, Laban refers to mythologies of all cultures and to philosophies, such as the Pythagorean cosmogony described in Plato's *Timaeus*, as well as to the beliefs of the followers of Dschella-eddin-Rumînû (the son of the founder of the order of dancing Dervishes whose tradition is known under the name of "Sufism"). Choreosophic attitudes are also found in the educational rituals of Confucius, which have a leaning towards dance, and in Nietzsche's view of the dancer as a complete being in his *Zarathustra*.[19] Laban presents another account of Choreosophy in his

Choreutics, describing it as the ancient wisdom of circles or circular motion in nature and life; there he divides it into three branches: Choreography, Choreology and Choreutics. While Choreography, the writing of dances or designing circles later becomes associated with dance planning and composition, Choreutics is also described as "the practical study of the various forms of (more or less) harmonized movement."[20] Laban's interpretation of the term "Choreology" is of particular interest. He describes it as a kind of grammar and syntax of the language of movement, investigating the unity of motion and emotion; it is based on the belief that motion and emotion, form and content, body and mind are inseparably united.[21]

For sources of the origins and Laban's subsequent interpretations of choreology, we have to refer back to *Die Welt des Tänzers*. Here under the heading "The Science of Dance," Laban points to common laws which govern organic and inorganic forms.

The task of the newly emerging science of dance will be to show that the whole of nature is ruled by the dynamic laws of harmony. The sources of the science of dance are:

1. The cognitive-theoretical, psychological, and physical determinants of the movement of living beings,
2. The geometrical and crystallographical theory of space,
3. The monuments of the visual arts in sculpture, painting, fine arts, including hieroglyphic and abstract signs for numbers and concepts as well as ornamentation,
4. The musical cognitive-theoretical research about harmony,
5. The written theoretic documents on old dances as well as on mantic religious ceremonial and ritual movement forms,
6. The theories of movement acrobatics, the art of fencing, and sports,
7. The mimetic tradition of acting,
8. The practical tradition of the European art dance as well as of folk and ethnic dances of all peoples.[22]

The above gives us an excellent insight into the complexity of Laban's scope, reaching into other arts and disciplines. We will consider each of the eight cited sources, tracing the emergence of Laban's insights into dance, drawn from multiple sources.

Laban's search for the first source, the psychophysical determinants of movement, resulted by the 40's in his concept of Effort, the inner impulse for movement, and its articulation into qualitative and quantitative components. This holistic approach to movement transpired from many considerations in his first book on the unity of motion and emotion. Laban proposes a schematic representation of the forms of human perception with the intent of clarifying the process of thinking about the dance experience.[23] The scheme shows some explicit references to Indian philosophy and some implicit ones to Wundt and Jung. The tripartite division of consciousness into thinking, feeling, and willing reflects Wilhelm Wundt's classifications from his physiological-psychology; the inclusion of conscious and intuitive forms of perception announces some Jungian influences. The synchrony between Laban's and Carl Gustav Jung's ideas is even more apparent in Laban's later association of the space, weight, time, and flow elements of human movement with man's powers of thinking, sensing, intuiting, and feeling, respectively. The latter are terms which Jung used in his division of consciousness. Accordingly, sensation or sense perception tells us that something exists; thinking tells us what it is; feeling tells us whether it is agreeable or not; and intuiting tells us where it comes from and where it is going to. These four functional types correspond to the means by which consciousness obtains its orientation to experience.[24]

Laban found another source for his investigations in the relationship between the perception of harmony and bodily structure: "It is noteworthy that the number 12 plays a role in man's perception of harmony: the European has built a tonal scale in music from 12 tones; the brain sends 12 pairs of nerves into various organs through cavities in the base of the skull. We find here a relationship between the perception of harmony and bodily structure."[25] Laban also considers the structure of the spine in terms of the numerical relationships of vertebra and its movement possibilities; further elaborations on flexion, extension and rotation of the joints pave the way for his correlations with crystalline structures. The following quotation summarizes these concerns and clarifies Laban's holistic view of the movement:

There is not a thought, feeling, or force which is not predesigned in the structure of the human body and fundamentally in the skeleton. The human skeleton is the crystal of crystals. The skeleton delineates in its functional as well as expressive movements the edges and inclinations of an invisible spatial crystal.[26]

Laban's investigations of the second source, the geometrical and crystallographical theory of space, became one of the major components of his "new choreography," later referred to as "choreutics" and "space harmony." Discussing the harmonic laws of form, Laban finds that the structuring of form, the growth of movement of all natural things including crystals, plants, and animals are subjected to the same spatial laws which man applies in his harmonic movement. Laban's resources for these investigations are manifold. Besides his correlations of the human skeleton with the structure of crystals, he refers to some writings on crystallography: "Modern crystallography explains that the structure of crystalline forms evolve from the same basic rule as the building of artistic harmonies in the art of dance, music, poetic writing, and thinking."[27] Geometrical ideas from Antiquity and the Renaissance are another strand of Laban's resources. In his *Choreutics*, Laban draws correspondences between the ancient knowledge of dynamic crystallization, which brought Plato to classify the five regular solids, and his own ideas on harmonic forms of movement. Laban uses the five polyhedra on the one hand as an aid for spatial orientation and as a kind of model for the design and practice of his choreutic dance sequences or scales. On the other hand, he draws close analogies between the proportions of the icosahedron (one of the five regular Platonic solids) and those of the human body, which, as found by Pythagoras as well as Leonardo, are constructed according to the laws of the Golden Section. In his first book, Laban already hints at these correlations:

> Anatomy and dance point to . . . numerous proportionalities of limbs, positions, sequences of movement, and angles of inclinations based on orders which can be divided according to the golden section.[28]

In discussing the foundation of Laban's ideas on movement harmony, certain authors have attempted to draw a direct and exclusive correpondence to Pythagorean cosmic harmonies as interpreted by Plato. In *The New Ballet*, A.V. Coton suggests that the point of departure for Laban's inquiry into the nature of bodily movement has been Platonic mathematic and scientific hypotheses. Without citing his sources, Coton states that Laban felt that some of Plato's observations on the proportional interrelationship among all forms of life should offer a clue to the discovery of the basic laws of bodily movement. He sees Laban's usage of the icosahedron as a system of relations and stresses corresponding to bodily tensions, oppositions and equilibria; he evaluates such an inquiry into organic and inorganic expression as far-reaching.

Gordon Curl's analysis of Laban's writings (expounded on in six articles in *The Laban Art of Movement Guild Magazine*), on the other hand, stems from a particular concern of British education in the late 60's dealing with the academic respectability of the arts, particularly dance.[29] In his comparison of Laban's texts to Plato's *Timaeus*, Curl deduces that all Laban's ideas originated from Pythagorean principles. Contrary to Coton, he evaluates Pythagorean and Platonic views as a "mythical mode of apprehension" which prevented Laban from forming a sound aesthetic theory. From the perspective of these deliberations, it appears that Coton's view of Pythagorean paradigms as a point of departure for Laban's investigations of dance space may be more acceptable than Curl's contention about Laban's exclusive inspiration from philosophical metaphors in *Timaeus*. Further, Curl's evaluation of the mystical and mythical dimensions of Laban's ideas displays a narrow view of the nature of insights and discoveries.

Laban's interest in and study of the third source — old symbols, alphabets, and ornamentation — led him to formulate the fundamental form elements — the line, wave, spiral and circle — linked both with basic functions of the joints as well as with some ways of perception.[30] He finds that "the script symbols . . . of all people, and all times are symbols of tensions through which a pictorial echo of the things of the environment is given . . . . A form element always corresponds to a concomitant symbolic and psychological component or differentiation."[31] One may suppose that underlying these considerations is the aesthetic theory of empathy, proposed by Theodor Lipps at the beginning of the century. This may be even more obvious from Laban's further considerations of a direct connection between form and its perceptual experience: "The straight line, when vertical, gives the motif of weight, sinking-rising (arsis-thesis). The horizontal gives a more suspended impression. The inclined line gives a restless impression through its risk of falling . . . . The bent line is swinging . . . . Strongly curved arches seem to embody the element of speed."[32] Laban even discusses the form of tools and furniture from a dance-like perception:

> When the dancer looks at an appliance . . . , the picture of movement and thoughts, even the feeling of the people that created these appliances, becomes immediately alive to him. Some appliances lack . . . any movement expression. One observes a typical straight chair of our time next to a rococco chair. Here exaggerated stiffness, there exaggerated movement. The leg of the rococco chair winds as if to allow the seated person all those poses he combines with the jumps of his thoughts and the turns which his feelings take . . . . The chair is mimo-plastic; it mimes the moving plasticity of the human body.[33]

It may be of interest to note that the aesthetic views of empathy have also influenced some other dance writers such as dance critic, John Martin. He formulated the notion of "metakinesis" to refer to muscular and kinesthetic sympathy as a link between the dancer's intention and the viewer's perception of it.[34]

Laban found that the fourth area, musical research about harmony, further corroborated his investigations of the dynamic laws of form in organic and inorganic matter. He maintains that "the examination of music has shown that forms, tensions, and the dimensions of a sound generating body are regulated according to the same rules as the building of form in crystals."[35] In his *Choreutics*, Laban traces parallels between harmonic relations in music and dance such as the seven fundamental cross-sections of space and the seven fundamental notes of Western music, or the peripheral movement scale in the icosahedron and the diatonic scale in music. He even suggests that the relationships of bodily rotation, flexion and extension are analogous to the relationships and measurement in acoustics. Laban sees the task of future choreutic research as investigating further the above structural congruities.[36]

Laban's approaches to dance-music relationships, however, differ from those of Dalcroze. While for Dalcroze movement and dance are stimulated through music, for Laban music originates from rhythmical movements of the body. Hans Brandenburg delineates the differences between the two reformers: "Laban does not intend to transpose musical rhythms into bodily rhythms [as does Dalcroze] but stimulates his students to draw rhythm from their own body movement. . . . rhythm with all its elements: swing, tempo, meter, order, articulation. . . . . The double function [of movement in space and time] creates such an endlessly rich material that the silent movement becomes for Laban the most fulfilled dance."[37] The article also refers to "free dance" as the expression of the new bodily culture; it is based on itself and its own rules regardless of whether it is with or without music. Wigman corroborates this statement by arguing that Laban liberated dance from a slave-like dependency on music and thus returned it to the absolute language of art.[38] Laban comments on the frequent link of music and dance in which "we see the musical values in the foreground while dance is supressed."[39] He sees attempts to affiliate the art of dance to either music or drama as arising out of the desire to interpret the ineffable in dance. Laban further argues that "dance is the art form out of which music and drama have evolved through differentiating and developing especially its psychic and formal fundamental principles. The new dance theatre now has the task to discover all the possibilities of dance-like expression and to draw them together again towards a synthesis."[40] Besides, he argues, that which moves us in dance is neither the accompanying music nor the plot. It is a selection of hidden forms of tension which are made visible in the rhythm of the dancers lifting, turning, bending which they inscribe in the environment.[41]

Laban's views of rhythm and Eurhythmy also have different starting points from those of Dalcroze. Dance rhythm is for Laban

> not time-duration divided by accents, as one tries to interpret this concept in music. Rhythm is the law of gesture according to which it proceeds at one time more fluently and at another less fluently. Tensing and relaxing of the body arise through this, which presents nuances of force. In addition the gesture needs a duration in time for its sequence in space.[42]

This early description of the components of rhythm announces Laban's later concept of Effort with its elements of flow, weight, space and time. The term "Eurhythmy" was used in the 20's not only by Dalcroze but also by Rudolf Steiner and Laban before he replaced it with "Eukinetics" and "Choreutics." Laban refers to Eurhythmy as one of the basic concepts in dance education. He describes this Greek term (meaning "good rhythm") as heightening simple harmonious forms such as regularity, symmetry, and proportionality. Without mentioning Dalcroze or Steiner, Laban criticizes the use of the term Eurhythmy for works of art, and he comments that its use for educational systems conceals the notion of dance.[43]

From many references to the fifth source, the significance of rituals, transpires Laban's emphasis on the power of gesture as its medium. He writes that old mantic, magic gestures "bring about changes in our inner imagery, i.e., an inner spatial adaptation of a plastic nature, whose cause and effect can for the time being only be surmised, although they unfold according to fixed laws of harmony."[44] Laban makes a further link between modern psychoanalysis, which examines the content of dreams in terms of their symbolic meaning, and the area of mantics and ritualistics, which is, he maintains, a rich treasure fund for the psychophysiological relationship of symbols. As Laban points out, "to the dancer all questions of psychology and theories of perception become a plastic representation of formal tensions through the experience of body-mind movement."[45] (Without directly referring to Sigmund Freud, Laban undoubtably had an acquaintance with his theories as is apparent from these views.) Laban further maintains that even

> ballet is of cultic origin and . . . has always been aware that human move-ment evolves only in a few definite form structures and swings. Ballet knows the primary phenomenon of motility in its *ouvert*, *tortillé* and *rond* just as the modern Eurhythmicist or the old Arabic writer of numerals. In the shapes of 1, 2, 3, and the letters of the Greek alphabet are given all the primary forms of flowing motion."[46]

Ouvert (open), *tortillé* (wavy), *rond* (circular), as well as *droit* (straight) as fundamental forms of step patterns are first cited in Feuillet's *Chorègraphie* from which Laban drew extensively.[47]

The sixth source of Choreology came from the martial arts and sport. Amongst photographs of dancers, Laban also included in his first book pictures of wrestlers. He had a great esteem for the unity of clear thinking, feeling and energy in combat: "Wrestling and other forms of combat are to me important means of cultic training."[48] As referred to above Laban found a correlation between his dimensional scale and sequences used in combat: "One can see particularly in fencing the performance of move-ments which have such typical directions . . . . The order is known in the gestures of defense (parries) of the art of fencing (as prime, second, terce, quarte, quint, and sixth) . . . . The swing scale moves in the order of up, down, left, right, backward, forward . . . . All types of defense since ancient times are based on this as much as are all expressive movements . . . . "[49]

While the mimetic tradition of the art of acting, the seventh source, is only touched upon in Laban's German writings, it is the starting point of his *The Mastery of Movement on the Stage*. This tradition is considered in terms of expressive movement which mirrors man's trend towards values; movement styles of particular periods and their aesthetic and utilitarian back-ground are discusssed.

The eighth source for Choreology is the theatrical, folk and ethnic dance tradition. Laban's references to the latter are global. One can gain a glimpse of his insights into ethnic dance traditions from considerations of rhythmic, melodic and harmonic tendencies in dance, music and poetry such as: "The art of the people of Asia has lyric-melodic characteristics . . . . Africa and Australia prefer rhythmical art creations. The European has been inclined up to now toward harmonious formulations in his creations. Mixed types occur at crossroads of culture: Polynesia is essentially rhythmic-melodic."[50] He elaborates on each type from the point of view of compositional and qualitative movement characteristics.

Laban's investigations of the practical tradition of the European art dance is, in contrast, very specific. In his *Choreographie* he analyzes the theory of ballet as systematized in Feuillet's treatise. "The so-called five positions have been handed down to us as the simplest means of spatial orientation in the art of dance."[51] Referring to forms of steps (the *droit, ouvert, tortillé,* and *rond,* mentioned above) and their notations, Laban maintains that the three-dimensionality of signs in the traditional ballet choreography represent form elements which are fundamental to all styles of movement.

The consideration of Laban's eight sources of Choreology have provided further insights into the origins of his ideas and roots of his theories. Together with Laban's explicit tribute to the heritage of dance, the discussion of the eight sources offers a historical perspective of his concepts and theories.

A brief survey of major philosophical paradigms derived from and in reaction to the tenets of the French philosopher René Descartes will preface the examination of Laban's awareness of some contemporary philosophical views. A common denominator of major paradigms deriving from views of post-Cartesian philosophy and science can be seen in the assumption that reality is separate from man. Space, time, and even movement are things "out there" or physical properties which are perceivable through our minds – according to rationalists – or our senses – according to empiricists. As a consequence of Descartes' main tenets in his *Meditations of First Philosophy*, movement is seen as a purely mechanical act which belongs to the realm of bodies, completely separate from the world of intelligent minds. This body-mind dichotomy has enforced the mechanistic view of human movement, explaining it according to the laws of inanimate motion. The implications of these philosophical views are the separation of the living person from the world, from the lived experience. A radical change in these concepts can be seen in the efforts of some individuals in the 20's and 30's, such as Husserl and Merleau-Ponty, to undo centuries of traditional thinking and bring together the person and the world, returning thus to what is directly given to us in experience. In that pursuit space and time are transformed from the status of physical properties to world dimensions which are created through the intent of human action, through movement.

Within the literature on dance theory of post-Cartesian times, i.e., the dance manuals of the eighteenth and nineteenth centuries, one can notice a separation of body space and dance space. The Beauchamp-Feuillet notation is conceived in terms of tract or floor patterns in the dancing area on which dancers perform their positions and steps. The notion of linear time extended through space which permeates Western music had infiltrated dance: "It is the time and tone of the music which fix and determine all the dancer's movement," exclaims Noverre.[52] The radical change of linear time concepts to the experience of its totality or simultaneity present with dance can be seen in some modern writings and choreographic embodiments. Merce Cunningham, for example, brings to dance composition the notion of dance as coexisting with music, and not depending on it. His structuring of dance events displays a simultaneity of several events.[53]

Laban's awareness of the clash of classical and contemporary views of movement, space and time is apparent in his writings. Discussing views of space, time, and movement he writes that "the conventional idea of space as a phenomenon which can be separated from time and force and from expression, is completely erroneous," and further that "movement is the life of space. Dead space does not exist, for there is neither space without movement, nor movement without space."[54] Laban also expressed his reservations that certain writings in aesthetics, history of art and criticism, as well as scientific literature, had arisen out of pure intellect and thus were not sufficiently comprehensive to contribute to insights about dance: "Purely rationalistic works do not serve to sharpen a clear judgement .... Scientific literature suffers from the same evil as do the fantasies of sectarianism. Only it is here not the sentimentality of feeling but of intellect which misrepresents all the dance elements present in knowing."[55] This statement seems to imply a kind of knowing which is based on a unified sense, the dance sense, which actively links the person with the world in the act of perception.

A clear account of the essential differences of the dance descriptions of eighteenth-century ballet and Laban's vision of the new dance seen through the prism of their respective notations is given in his *Choreographie* in the form of a comparative table:

... Ballet:	New dance notation:
movement of the legs	unified movement of the whole body
...	...
division of the body space from dance space	unified view of space
...	...

[a two-partite articulation of movement phenomena into the manner of performing & form] Further: elements of direction and rhythm	referring articulation to spatial causes
. . .	. . .
indication of body parts and body sides	notation of the complete plastic form of a particular movement sequence, from which the movement of particular limbs can be seen
. . .	. . .
dimensionally stable orientation	diagonally labile orientation [56]

This comparison indicates several opposing views:

1. In contrast to the fragmentation of the body, which in ballet is reduced predominantly to leg movement, *pas* and *port des bras*, arm gestures, Laban juxtaposes a unified, total movement which includes equal participation of the whole body.
2. To the separation of body space and dance space in ballet, Laban juxtaposes a view of body movement as creating space.
3. While in ballet the rhythm of movement is derived from music or musical notation, rhythm in Laban's new dance is articulated from the point of view of unfolding movement in space and time. As discussed in Chapter III, Laban's movement symbols unify the indication of direction and level — i.e., space — with the indication of duration — i.e., time — of movement. One may suggest a synchrony between Laban's approach and Einstein's interpretation of the universe as a space-time continuum.
4. With regard to the aspects of stability or equilibrium and lability/mobility or loss of equilibrium, the more stable, positional, dimensional orientation of ballet is juxtaposed to the more dynamic, movement-oriented mobility of the diagonal orientation of the new dance.

One can see from these considerations that Laban was not only keenly aware of paradigms which underlie classical dance tradition but was also clearly formulating theoretical perspectives of the new dance. While these views were revolutionary in the 1920's, they have been perceived as hampering progress in the British tradition of Laban's teaching during the 50's and 60's, as will be discussed below. The examination of paradigms behind major systems of body culture and views of modern dance pioneers will preface this discussion.

The idea that each movement which involves the whole body should be initiated from the centre of gravity and flow easily to its periphery creating the resulting movement had already been entertained by the German poet Heinrich von Kleist in 1810.[57] The initiation from the centre of gravity is a common assumption in the gymnastic systems of Mensendieck, Loheland and Bode. It also bears resemblence to Duncan's discovery of the solar plexus as the central spring of all movement and motor power, further with Graham's principles of central contraction and its release toward the body periphery, and with Laban's view of the centre of the body as the focal point of irradiating spatial directions, as well as his principle of sequence. In fact, central initiation of movement became somewhat normative in the tradition of Laban-based teaching, implying that a movement initiated by distal body parts is less harmonious. A similar judgment is implicit in the preference for large or total body movement over isolations. Bode dogmatically states that only movement which engages the whole body is *right* and so are only such exercises which tackle the center of gravity as the central point of depature. Such a view in body culture may have sprung initially from the need for counteracting the reduced body-mind involvement in factory work. Its preference in the new dance over the fragmentation of the body in ballet has been pointed out by Laban in the above comparison from *Choreographie*. (These two related paradigms also underlie Warren Lamb's movement observation and assessment, the action profile. While an action which involves a continuous adjustment of the entire body is referred to as posture, gesture is an action confined to a part or several parts of the body.[58] The latter has also been associated with learned, acquired, rather than natural movement patterns. Because the natural movement qualities are seen to prevail in the fusion of posture and gesture, "it is only posture-gesture merging that is used as a basis for analysis and construction of the action profile.[59])

The rhythmic exchange of tension and relaxation over predominant muscular contraction is another common view initially intended to counteract both life conditions caused by increasing industrialization and the predominant light tension in the style of classical ballet. For instance, Graham's principle of central contraction and release unifies both the requirement of central initiation and of the rhythm of tension and relaxation. The German notion of *Anspannung* and *Abspannung* are words which better express the process of increasing and decreasing tension. For the latter, Graham's term "release" is more appropriate than "relaxation" which may imply passive limpness. Abspannung or Entspannung in the context of Laban's "Tänzerische Körperkunst" ("Dancer's body art") should also influence both mind and body.[60]

This brings us to another belief common to gymnastics and dance in the early 1920's and that is the inherent correspondence among the physical, and the spiritual, emotional, and conceptual. Humphrey's statement that a movement without motivation is unthinkable had been anticipated by

Delsarte's view of the unity of motion and emotion, Duncan's view of dance as the divine expression of the human spirit, and was contemporary with the trends of German "expressive gymnastics" (Bode) and Laban's eukinetics and choreutics.

The search for the intrinsic rhythm of bodily movement rather than the following of rhythm imposed by music can also be seen as a reaction to both the predominant slavery to music in ballet and to the rhythmic gymnastics of Jacques-Dalcroze which aimed at expressing music through bodily movement. It had already been clearly stated by Laban in his search for the "free dance" as well as in the above comparison; it is also visible in the work of Wigman, and of Graham and Humphrey (to a certain extent) in response to the Denishawan "music visualizations."

Finally Laban's point about the more dynamic, movement-oriented mobility of diagonal directions of the new dance as a reaction to predominantly stable dimensional directions of ballet had prompted Valerie Preston-Dunlop to find Laban guilty of dismissing the set of predominantly stable choreutic forms, thus jeopardizing the use of his choreutics for a comprehensive analysis in choreography.[61] By adding six form groups to Laban's existing nineteen, Dunlop was, however, able to use this theoretical model in her analysis of contemporary choreography. She believes that broadening and reassembling Laban's choreutic concepts can make them a central resource for an analysis which reveals the choreutic content and style of a work.[62]

The above discussion indicates that Laban's theoretical foundations were based on multifarious resources. Philosophical tenets from antiquity, ideas from eighteenth and nineteenth century dance theories, and contemporary points of view were integrated within his own interpretations of all life phenomena in dance-like terms and conceptualizations. On the other hand, the discussion of the common basis of Laban's notation and his other theories in Chapter III has shown the universality of his major concepts. In addition, some of Laban's principles creatively unify old and new paradigms: his system of Kinetography/Labanotation may be seen as departing from the Beauchamps-Feuillet concepts towards the Einsteinian unity of space-time created through bodily movement. One may, therefore, suggest that the process of unraveling inherited paradigms from Laban's intuitive insights offers yet another perspective on his concepts, principles and classification. It provides grounds for more clearly seeing Laban's creative assimilations as a synthesis of all the above strands.

Notes to Chapter V

1. *Die Welt des Tänzers*, p. 260.
2. Ibid., pp. 260-261.
3. Cf. "Der Tanz als Eigenkunst," *Zeitschrift fur Aesthetic und Allgemeine Kunstwissenschaft*, XIX Band, Stuttgart, 1925, p. 356.
4. *Gymnastik und Tanz*, p. 155.
5. Ibid., p. 157.
6. Source in note (3), p. 359.
7. Cf. *Modern Educational Dance*, p. 3-4.
8. Cf. *Principles of Dance and Movement Notation*, p. 16.
9. *Gymnastik und Tanz*, p. 129.
10. *Modern Educational Dance*, p. 5.
11. Cf. *Die Welt des Tänzers*, pp. 262-264.
12. Cf. Source in note (3), pp. 358-359.
13. Cf. *Des Kindes Gymnastik und Tanz*, p. 34.
14. Cf. Source in note (3), p. 362.
15. Cf. Ibid., p. 357.
16. Cf. Ibid., p. 362; *Choreographie*, pp. 54-64; *Principles of Dance and Movement Notation*, p. 7.
17. *Gymnastik und Tanz*, p. 157.
18. "Tanzkomposition und Schrifttanz" ("Dance Composition and Script-Dance"), *Schrifttanz*, Heft II, 1928, p. 20.
19. Cf. *Die Welt des Tänzers*, pp. 13-14.
20. *Choreutics*, p. viii.
21. Cf. Ibid., p. vii-ix.
22. Op. cit., pp. 64-65, translated by Lisa Ullmann.
23. Cf. Op. cit., pp. 10-11.
24. Cf. Carl Gustav Jung, *Man and His Symbols* (New York: Doubleday & Co., Inc., 1964,) p. 61.
25. *Gymnastik und Tanz*, p. 87.
26. Ibid., p. 121.
27. *Die Welt des Tänzers*, p. 32.
28. Ibid., p. 37.
29. Cf. "Philosophic Foundations" I-VI, *The Laban Art of Movement Magazine*, Nos. 37-39, 40, 43, 1966-69.
30. See Chapter I.
31. *Die Welt des Tänzers*, pp. 31, 38.
32. Ibid., p. 209.
33. Ibid., pp. 149-190; translated by I. Bartenieff in *Four Adaptations of Effort Theory* (New York: Dance Notation Bureau, 1970), p. 24.
34. Cf. John Martin, *The Modern Dance* (New York: Dance Horizons, 1935), p. 13.
35. *Die Welt des Tänzers*, p. 36.
36. Cf. *Choreutics*, pp. 117-122.

37. Hans Brandenburg, "Der 'Freie Tanz'; Mary Wiegmann," *Tagblatt*, Bern, 24. II. 1916.
38. Cf. Mary Wigman's, "Rudolf von Laban zum Geburtstag," *Schrifttanz*, Heft IV, 1929, p. 65.
39. *Die Welt des Tänzers*, p. 211.
40. *Gymnastik und Tanz*, pp. 148-150.
41. Cf. Source in note (3), p. 362.
42. *Die Welt des Tänzers*, p. 55.
43. Cf. Ibid., p. 258.
44. Ibid., p. 59.
45. Ibid., p. 42.
46. *Gymnastik und Tanz*, p. 165.
47. Laban called his first publication on space analysis and its notation *Choreographie* honoring his debt to Feuillet's *Chorégraphie* (1701). Cf. *Choreographie*, p. 54.
48. *Die Welt des Tänzers*, p. 260.
49. *Gymnastik und Tanz*, pp. 85-86.
50. *Die Welt des Tänzers*, pp. 199-201; translated by I. Bartenieff, see note (33).
51. *Choreographie*, p. 6.
52. *Lettres Sur la Danse*, first published in 1760 (Paris: Éditions Lieutier, 1952), p. 71.
53. Cf. *Changes, Notes on Choreography* (New York: Something Else Press, 1968).
54. *Choreutics*, p. 67.
55. *Die Welt des Tänzers*, p. 262.
56. Cf. *Choreographie*, p. 64.
57. Cf. Heinrich von Kleist, "Puppet Theatre," *Salmagundi*, No. 33-34, pp. 83-88; Cf. also Martin Gleisner, *Tanz für Alle*, p. 39.
58. Cf. Warren Lamb, *Posture and Gesture*, pp. 12-16, and 65-68. There is yet another assumption which underlies Lamb's design of the action profile and that is the correlation of the Effort movement pattern components to the Shape or Shaping components. This correlation had intially been based on Laban's observation of affinities between Effort elements and dimensional directions as discussed in Chapter I (pp. 77-79 above). Further research in nonverbal communication and anthropology may challenge these assumptions. Also, Laban's concept of affinities cannot be normative for dance as an art form which differs from behaviour even in its "pedestrian" phase during the 1960's in the U.S.A.
59. Pamela Ramsden, *Top Team Planning: Individual Motivation and Management* (London: Cassell/Associated Business Programes Ltd., 1973), p. 89.
60. In an article titled "Wie unterscheiden sich die Gymnastische Systeme?" ("How do Gymnastic Systems differ?") in the *Berliner Tageblatt* from 1926, Laban's system is referred to as "Tänzerische Körperkunst" (Laban Archives).

61. Cf. Valerie Preston-Dunlop, "Choreutics: The Study of Logical Spatial Forms in Dance," *Dancing and Dance Theories*, 1979, pp. 131-154.
62. From the abstract of Preston-Dunlop's doctoral thesis titled "The Nature of Embodiment of Choreutic Unites in Contemporary Choreography," as cited in "Going for a Walk with a Line," *Movement and Dance: Magazine of The Laban Guild*, No. 69, 1982, pp. 3-34.

CHAPTER VI

Open-Ended Conclusions

As announced in the Preface a definitive work on Laban might be in a state of constant making and re-making. In the final chapter, however, an attempt is made to summarize all the strands of this multilateral study.

Rudolf Laban formed his theoretical framework on the basis of his multiple experiences as artist-designer, dancer, choreographer, director, teacher, and work-study adviser. His acquaintance with the heritage of dance and traditional thinking, on one hand, and his exploration of anatomy, psychology, and crystallography, on the other, significantly contributed to the forming of his theories. In contrast to traditional approaches to the study of movement in terms of examining phenomena in isolation, Laban believed that the underlying principles of movement and dance must be understood. His view of modern dance as human expression connected with universal forms of movement directed him to seek movement elements as common denominators in all types of movement.

Several significant features constitute Laban's particular approach to the examination of movement and dance: (a) the view of movement as dynamic process, (b) the correlation and unity of all movement components, (c) the concern with the experience of movement and its perception based on the view of mind-body unity, and (d) the description of movement and dance in its own terms.

Already in his first attempts to formulate a language for dance description, Laban argues that "the explanation of the world of dance forms should not be limited to the enumeration of rigid states. It should rather be considered as a wave of living, changing transformations."[1] Hence, in contrast to the "static form theory" the "dynamic form theory" investigates and describes progressions by following the process of movement from its beginning to its terminating stages; the phases in between constitute the actual movement.[2] This view of movement as dynamic process was to become the continuum of Laban's entire theoretical framework; it is reflected in all concepts and the movement symbology.

Although Laban articulated movement and dance forms into component parts, these are considered interdependently from the onset. That the systematization of movement into time, force, space, and flow elements is arbitrary, and that one cannot discuss these without also considering bodily participation had already been expressed in Laban's German writings.[3] It is the movement's complexity and its countless variables which justify the separate examination of its spatial and dynamic strands.[4] Hence, the correlation and unity of all movement components formed the basis for Laban's comprehensive classification of movement and dance generating a sound language for its description and analysis.

In Laban's movement concepts the link between the physical and mental aspects of movement is a constant, reflecting his view of mind-body unity: "There is no emotional arousal or mental effort without body movement and vice versa."[5] Dance is seen as unifying "the clarifying thought of imagery, the rousing element of irrational confluences, and at the same time the physicality of the actual rhythm."[6] The movement and dance expression can also be shared by the performer and the viewer/observer in an immediate or more analytical way. Although not the first one to have conceptualized the links between the mental and physical, as well as the performer and the perceiver, Laban proposed to outline a contemporary choreology as "a kind of grammar and syntax of the language of movement, dealing not only with the outer form of movement but also with its mental and emotional content."[7]

Laban's choreology is based on the discipline of movement and dance itself; it defined common denominators of all types of movement and provided means of differentiating them through description, classification and notation. It can serve as a foundation for research in movement and dance without borrowing from conceptual frameworks in other disciplines.

These major systems of movement classification constitute Laban's theoretical framework:

1. a general, objective movement classification and description which also underlies his system of notation (Kinetography Laban or Labanotation);
2. the theory investigating spatial structure and relationships of movement and dance referred to as Space Harmony or Choreutics;
3. the theory dealing with the dynamic structure and rhythm of movement and dance known as Eukinetics and Effort; and
4. the concept of movement harmony reflecting the idea of affinities between the movement's energy or Effort and its spatial unfolding.

General Movement and Dance Classification

In creating a descriptive vocabulary and classification of the components of movement and dance, Laban provided the possibilities for two applications

— a descriptive and a prescriptive one. While the process of observation, recording, and analysis can describe individual, cultural, period and/or choreographic styles, the awareness of the whole range of bodily-spatial dynamic rhythms can facilitate an expansion of expression or efficiency. The perscriptive aspect of dance notation and classification can also offer an acquaintance with a variety of movement styles, thus widening the performer's idiosyncratic range.

Laban sees style as a special selection of movement: "In dance a few significant bodily actions are selected which form the characteristic patterns of a particular dance."[8] He maintains that the motivation for the particular selection of movement originates from "racial, social, period and other characteristics."[9] Detailed guide-lines are provided for observing bodily actions from the point of view of the subdividions of body, time, space, and energy, as well as relationships. Laban firmly believes that "thinking in terms of movement" underlies the analysis of all movement style from individual behavior to bodily actions in work, sport, play, acting, and dance. He also points to the universal basis of the logical order of movement observation: "Dancers in every age and in all countries have thought, and still think, in terms of movement which are essentially space, time, and energy indications."[10]

Laban's concern with an objective movement analysis is visible from his first publications in Germany, particularly those dealing with his system of notation, such as *Choreographie* (1926), and "Fundamental Principles of Movement Notation," in *Schrifttanz* (No. I. 1928). The identification of body symmetry or asymmetry, of spatial direction in relation to the vertical including the type of balance, and of temporal sequencing of movement, are considered as the most important components of observable movement.[11] The analysis of simple and complex bodily actions is the topic of two chapters in *The Mastery of Movement on the Stage* (1950) and the subsequent *The Mastery of Movement* (1960). The intent is "to give the student of movement an introduction to exercises designed to train the body as an instrument of expression. In this it is important not only to become aware of the various articulations in the body and of their use in creating rhythmical and spatial patterns, but also of the mood and inner attitude produced by bodily actions."[12] The link between mental and physical aspects of movement is explicitly stated here.

Bodily actions are seen as consisting of "one of the various combinations of the subdivision of body, time, space, and muscular energy."[13] The movement of the whole body and its parts is analyzed from the point of view of its anatomical structure including the consideration of torso and extremities, functions of the joints, bilateral symmetry, forward-backward, and upper-lower body articulations. Gestures are observed in their bending, extending, rotating, tilting and shifting variations, and the simultaneity or succession of their movement flow is also analyzed. Transference of weight is described as changes of support on various body parts, steps, and jumps. Movement related to people and objects is equally described as an important aspect of bodily action.

The temporal dimension of movement can be related to time units of varying choices such as meter and tempo of Western classical music, as well as clock time (an important measurement both in industry as well as in post-modern dance); the timing relative to the perception of the performer or an *ad libitum* timing is also considered particularly in the context of Laban's concept of Effort.

Spatial direction and level are assessed in relation to the vertical as a gravity-determined constant. Laban places the dividing point between the main directions in the centre of gravity of the upright body facilitating directional orientation from the mover's or dancer's front. Verticality and the centre of gravity are also references for determining aspects of equilibrium: a predominantly stable, in-balance one which induces stillness, and a mobile, off-balance one promoting movement. Laban's more detailed analysis of spatial relationships of body movement has been discussed in Chapter I. The qualitative aspects of space in terms of a direct, linear, one-dimensional path and/or focus, and a flexible, three-dimensional multifocal movement are part of the concept of Effort.

Muscular energy or force used in resistance to weight can be described in predominantly quantitative terms such as degrees of muscular tension and in terms of accents. The qualitative dimensions of weight in terms of strong, firm, and light, fine touch attitudes in movement performance are also part of Effort actions discussed in Chapter II.

Laban saw the energy, time and space components of bodily actions in sequences constituting rhythms: "One can discern *space-rhythms, time-rhythms*, and *weight-rhythms*. In reality these three forms of rhythm are always united,though one can occupy the foreground of an action."[14] Space rhythm consists in the alternative use of various directions resulting in various forms and shapes, such as straight, rounded and twisted, and their combinations. The distinction of the successive, sequential or "melodic" development of forms, and the simultaneous or "chordal" creation of shapes can be significant. The division of the continuous flux of movement into parts of duration in time creates time-rhythm which can either be metrically regular or free, irregular. In associating time-rhythm with weight-rhythm of accented and unaccented parts of movement sequences, Laban refers to six fundamental rhythms which had already been found in Greek metrics (trochee, iambus, dactylus, anapestus, peon, and ionian). Related to the area of rhythm is also the consideration of phrasing which can be distinguished through various emphases of the space, time, weight components. These considerations clearly indicate Laban's view of the inseparability of movement components; some elements can be emphasized more than others in a particular movement or dance style, and they can be isolated only by means of our attention for study purposes.

Spatial Relationship/Order of Movement – Space Harmony/Choreutics

The comprehensiveness and depth of Laban's classification of spatial components of movement is particularly obvious when compared with any classical or modern dance theory. Here again the descriptive and prescriptive approaches are applicable. Spatial description is an integral part of Laban's notation, on one hand, and the prescriptive aspect of moving into 26 directions and acquiring a greater variety of size and shaping can expand a personal movement range and complexity.

Laban maintains that "there is no limit to the possibilities of the study and practice of choreutics. It penetrates every human action and reaction, since all actions and reactions spring from movement within us."[15] Such a global view underlies the elaborations of spatial relationships and structures of movement. That the recording and analysis of choreutic units can reveal the nature of the embodiment of choreographic ideas is the premise of Preston-Dunlop's research, cited above.[16] The potential of its prescriptive use is also vast. If we take as an example just the notion of Laban's dimensional and diagonal directions (discussed in Chapter I), one can find numerous possibilities for drawing technical and compositional ideas from their nature. For instance the mastery of a greater range of "daring," off-vertical, mobile movements and of various stable, balancing situations can provide both skillful performance and an extended vocabulary for movement invention. Both scales form a basis for the compositional invention of movement and dance motives and themes. The choreographer can select and organize the order of directions and design the performance either sequentially, creating various shapes, or simultaneously, creating several sequences or chords of spatial tensions at the same time. Laban refers to these two different types of movement sequencing as *monolinear* and *polylinear*.[17] Shorter sequences, so-called *rings*, can also be formed, creating circuits of three, four, six, etc., links. On the other hand, the dimensional and diagonal crosses can also be used as references in style analysis, facilitating the distinction of characteristic spatial structures in movement and dance.

While the compositional application of the dimensional and diagonal scales can be likened to that of major and minor scales in Western traditional music, the scales and rings within the icosahedral structure can be compared to the twentieth century twelve-tone or serial compositions. The order of the scales and rings is kept constant, and various contrapuntal compositional manipulations are applied. A few examples are: relating the spatial axis to the form, enhancing a particular inner harmonic structure, and performing simultaneously various parts of the form; variations with regard to bodily performance, size, rhythmic-dynamic qualities are innumerable. Identifying various forms of the icosahedral structure of its parts further contributes to the classification of spatial structures in movement and dance for purposes of style analysis.

When formulating the organizing principles of movement in space, Laban drew from many resources such as the theory and notation of ballet, and the geometrical and crystallographical theory of space. His observation that the same spatial laws which underlie the harmonious movement of man also govern all growth in nature was confirmed by contemporary investigations. On the other hand, the ancient knowledge of dynamic crystallization which brought Plato to classify the five regular solids (cube, octahedron, tetrahedron, icosahedron, dodecahedron) supported Laban's view of bodily movement as a continuous creation of fragments of crystalline forms. Laban believed that moving into various spatial directions contains a form-building force, similar to the building of crystalline forms, and that muscles which are to move particular body parts into various directions degenerate when they are not exercised. Basic ordering principles were thus found in movement sequences including particular sets of directions and counter-directions within crystalline structures such as the octahedron, cube, and icosahedron. Laban referred to the theory and practice or ordering movement in space as "Space Harmony" and also coined the term "Choreutics" (*Choros* – circle/dance, and *Eu* – good/harmonious).

Laban's principles of Space Harmony can be drawn from several works. His 1926 *Choreographie* presents the first outline of Laban's theory of movement in space. The manuscript for his major book on Space Harmony, written in England in 1939 and published posthumously as *Choreutics* in 1966, was republished in the United States under the title *The Language of Movement: A Guidebook to Choreutics*. A succinct survey of his theory of movement in space can also be found in Chapter IV, "The Conception of the Sphere of Movement," of *Modern Educational Dance*, 1948.

Not unlike the relationship of the theory of music to harmony and counterpoint, the prerequisites for choreutics or space harmony are the awareness and mastery of directional orientation with its inherent stabilizing and mobilizing tendencies, and the appreciation of shape and extension of movement.

– Particular features of Laban's *directional orientation* are:

(a) directions are related to the centre of the body or are judged from the mover's/dancer's front rather than from the environment/performing space.

(b) The main 26 directions are classified in three systems of orientation: 6 dimensionals, 8 diagonals, and 12 diametral directions. (An analogy with musical keys may be drawn.)

(c) directions are associated with two states of equilibrium: dimensionals are predominantly stable and diagonals predominantly labile/mobile; diametral directions oscillate between stability and lability/mobility.

– The notion of *extension* and *size* of movement is connected with the structure of the human body, such as the vertical and bilateral extensions, and with the notion of the sphere of movement – kinesphere – which can grow and shrink by means of stretching and bending the joints.

– The classification of *shape* or *formal elements* into straight – *droit*, curved – *ouvert*, twisted – *tortillé*, and rounded – *rond* is based on movement possibilities of the joints, as well as on movement forms of the ballet tradition.

The interrelatedness of bodily structure and spatial structure is evident from all the above fundamental considerations.

Choreutics/space harmony deals with the theory and practice of the spatial relationships of bodily movement. These relationships are established by means of harmonic principles and are embodied in choreutic forms, such as spatial scales and rings.

– An intermediary step towards choreutics is the linking of directions *centrally* or spoke-like from or through the centre, *peripherally* – moving around the centre, and *transversally* – traversing the kinesphere in bypassing the centre of the body.

– Major *Harmonic Principles* or *laws* which underlie the structure of spatial scales and rings are:

(a) *relatedness to the centre* of the body and the kinesphere from which spatial directions are derived, and which determines the nature of central, peripheral, and transversal movements;

(b) principle of *counter-movement* or *opposition* which underlies all spatial scales;

(c) principles of *parallelism* and *trialism or triad* which underlie icosahedral scales and rings;

(d) principle of *complementarity* which is implied in the relationship of diagonal axes to the structures of the A and B scales; each choreutic configuration is actually complemented by one of the four spatial diagonals, six diameters, or three dimensions as the axis;

(e) *sequential laws* forming the spatio-temporal structure of scales and rings are a confluence of principles of opposition, parallelism and trialism (as illustrated by the example of the inner structure of the A-scales in Chapter I).

— The *logical order of scales and rings* can be approached from several points of view, such as:

(a) the relationship to the diagonal, diameter or dimension creates a series of configurations around the common axis. For example, each of the four space diagonals is the axis of a peripheral and transversal standard scale, and axis and equator scale, and two peripheral and transversal three-rings.

(b) the formation of choreutic forms can also be derived from the intervals or distances between directions on the basis of numerical relationships. If the directions of a peripheral standard scale are numbered from 1-12, the series of odd numbers creates the structure of the axis scale, and the sequence linking even numbers creates equator scales. The three-dimensional planes are created by linking each third number, peripheral three-rings are created by linking each fourth odd number, and transversal three-rings by connecting each fourth even number. Transversal standard scales arise from the linking of each fifth number.

A very simple level of distinction of choreutic forms can also be found in the classification of peripheral and transversal circuits, as well as mixed peripheral and transversal ones (such as the four-ring).

The Theory of Dynamics – Eukinetics-Effort

The purpose of Laban's theory of Effort was to create a means whereby to describe the motivating power for movement or the myriad of individual and collective mind-body strivings. The concept of Effort is linked with emotion and with the human psyche, as well as with functional and/or operational intentionality. While Eukinetics focussed on the expressive qualities in dance (as referred to in Chapter V one may also speculate that Laban devised the term to differentiate his work from Dalcroze's and Steiner's), Effort is concerned with all human movement and its term indicates that unlike energy which exists in all nature in many different forms, Effort can only be found in living organisms and is clearly linked with motivation/intentionality. Although not a measurable but classifiable movement description, the concept of Effort had so far been integrated into other theoretical frameworks more frequently than has Laban's exact analysis of the spatial structure of movement.

In his early explorations Laban drew from traditional ways of describing basic forms of dynamic movement such as the *battu*, *fouetté*, and *glissé* of the French ballet terminology which corresponds to thrusting, slashing, and gliding — descriptive terms which were used within the framework of both Eukinetics and Effort.[18] Eukinetics, along with Choreutics, is also seen as an integral part of Choreology, the science of dance. While Choreutics considers laws of structuring movement within the rhythm of forms, Eukinetics deals with temporal and dynamic occurrences within the rendering of expression; it is the fusion of the three factors of movement – the sequentiality of time, strength of force, and extension of space – which give movement the intended expression.

Complementary to Eukinetics, Laban developed in the 40's the Effort theory which considers the various qualities of mind-body movement involved in human exertion in general. The concept of Effort and its theory are developed in several of Laban's books. While his first book *Effort* (1947) focuses on Effort in work and industry, his *Modern Educational Dance* (1948) proposes a new dance education or a "free dance technique" based on the practice of Effort sequences. *The Mastery of Movement on the Stage* (1950) and the subsequent *The Mastery of Movement* (1960) elaborate on Effort expression in mime, acting, and dance.

The term Effort differs from its current usage as denoting activity which requires substantial expenditure of energy. Laban sees Effort as the inner impulse – a movement sensation, a thought, a feeling or emotion – from which movement originates; it constitutes the link between mental and physical components of movement. The manifestations of this inner impulse or movement motivation can be described in terms of movement factors. There is no movement which does not evolve in space as well as in time, bringing the weight of the body into the flow of change. Hence, every human movement engages the Four Motion Factors – Space, Weight, Time, and Flow – in a more or less active or clear fashion. The particular emphases on, or selections from, these factors make up what Laban calls the characteristic Effort patterns of a person. More specifically, the Effort patterns result from mental or inner attitudes of resisting or accepting the physical conditions influencing movement: the mover's attitudes of fighting against or of contending with the Four Motion Factors result in polarities of opposing Effort Elements of Space – *direct* and *flexible/indirect*, Weight – *Strong/firm* and *light/fine touch*, Time – *sudden* and *sustained*, and Flow – *bound* and *free*. The attitudes of accepting or resisting, however, may not always be voluntarily exercised but can also occur automatically.

Laban also correlates the attitudes toward the Motion Factors to the various levels of consciousness. Attitudes toward Space are associated with *attention* and man's powers of *thinking*, attitudes toward Weight with *intention* and with *sensing*, attitudes toward Time with *decision* making and *intuiting*, and attitudes toward Flow with *progression* and *feeling*. (The link between Laban's concept of Effort and C.G. Jung's divisions of consciousness has been discussed in the previous chapter.)

The potential variety of dynamic qualities of movement thus arises from the innumerable variety of the moving person's situations or actions, and therefore varies the choices among attitudes of accepting or resisting (which may be deliberate or not). These attitudes are also visually represented in the design of the Effort Graph which facilitates the descriptive or prescriptive application of the Effort theory. For example, while a gesture of dismissal may be described as flexible/indirect and sudden (space and time), a stalking pursuit may require a direct, light, and bound quality (space, weight, and flow). In dealing with Laban's Effort theory, one has to keep in mind that the dynamic structure or the quality of a particular movement gains its full significance or meaning only when it is related to what precedes and what follows. In other words, one has to view it within a movement sequence or the context of phrasing. The significance of particular predominant combinations of Effort elements has been discussed in Chapter II. The performance and observation of these rhythms may, after specialized training, allow for a variety of applications. For instance idiosyncratic Effort patterns of a performer, choreographer, and teacher may be expanded through their prescriptive use. On the other hand the observation of individual patterns for purposes of vocational guidance, action profiling, and style description effectuate its descriptive application.

The Concept of Harmony or Effort-Space Affinities

The interrelationship of Eukinetics and Choreutics or of Effort and Space Harmony is manifest in Laban's view of harmonic relationships of the dynamics of bodily actions and of their spatial patterns. His "correlations of dynamic nuances with the spatial directions and this reciprocal relationship [which] rules harmonious movement in the kinesphere" gave rise to the concept of movement Harmony also referred to as Effort — Space affinities.[19] Laban found close correlations between Effort elements and Dimensional directions. These were based on his observation that a *light* movement has a tendency *upward*, and a *strong* aims *downward*; a straight, *direct* movement is correlated with the movement *across* the body, and a roundabout, *flexible* movement is correlated with an opening *outwards*; a quick, *sudden* movement tends toward a *backward* direction, and a slow, *sustained* one reaches *foward*.[20] Elaborating compounds of these, Laban arrived at the "eight basic Effort actions" which correspond with the eight Diagonal directions. Accordingly, a light-flexible-sustained movement is associated with the high-open-forward diagonal, and a strong-direct-sudden one with the down-across-back diagonal, etc.[21] That these observations gave rise to Warren Lamb's Effort-Shape concept had been discussed in previous chapters (II and V).

Laban's Collaborators

When designing his classification and notation of movement and dance, Laban frequently established creative collaborations with his students. In Part One Mary Wigman's and Suzanne Perrottet's collaborations between 1913 and 1920 were discussed. In the 1920's, Dussia Bereska and Kurt Jooss assisted with the formulation of Eukinetics and of Kinetography. Gertrud Snell compiled the emerging theories in several articles and in what was to become the second part of *Choreutics*. There was an extensive number of student-collaborators in the context of Laban's socio-pedagogical ideas in Germany during the 20's and early 30's; particularly instrumental in formulating methodologies for and conducting movement choirs were Albrecht Knust and Martin Gleisner. Knust's contribution to the development of Kinetography has been discussed in Chapter III.

During the 30's and 40's due to the rise and spread of Nazism several Laban students transferred their activities to England and the United States. While Jooss and Ullmann found a supportive environment in the English arts centre and progressive school — Dartington Hall, Irmgard Bartenieff and Irma Otte-Betz introduced Laban's principles and notation to American audiences.[22] Sylvia Bodmer transferred her pedagogical and choreographic activities to England in the 40's and became the co-founder and artistic director of the Manchester Dance Circle (1974, 1979). Laban's chief collaborator in England and annotator of his manuscripts, Lisa Ullmann, founded the Art of Movement Studio in 1946 (first in Manchester, the Studio was incorporated into the Laban Art of Movement Centre, moved to Addlestone, Surrey in the 50's, and in the 70's merged with the University of London Goldsmith's College). Further Laban student-collaborators were trained in the Manchester and Addlestone Studio, such as Warren Lamb, Valerie Preston, Geraldine Stephenson, Marion North, and Joan Russell. Ullmann (1952-1956, and 1971), Preston (later Preston-Dunlop) (1963, 1980), North (1959, 1961, 1973a), and Russell (1965, 1969) applied and elaborated Laban's ideas and movement classification within recreational and educational frameworks; Stephenson continued Laban's link between movement and drama and currently works in the theatre and for the BBC. Lamb and North expanded Laban's Effort theory through personal investigation in behavioral sciences: Lamb in management consultancy — action profiling and top management team building (Lamb and Turner, 1969, and Ramsden, 1973), and North in personality assessment through movement in children and babies (1972, 1973b). Preston-Dunlop also developed Motif Writing for purposes of describing movement ideas (1967, 1973); more recently she has been conducting research in choreographic style based on choreutic analysis (1979, 1982). (Survey charts of how Laban's students-collaborators interpreted and developed his concepts are presented in Appendix II.)

Pointing to the Future

That several of Laban's propositions can be seen as either germinal ideas or as areas in need of further development had been entertained by him throughout his life. In concluding his first book, he wrote:

> I don't praise myself for being a creator of words. On the contrary, I hope that my presentation is going to fall on fruitful grounds and that those more qualified than myself shall form word-structures which can give a valid language background to seeing from the point of view of dance. Thought processes have to be built and improved. This is particularly relevant to philosophical, scientific and other excursions which I undertook as a layman and not as a professional researcher. My aim is not to establish norms and dogmas but to awaken dance insights.[23]

In the 1940's Laban maintained that he was not interested so much in spreading his personal methods of mastering movement as he was in conveying them to those individuals who might apply them in education, industry, recreation, and science: "My methods might be developed or better forms might be found; the outlook on life, however, which is connected with the striving after the mastery of movement remains fundamental as long as the human race exists."[24]

Toward the end of his life he summarized his endeavors to encourage and guide people towards the freedom of a contemporary movement consciousness. In that pursuit:

> I have invented a few means and instruments to serve as a starting point in the exploration of the world of movement and to stimulate the understanding of harmony of movement.
>
> My tools can be better or worse than other people's, and more suitable for some people than for others. They are in no way a means to establish a method, or to replace other methods, or to attract people to "Labanism" to form Labanites or Laban folk and all this nonsense.[25]

In several instances Laban pointed to necessary future developments. Discussing the harmonic relations of choreutic forms (also in relation to those in music) he wrote that "it is the task of future choreutic research to investigate these amazing relationships. The results will give much more than an aesthetic satisfaction, for the building of symbolic forms with their dynamic transformations into different planes and plastic shapes, is one of the most profound inventions of man's imagination."[26] (We have seen above that Preston-Dunlop is actually pursuing research in this area.)

Choreography in terms of planning and writing a dance composition was described by Laban as a new profession "which offers those who are in it enjoyable and interesting pioneerwork."[27] Laban also suggested that in the near future choreographers would be able to notate their works and performers would be able to study their parts from the scores.[28] While this ideal has not yet been achieved one can find that Paul Taylor's dance company has on its regular staff a company dance notator, Jan Moekle, who also serves as rehearsal assistant; on the other hand, several masters projects in The Ohio State University Department of Dance (U.S.A.) include reconstructing and directing pieces from dance scores. Laban also found that the composition and notation of movement in theatre plays is of equal importance. He believed that it will become possible to study and reproduce directing innovations of Max Reinhardt and others even after centuries.[29] Dance, however, is still lagging behind music and theatre in the area of criticism where, unlike the music and theatre reviewer, the dance critic is not yet able to study a ballet or a dance piece from the score and compare it with the actual interpretation of the performers.[30] Many items which Laban listed as necessary in a dance notation library of the future, such as textbooks and training manuals, are today provided; the notation of movement in industry and therapy indicating possibilities for scientific research in other fields has so far not been represented to any extent.[31] Laban's suggestion that early symbols in anthropology be transcribed into modern dance notation has, however, been attempted.[32] Laban actually attributes the reawakening of the awareness of dance heritage to ethnography and comparative anthropology which "have found means of reconstructing certain prehistoric facts and helped to tap a once prodigious source of human experience."[33] He also felt strongly about the need to reform the study of dance history:

> The history of dance can give us more than somewhat perfunctory information about dances and dance-steps of the past or about the names and lives of some famous ballerinas. The history of dance is the history of the intuitive life of mankind. It is a deeply touching poem on human function which unveils more of the hidden motives of man's aspirations and of his destiny than do many other legends or reports on the facts of the past. . . . . It is the task of modern dance science to discover and collect such dispersed information [about dances and dance customs which can be drawn from the general history of civilisation].[34]

Laban argues that in the future the history of dance should become a part of the science of dance which "will incorporate besides data about historic facts an analysis of principles of movement as a human expression, of the laws of harmony as inherent in dance, as well as of the various theories and methods of dance education."[35]

But even more recently, evidence for the significance of Laban's classification can be found in several statements such as those of Siegel and Cohen. Dance critic Marcia Siegel writing in the 70's felt that

> the definition of style, one of the most fascinating subjects in all dance scholarship, is in its rudimentary stages . . . . Rudolf von Laban the inventor of Labanotation did outline a systematic way of looking at and talking

about many of the elements that contribute to "Style" the individual quality of any movement phenomenon.[36]
Siegel's article is titled "Waiting for the Past to Begin" and within its context Laban's classifications appear to be pointing towards the future. One can also agree with Selma Jeanne Cohen that because of its systematic classification Laban's theory is "one of the most important for modern thought."[37]
In conclusion one may suggest that due to the breadth of his original conceptions, Laban's movement classification provides a sufficiently broad basis for both further development of his germinal ideas and for its application within other theoretical frameworks.

Notes to Chapter VI

1. *Choreographie*, p. 1.
2. Cf. Ibid., p. 3.
3. Cf. Introduction to Part Two.
4. Cf. pp. 53-55 above.
5. *Die Welt des Tänzers*, p. 20.
6. Ibid., p. 211.
7. *Choreutics*, p. viii.
8. *The Mastery of Movement*, p. 25.
9. Ibid., p. 53.
10. Ibid.
11. Cf. *Choreographie*, pp. 3-5.
12. *The Mastery of Movement*, 1960 edition, p. 25.
13. Ibid., p. 52.
14. Ibid., pp. 127-128.
15. *Choreutics*, p. 114.
16. Cf. Chapter V, notes (61, 62).
17. Cf. Chapter III, p. 116.
18. Cf. *Choreutics*, p. 30.
19. Ibid., p. 31.
20. Cf. Ibid., pp. 30-32.
21. Cf. Ibid., pp. 33-34.
22. Cf. Source in note 127, Part One.
23. *Die Welt des Tänzers*, p. 9.
24 *A Vision of Dynamic Space*, compiled by Lisa Ullmann (London: Falmer Press in association with Laban Archives, 1984), p. 6.
25. Unpublished manuscript from 1957, Laban Archives.
26. *Choreutics*, p. 117.
27. Flyer of the Choreographic Institute Laban, Würzburg, 1929 (Laban Archives).
28. Cf. "Über die Tänzerische Berufe" ("On Dance Professions"), *Der Tanz*, Heft 14, 1929, pp. 2-4.

29. Cf. "Choreographie und Theater," *Der Scheinwerfer*, Heft 11/12, 1928, p. 22.
30. Cf. *Principle of Dance and Movement Notation*, p. 15.
31. "Foreword by Rudolf Laban," *Labanotation* by Ann Hutchinson, p. xvi.
32. Cf. Gertrude Kurath and Samuel Marti, *Dances of Anahuac*, (Chicago: Aldine, 1964).
33. "Dance in General," *Rudolf Laban Speaks about Movement and Dance*, edited by Lisa Ullmann, 1971, U.K., p. 67.
34. Ibid., p. 66.
35. Ibid., p. 67.
36. Marcia Siegel, "Waiting for the Past to Begin,"*Arts in Society*, Summer-Fall 1976, vol. 13, no. 2, pp. 233-234.
37. Selma Jeanne Cohen, "Dance as an Art of Imitation," *What is Dance*. Roger Copeland and Marshal Cohen, editors (New York: Oxford University Press, 1983), p. 19.

APPENDIXES

Appendix I

The Lived Body-Space-Expression

This appendix is an expansion of Chapter V which examines the paradigms underlying Laban's ideas, concepts, and classifications. It was the publication of papers for the 1974 symposium on "The Significance of Movement" (organized by the Center for Integrative Education and the Dance Notation Bureau in New York) which ignited this author's interest in further investigation of correspondences and differences between Laban's tenets and those of writers of phenomenological orientation.[1] Although this appendix represents an investigation in progress, it is believed that the appendix itself will help to clarify the dimensions of Laban's concepts.

Several fundamental views appear to be shared by Laban and the phenomenologists,[2] the first being the view of the significance of movement in our present understanding of the world. The unity and structure of this world prior to its division and separation, as well as the understanding of the living process in its expressive diversity of forms and its underlying unity of being, is further demonstrated both in Laban's and in phenomenological points of view.[3] The view of space, time, and movement as constituting dimensions and conditions which underlie the region of experience are articulated by both. In fact, as Patrick Milburn contends, "Laban was close to the phenomenologists in his recognition that perceived space originates in movement"; his "constructions" of polyhedra are not carried out in a neutral space but in a polar field of basic orientations.[4] Moreover Laban's concept of Effort arose primarily from his analysis of the quality of lived or living movement.[5] This space-time-quality of movement is seen as created in human action or through movement.

In the following discussion, writings of Ervin Straus, Maurice Merleau-Ponty, and F.J.J. Buytendijk are examined, and their notions of body, perception, motility, spatiality, and temporality are correlated to Laban's views. Straus, for example, by giving the title *Phenomenological Psychology* to his selected papers (written between 1930 and 1966), displayed a gesture of affiliation with the phenomenological movement. His attempt "to explore human experience, revealing its depth and wealth instead of reducing it, complies with Husserl's appeal: 'Back to the things themselves!'"[6] Straus believes that scientific reductionism leads not only to a disdain of the basic axioms of everyday life but also to catastrophies, such as Hiroshima.[7] While in his *Structure of Behavior*, Merleau-Ponty elaborates his views in a debate with the "scientific experiences" of behaviorism and Gestalt psychology, in *Phenomenology of Perception*, he presents the interpretation of the "natural experience" against the background of some studies in laboratory psychology and psychopathology. He argues that "to return to things themselves is to return to the world which is prior to knowledge, of which knowledge always *speaks* and with regard to which every determination is abstract, signicative and dependent . . ."[8] Hence the original perception of the surrounding world in fact articulates the world. In his *Allgemeine Theorie der menschlichen Haltung und Bewegung* (General Theory of Human Posture and Movement), Buytendijk refers to views of man in physiology and psychology as a "psychochemical system in which something is happening."[9] He therefore chooses a different point of departure, namely that of "being" — the existence and its full concreteness: "The continuous contact with the fertile ground of experience should thus offer a defense against lapsing into a concept schematism which is only deductive and sterile and hampers the advance of science rather than promotes it."[10]

All three authors departed from the critique of the various scientific disciplines, particularly psychology, and the survival of idealist and realist philosophies. Such a posture, although not in any systematic way, can also be found in some of Laban's writings, such as his comment that scientific literature misrepresents all that is dancerly (das Tänzerische) and a part of knowing,[11] that purely rationalistic works do not contribute to a clear judgement,[12] that rationalistic theories of experience, as well as abstract philosophies, are based on one-sided presuppositions and frozen concepts.[13] Common to all four authors is the conviction that one has to seek the ground of all knowledge in experience.

The following examination will consist of three major topics: (a) a discussion of Merleau-Ponty's notion of the "lived body" and of Laban's "gesture" as the basis for all perceptual experience, (b) a correlation of Laban's concept of Effort to Merleau-Ponty's views of motility and intentionality, and (c) an examination of the correspondences and differences in all four author's views on spatiality and temporality.

Merleau-Ponty perceives the body as our means of belonging to the world and facing our tasks. He refers to it as the "lived" or "phenomenal" body as different from scientific investigations of the body as a natural object. The lived-body is the source of all action-perception-consciousness: "to move one's body is to aim at things through it, it is to allow oneself to respond to their call, which is made upon it independently of any representation."[14] He contends that "our body, as the potentiality of this or that part of the world surges towards objects to be grasped and perceives them."[15] Laban's metaphor for the lived-body is the power of gesture (Gebärdenkraft) and/or the sense for dance (Tänzerischer Sinn) which perceive the gestures of the environment (Umweltgebärden): "One perceives this whole interwoven complex [of man and the world] as I, as a thing, as a phenomenon. The stirring or excitation of the I is timed by the densities which we experience as matter, body, the touchable. The unifying basis is the eternally changing power of gesture."[16] Having stated that man perceives his environment through his sense of dance, Laban refers to the subdivisions of sensation made by the science of physiology and suggests that it is the unified sense or the dance sense which perceives the gestures of the environment.[17] He even goes as far as to articulate this phenomenon: "Each impression is a confluence (Mitschwingen) of an experienced thing with an expressive gesture leading into our inside. The remembered gestures, on the other hand, are projected towards the outside and find there a going with the confluence as soon as a relevant power of gesture is ready for reception. Receiving the impression, it will keep it in its inside, transform it into remembrance and preserve it for the relevant expression."[18] Aware of the limitations of the language, Laban comments that such a schematic description renders the occurrence as distinct as it is possible in words.[19] He also describes this phenomenon in terms of outer and inner tensions: "What we see, hear, touch seems to us an image of an inner form tension which lives in the perceived object . . . . The same inner tension arises in us as in the perceived object by mediation of our senses which awaken and realize the image of the external bodily tension. In that way, we do become aware of a particular event, equally so if this awareness were a thought, feeling or will. An *inner* symbol, experience [Erlebnis] emerges."[20]

The lived, phenomenal body, and the gesture are then a means by which we perceive the world and at the same time respond to it. The body carries the *intentionality* of consciousness which underlies all movement.[21] We have referred to Merleau-Ponty's view of our body potentially surging towards objects to be grasped while perceiving them.[22] Laban also maintains that "only movement can be perception, experience, consciousness."[23] In broad terms, Merleau-Ponty refers to the "intentional arc" (a term borrowed from another framework) which buttresses the life of consciousness, cognition, and perception: "It is this intentional arc which brings about the unity of senses, of intelligence, of sensibility and motility."[24] The lived body and the power of gesture are also a means by which we are situated in space and time or inhabit them: "In so far as I have a body through which I act in the world," writes Merleau-Ponty, "space and time are not, for me, a collection of adjacent points . . . . The space and time which I inhabit are always in their different ways indeterminate horizons which contain other points of view. The synthesis of both time and space is a task that always has to be performed afresh."[25] In Laban's view, "space and time structures, as well as time and energy phenomena, are for the dancer concrete unities, which are constantly renewed through the power of gesture."[26] "Dancer," in this context, refers to a person alert to the world, self and others.

Inspite of the different contexts of Merleau-Ponty's and Laban's elaborations, some correspondences between the concept of Effort and intentionality are worthy of discussion. Merleau-Ponty comments that it is not easy to reveal motor intentionality because it is concealed behind the objective world which it helps to build: "Motility, then, is not... a handmaid of consciousness, transporting the body to that point in space of which we have formed a representation beforehand. In order that we may be able to move our body towards an object, the object must first exist for it. ..."[27] The awareness of the existence of an object, a person, or a situation, as well as the intent and the movement in response to it, is embodied in Laban's concept of Effort: "Effort is the common denominator for the various strivings of the body and mind which become observable in . . . activity."[28] In other words, Laban calls Effort our inner function from which originates living movement — as different from mechanical motion — with which we purposefully control mechanical happenings. Thus, "every human movement is indissolvably linked with an effort which is, indeed, its origin and inner aspect."[29] The visible or observable qualities of the living movement are referred to as Effort elements and Effort attitudes and actions. The manifestations of inner Efforts or movement motivations are described in terms of our inner attitudes engaging the four factors of motion — space, weight, time, and flow — and their eight polarities of Effort elements. The seventy-two basic combinations of the latter (discussed in Chapter III) constitute a comprehensive articulation of the qualities of lived movement. Also "Effort and its resulting action may be both unconscious and involuntary, but they are always present in any bodily movement; otherwise they could not be perceived by others or become effectual in the external surroundings of the moving person."[30] This Laban dictum brings to mind Merleau-Ponty's statement that "even 'automatic' movements must announce themselves to our consciousness, which means that there never occur, in our bodies, movements in themselves."[31]

From the above discussion, we see that the lived body not only inhabits space and time but also sythesizes them in movement (Merleau-Ponty) and that space-time-energy are constantly renewed through the power of gesture (Laban). Further understanding of spatiality and temporality according to Laban and Merleau-Ponty, as well as Straus and Buytendijk, will be examined below. While we have already presented and analyzed Laban's concepts, a brief reference to the context of the views on spatiality and temporality in the writings of the other three authors will preface this examination.

Ervin Straus' thinking about space is linked both with the phenomenon of sound, which implies temporality, and with the upright posture and gait in the gravitational field imbued with the body interaction with energy. In his pursuit of the primary lived experience of space, Straus warns against the physical and mathematical concepts of space which are posterior to its lived experience. He also fends against concerns "with psychological genesis and dominance of particular sensory fields, like optical or tactile, over others."[32] On the other hand, Straus differentiates the "optical space of color,"[33] which is also the "space of directed or purposive movement,"[34] from the "accoustical or temporal space of tones"[35] which he sees as the space of dance and of symbolic qualities of the presentic movement.[36] The notion of "presentic space" is created in contrast to the "historical space," the space of directed actions:

. . . Historical action is suspended while dancing; the dancer is lifted from the stream of historical becoming. The dancer's experience is a mode of being present that does not point to any future end and is thus spatially and temporally unlimited . . . . Dance space is not a part of directed, historical space, but is the symbolic region of the world. It is determined not by distance, direction and magnitude but through the "wide openness," loftiness, and autokinesis of space . . . "wide openness" is neither here nor on the horizon, nor is it on a line connecting the here with any other points of space or such points with each other; it is not quantifiable but is rather a quality of space. Thus, we can legitimately say that dance movement is ordered according to the symbolic qualities of space.[37]

These qualitative aspects of Straus' consideration of dance space in the context of his "Phenomenological Studies" in *Phenomenological Psychology*, differ somewhat from his approach in his "Anthropological studies" of the same book.

In the latter context, the action space and the space of the dance are also experienced space which differs from the homogenized space of Cartesian coordinates. The action space, however, constantly refers to the up-down in relation to the gravitational field, to the laterality of body structure and to distance in interaction.[38] In elaborating on distance, Straus refers explicitly to the interrelationship of space and time which he calls the space-time form of living movement.[39]

In his General Theory of Human Posture and Movement, F.J.J. Buytendijk introduced the notion of "self-movement" (Selbstbewegung) or "vital movement in physics and psychology. "Self-movement" is seen as a realization of the possibility to move in relation to the environment, to the being-in-the-world. This requires a consciousness of the space and time of the execution. Buytendijk considers the environmental space to be a field for perception and action. It has some common characteristics, such as polarities of up and down, right-life, and forward-backward conditioned by the orientation of eyes, ears, head, hands, and feet. Our environmental space coincides with our optical space. The phenomenon of size and form constancy confirms and demonstrates the vital space: "The near space unfolds around us and is at the same time the movement space. It is governed by the size and form constancy. It is space in which things represent themselves as such . . . with their constant properties related to the subject."[40] Buytendijk's notion of "vital space" relates both to our perceptions as functions of self-movement and to our possibilities of movement as the foundation for our movement organization. He finds the interrelationship of vital space and vital time in the "natural" situation, which forms the starting point of self-movement: "Time is always a *moving time* in our relationship to the outside world, and as such forms spatial changes. *When nothing happens and there is no self-movement, there is no time.*"[41] Buytendijk also argues that "*the living function evolves in another space-time system from the psychical and physical processes,*"[42] and that "*movement imprints definite relationships on space and time.*"[43] In his considerations of the structures of space and time, Buytendijk relies heavily on Straus' contentions referred to earlier.

Maurice Merleau-Ponty articulates his views on space in two chapters of *Phenomenology of Perception.* In "The Space of own Body and Motility" Part I, Chapter 3, he sets forth his views in critique of various psychological theories on body image, considering the Gelb-Goldstein study of "psychological blindness." In "Space" Part II, Chapter 2, Merleau-Ponty juxtaposes his views to those of Berkley, Descartes, Kant as well as the Gestalt-Psychologists, which he finds are reflected in reports on experiments with distorted vision made by Stratton, Wertheimer and Nagel. Merleau-Ponty's view of bodily spatiality as "spatiality of situation" (rather than of "position") is rooted in his contention that body motility manifests itself in action ("in face of its task" and in "pursuit of aims"), as discussed above. Bodily space, therefore, cannot be analysed simply as a figure (object) without its background (situation, context). It is thus "in action that spatiality of our body is brought into being."[44] He refers to the immanent background of movement, "inspiring and sustaining it at every moment,"[45] which can be seen as the motoric equipment of man. The "plunge into action," or truer to the French text − "the kinetic initiation" (*l'initiation cinétique*), of the person/subject relating to the object is on equal footing with perception.[46]

On several occasions Merleau-Ponty points to the difficulty of reflecting upon and observing spatiality and the act of perception: "Space and perception generally represent, at the core of the subject, the fact of his birth, the perpetual contribution of his bodily being, a communication with the world more ancient than thought. That is why they saturate consciousness and are impenetrable to reflection."[47] And further, space "can neither be observed, since it is presupposed in every observation, nor seen to emerge from a constituting operation since it is of its essence that it is already constituted."[48] Space can be seen as having its basis in our facticity and can confer its own spatial particularization upon the landscape without ever appearing itself.[49] From this perspective then

> it is clearly in action that the spatiality of our body is brought into being, and analysis of one's own movement should enable us to arrive at a better understanding of it. By considering the body in movement we can better see how it inhabits space (and, moreover, time) because movement is not limited to submitting passively to space and time, it actively assumes them, it takes them up in their basic significance which is obscured in the commonplaceness of established situations.[50]

It appears that this "commonplaceness" of human activities — seen as situations to be responded to or as "facticity" — underlies all of Merleau-Ponty's elaborations. Space then is "not a setting in which things are arranged but the means whereby the positing of things becomes possible."[51] The space of one's own body is constantly created and recreated through its motility in time. It is rooted in existence. Therefore, the synthesis of both time and space is a task that always has to be performed afresh.[52] Because spatial synthesis is based on its unfolding in time, "[the] body takes possession of time; it brings into existence a past and a future for a present; it is not a thing, but creates time instead of submitting to it."[53]

A comparative examination of the above approaches to spatiality and temporality is hereby proposed from the point of view of selected topics. All four authors share *the view of the interdependency of body movement in space* but approach it from different premises. Laban maintains that movement is a life of space and that "dead space does not exist, for there is neither space without movement, nor movement without space."[54] Merleau-Ponty argues that the body is far more than a fragment of space and that "there would be no space at all for me if I had no body."[55] For Buytendijk, the environmental space exists only for the living man: "It relates to our organization as a body-able-to-move-itself and to our perceptions of self-movements as functions, but not to a rational point of view."[56] Straus differentiates the homogeneous space of equivalent dimensions and a space in which "the cardinal directions are directions of movement determined by the organization of our live body within an ever present field of gravity to which it is opposed."[57]

While Straus and Buytendijk confront in their views spatial paradigms of scientific rationalism, Merleau-Ponty argues against certain definitions of the "body image" in psychology, maintaining that the bodily space is created within the spatiality of situations rather than positions. Laban's stance has emerged from his view that the illusory static appearances of life are transformed into clear spatial dynamism.

Concern with *the existential foundation for orientation* has been hinted at by Straus' differentiation of the space we do not live in and the "terrestrial space, the space of human action, [in which] each of the three different pairs of cardinal dimensions has its special character."[58] Buytendijk maintains that in the space in which our everyday movements evolve we always distinguish up and down, forward and backward, right and left:

> We thus relate directions with regard to our own person; they are, however, determined through our *movement possibilities* on the basis of our movement organization . . . . Man's world has right and left halves, not on the basis of experience with acquired impressions and accomplished movements, but rather, on the basis of the relationship of right and left which enables first the functional relationship towards the environment and is an *a priori* basis to all our vital experiences and movements.[59]

While the dimension of depth for Merleau-Ponty immediately reveals a link between the subject and the space, height and breadth appear to be concerned with the relationship of things among themselves. But "in reality vertical and horizontal too are ultimately to be defined as the best hold our body can take upon the world. Breadth and height . . . are 'existential' dimensions . . . . The vertical and the horizontal, the near and the far are abstract designations for one single form of being in a situation, and they presuppose the same setting face to face of subject and world."[60] We are familiar with Laban's view of the centre of gravity of the upright body as the crossing-point of the three dimensions and the centre of our kinesphere. Laban does not feel the need to separate the notions of geometrical space from movement space: "The basic elements of orientation in space are the three dimensions: length, breadth, and depth. Each 'dimension' has two directions. With reference to the human body, length or height has the two directions up and down; breadth has the two directions left and right; depth has the two directions forward and backward."[61]

The concern with spatial orientation rooted in the existential foundations of man, such as the gravitational field, the body structure and the centre of gravity, and the movement organization and movement possibilities, is common to the four authors. While the distinction between the objective, geometrical, and the action space is again inferred in the statements of Straus and Merleau-Ponty, Laban sees no difficulty in unifying the action space and the geometrical space. The link between crystalline and organic is, in fact, the basis of his dynamic crystallography of movement.

Action space is also *the space of interaction* with a partner, another person. Here the interplay of spheres which surround the body and the human space of distance is significant. In the following passages, Laban refers to a specific sequence of attack and defense in sword fencing, while Straus considers both the defensive as well as the welcoming attitudes of interaction. In the sphere which surrounds his body, Straus writes,

> I can meet the other as the other, join him as my partner, arm in arm or hand in hand, and yet leave him in his integrity . . . . It is the space of the linking of arms or embracing but also crossing the arms, a motion in which we keep distance, "circumwalling" ourselves in an attitude of defence or of fortification.[62]

Laban sees the thrusts and parries of two opponents as an interplay between their respective kinespheres:

> The general spatial orientation of the attacker shows a confluence of his movements approximately in front of himself no matter from which area they come. The spatial orientation of the defender is dispersed into a number of directions of his kinesphere. The kinesphere of the one will at times overlap with that of the other since the attacker will always attempt to reach his opponent's body with his strokes, often involving one or more steps towards it.[63]

The context of Merleau-Ponty's consideration is the human space built by abstract, centrifugal movement as different from the concrete movement of the physical space:

> . . . When I motion my friend to come nearer, my intention is not a thought prepared within me and I do not perceive the signal in my body. I beckon across the world, I beckon over there, where my friend is; the distance between us, his consent or refusal are immediately read in my gesture; there is not a perception followed by a movement, for both form a system which varies as a whole.[64]

The sphere of movement and of interaction can grow and shrink in size. Straus considers the "three-mile zone" of the sphere surrounding our body as a border with fluctuating frontiers which expand or shrink: "Corresponding to our conation, space itself loses its static character, opens endlessly before us, and expands or represses us."[65] Laban refers to the general possibilities of the changing expansion of movement space: "The conception of a shrinking and growing kinesphere in addition to the normal one makes it possible to describe innumerable variations of traceforms."[66]

Both Laban and Straus perceive human movement as an *interplay of balance and loss of balance.* We are familiar with Laban's concept of stability and mobility/lability according to which movement containing dimensional tensions (i.e., vertical or horizontal) provides a feeling of stability, while movement following space diagonals produces a feeling of growing disequilibrium or of losing balance.[67] Straus refers to the upright position which is never fully accomplished and perfect: "As a state of becoming open to the future, it demands my continuous effort, counteracting the permanent forces of gravity. In this precarious equilibrium, oscillating between vertical and perpendicular tendencies we never reach security, firmly established."[68] A view of perpetual oscillation between equilibrium and its loss is common to both statements. However, every movement is a composite of stabilizing and mobilizing tendencies and, consequently, the act of balancing constantly exists.

Particular action and *spatial tendencies* in carriage and movement are seen as *having expressive connotations*. Straus refers merely to posture and accounts for verticality only:

> . . . the strict upright posture expresses austerity, inaccessibility, decisiveness, domination, majesty, mercilessness, or unapproachable remoteness, . . . (p. 145) . . . When we lower our heads or kneel in prayer, when we bow or bend our knees in greeting, the deviation from the vertical reveals the relation to it. . . . There is only one vertical but many deviations from it, each one carrying a specific, expressive meaning.[69]

Laban describes expression accompanying movement between vertical and horizontal dimensions:

> Dimensional axial sequences give the opportunity to describe a less active and more meditative kind of inner attitude. Movement or gestures of admiration, benediction or submission, for instance, ...[70]

Merleau-Ponty refers to expressiveness of movement both in spontaneous action and in symbolic gestures:

> It [our body] is the origin of . . . expressive movement itself . . . sometimes it is restricted to the actions necessary for the conservation of life . . . . At other times, elaborating upon these primary actions and moving from their literal to a figurative meaning, it manifests through them a core of new significance: this is true of motor habits such as dancing . . . . At all levels it performs the same function which is to endow the instantaneous expression of spontaneity with "a little renewable action and independent existence."[71]

Dancing, of course, is a true model in which the expressive body-movement-space is most obvious.

The discussion of seven topics related to spatiality and, tangentially, to temporality has shown a basic concordance among the four authors in their views on the interdependency of body movement and space, the existential foundation for orientation, the action in space and the space of interaction, the changing size of space, the inter-play of balance and loss of balance in every movement, and of expressive space. Choreographer-inventor Laban, however, saw no need for a separation of the geometrical space, the space of the mind, from action space or the lived (Straus), vital (Buytendijk), and phenomenal (Merleau-Ponty) space. It is as though the crystalline tendencies, which Laban saw as the "light" side, and the dynamospheric or dynamic nuances, the "shadow" side, form a "yang – yin" harmonious unity.[72] Their synthesis occurs in "any action . . . within the bounds of dynamic cystallization."[73]

The close juxtaposition of texts deriving from philosophical investigations into the structure of behavior and perception to Laban's first ruminations on the world of dance and to his applied theories of space and Effort may, on one hand, appear debatable. On the other hand, this correlation has illuminated further possibilities for cross-fertilizations. While some of Laban's language does not consistently reflect the mind-body inseparability (such as the "body as an instrument of expression"), such references could be clarified through a conscious phenomenological stance. Merleau-Ponty's view of the intentionality of body motility and the body's spatiality could also be articulated further through Laban's structural differentiations within his Effort and Choreutic frameworks, an application which could efficiently describe the range of possibilities of the phenomenal body and the aspects of its background or horizon which all humans share.

Notes to Appendix I

1. Cf. *Main Currents in Modern Thought*, Sept.-Oct., 1974, Vol. 31, No. 1.
2. Cf. Chapter V above, pp. 162-164.
3. Cf. Algis Mikunas, "The Primacy of Movement," (pp. 8-12), and "The Significance of Movement" (unsigned editorial, p. 3) in *Main Currents in Modern Thoughts*, Vol. 31.
4. Cf. Patrick Milburn, "Movement and the Idea of Organism," ibid., p. 35.
5. Cf. Ibid., p. 34.
6. Erwin W. Straus, *Phenomenological Psychology* (New York: Basic Books, 1966), p. xi.
7. Cf. Ibid., p. x.
8. Maurice Merleau-Ponty, *Phenomenology of Perception*, translated from the French by Colin Smith (London: Routledge & Kegan Paul, 1962; originally written in 1945), p. ix.
9. F.J.J. Buytendijk, *Allgemeine Theorie der Menschlichen Haltung und Bewegung* (Berlin: Springer Verlag, 1956; originally published in Antwerpen, 1948), p. 4.
10. Ibid., p. 57.
11. Cf. *Die Welt des Tänzers*, p. 262; see also Chapter V.
12. Cf. Ibid.
13. Cf. Ibid., p. 28.
14. *Phenomenology of Perception*, p. 139.
15. Ibid., p. 106.
16. *Die Welt des Tänzers*, p. 50.
17. Cf. Ibid., p. 48.
18. Ibid., pp. 56-57.
19. Cf. Ibid.
20. Ibid., pp. 39-40.
21. Merleau-Ponty has extended Husserl's notion of intentionality (an

activity of consciousness tied to the world) to a fundamental activity underlying all motility.

22. Cf. *Phenomenology of Perception*, p. 106.
23. *Die Welt des Tänzers*, p. 205.
24. *Phenomenology of Perception*, p. 136; Merleau-Ponty refers to F. Fisher's article in *Neurologie und Psychiatrie*, 1930.
25. Ibid., p. 140.
26. *Die Welt des Tänzers*, p. 56.
27. *Phenomenology of Perception*, p. 139; cf. also note (2) on p. 138.
28. *Modern Educational Dance*, p. 18.
29. *The Mastery of Movement on the Stage*, p. 23.
30. Ibid.
31. *Phenomenology of Perception*, p. 123.
32. *Phenomenological Psychology*, p. 4.
33. Ibid., p. 7.
34. Ibid., p. 23.
35. Ibid., p. 7.
36. Cf. Ibid., pp. 23 and 35.
37. Ibid., p. 35.
38. Cf. Ibid., pp. 152, 156.
39. Cf. Ibid.
40. *Allgemeine Theorie der Menschlichen Haltung und Bewegung*, pp. 49-50.
41. Ibid., p. 52.
42. Ibid., p. 54.
43. Ibid., p. 56.
44. *Phenomenology of Perception*, p. 102.
45. Ibid., p. 110.
46. Cf. Ibid., pp. 110-111.
47. Ibid., p. 254.
48. Ibid.
49. Cf. Ibid.
50. Ibid., p. 102.
51. Ibid., p. 243.
52. Cf. Ibid., p. 140.
53. Ibid., p. 240.
54. *Choreutics*, p. 94.
55. *Phenomenology of Perception*, p. 102.
56. *Allgemeine Theorie der Menschlichen Haltung und Bewegung*, p. 46.
57. *Phenomenological Psychology*, p. 117.
58. Ibid., p. 30.
59. Source from note (56) above, p. 47.
60. *Phenomenology of Perception*, p. 267.
61. *Choreutics*, p. 11.
62. *Phenomenological Psychology*, p. 153.
63. *Choreutics*, pp. 38-39.

64. *Phenomenology of Perception*, p. 111.
65. *Phenomenological Psychology*, p. 154.
66. *Choreutics*, p. 42.
67. Cf. *Choreutics*, p. 90.
68. *Phenomenological Psychology*, pp. 142-143.
69. Ibid., p. 146.
70. *Choreutics*, p. 133.
71. *Phenomenology of Perception*, p. 146; at the end of the quotation Merleau-Ponty quotes from an article by Paul Valery.
72. Cf. *Choreutics*, p. 91.
73. Ibid., p. 114.

Appendix II

British Applications of Laban's Concepts: Survey Tables

Laban's chief collaborator Lisa Ullmann and his student-collaborators Valerie Preston-Dunlop, Marion North, and Joan Russell applied and elaborated Laban's ideas and classification within various educational frameworks as practiced in schools, colleges and recreative courses in Great Britain. In their publications, the content for teaching and the teaching methodology are drawn from Laban's concepts (particularly as presented in his *Modern Educational Dance*). Laban's classification of movement and dance frequently serves as a means for observation with the purpose of assisting students' movement and dance invention and mastery in performance. In addition to this educational emphasis, Warren Lamb and Marion North developed several aspects of Laban's concepts within their own methods of personality assessment and action profiling.

The five survey tables below show concordance with and variance from Laban's classification and terminology. While the analogy sign (≠) shows the use of the same concept and terminology, the asterisk indicates elaborations of a new concept or the development of an existing one. The survey is drawn from key publications which have served either as texts or were germinal works for further investigations: Lisa Ullmann, "Some Preparatory Stages for the Study of Space Harmony in Art of Movement," (1952-55/71); Valerie Preston, *A Handbook for Modern Educational Dance* (1963), and its second edition, *A Handbook for Dance in Education* (1980); Marion North, *A Simple Guide to Movement Teaching* (1959), *Composing Movement Sequences* (1961), and *Personality Assessment through Movement* (1972); Joan Russell, *Creative Dance in the Secondary School* (1969); and Warren Lamb, *Posture and Gesture* (1965).

1. *Survey of Interpretations of Laban's SPATIAL Concepts*

LABAN's CLASSIFICATION	Ullmann (1952–1956/71)	Preston (1963) Preston-Dunlop (1980)	North (1959, 1972)	Russell (1969)	Lamb (1965)
EXTENSION – narrow-wide small-large – Kinesphere-General space	Kinesphere	extension: near-far small-large Kinesphere	size: normal, reduced, exaggerated (1972)	extension: small (near) large (far)	growing shrinking
ORIENTATION – 26 directions: 6 dimensional 8 diagonal 12 diametral – 3 dimensional planes – Polyhedral-scaffoldings	directions "door," "table," "wheel" planes	levels, areas, body zones, orientation: dimensional & diagonal cross, three planes: "door," "table," "wheel"	zones around body, levels, orientation: dimensional, diagonal, icosahedral (1972)	levels directions (26) "door," "table," "wheel" planes	three planes: horizontal, vertical, sagittal
STABILITY-LABILITY stabilizing mobilizing	stability (bound fluent)* mobility (bound fluent)*	stable scale mobile scale/ labile scale (1963)	stability-instability or balance-off-balance	(stable, mobile)	

(To be Cont'd.)

(Cont'd.)

LABAN's CLASSIFICATION	Ullmann (1952-1956/71)	Preston (1963) Preston-Dunlop (1980)	North (1959, 1972)	Russell (1969)	Lamb (1965)
SHAPE					
– 4 basic formal elements or shapes: straight, curved, round, twisted		basic space patterns: straight, round, twisted;	simple shape discernment: zig-zag, angular, rounded, twisted	4 air patterns: straight, angular, curved, twisted	shape: growing shrinking
– linear, plane-like plastic (3-dim.) forms			linear, plane, plastic; one-two-three-dim. (1972)		spreading – enclosing horizontal
– path: straight, angular, curved		floor and air patterns	air patterns	4 body shapes	rising – descending vertical
– 4 shapes of body carriage		4 body shapes	4 body shapes (1959)		advancing – retiring sagittal

2. *Survey of Interpretations of SPACE HARMONY – CHOREUTIC FORMS – HARMONY*

LABAN's CLASSIFICATION	Ullmann (1952-1956/71)	Preston (1963) Preston-Dunlop (1980)	North (1957, 1972)	Russell (1969)	Lamb (1965)
PATH					
– central, peripheral transversal; inclinations (steep, flat, flowing)	central, peripheral, transversal; inclinations: (flat, steep, flowing)	central, peripheral, transversal; inclinations: flat, steep, flowing	central-spoke like, peripheral-edge (1959), transverse (1972)	(central, peripheral, transversal)	
SPACE HARMONY					
– symmetry-asymmetry	alternation of stabilizing mobilizing forces;	symmetry-asymmetry (body); counter-direction;	symmetry-asymmetry counter-direction (chordic, melodic, complex-melodic)* (1972)	symmetry-asymmetry (body)	
– counter movement or direction					
– balance, equilibrium					
– harmonies of scales and rings	harmonies of scales and rings				

(To be Cont'd.)

(Cont'd.)

LABAN's CLASSIFICATION	Ullmann (1952-1956/71)	Preston (1963) Preston-Dunlop (1980)	North (1957, 1972)	Russell (1969)	Lamb (1965)
CHOREUTIC FORMS — rings: two- three- four, five, six- seven-rings; scales: dimensional, diagonal, primary, axis, equator, A & B scales	peripheral rings; 3-dimensional 4-diagonal	harmonies of scales and rings: Octahedral forms (dim. cross; 3-rings; 6-rings; 12-rings) Cubic Forms (diag. cross; 3-rings; 6-rings; 12-rings) Icosahedral forms (a) w/h diagonal axes (b) w/h axes through corners (c) w/h diametral axes* (d) w/h diag. axes twisted* (1980)			

(To be Cont'd.)

(Cont'd.)

LABAN's CLASSIFICATION	Ullmann (1952-1956/71)	Preston (1963) Preston-Dunlop (1980)	North (1957, 1972)	Russell (1969)	Lamb (1965)
DYNAMICS OF HIGH MEDIUM and DEEP MOVERS			High, medium low movers		
HARMONY between KINESPHERE and DYNAMOSPHERE (AFFINITIES)	6-dimensional directions and "inner experience"	the effort cube (1963) natural affinities between effort . . . and spatial use (1980)	the effort cube refers to areas around the body where effort actions are placed most easily		Affinities between shape & effort* horizontal-space vertical-force sagittal-time flow of shape flow of effort

3. *Survey of Interpretations of Laban's Classification of EFFORT and its Terminology*

LABAN's CLASSIFICATION	Preston (1963) Preston-Dunlop (1980) North (1972)	Russell (1969)	Lamb (1965)/ Ramsden (1973)
MOTION FACTORS	✓	✓	three components
Weight, Space, Time, Flow	✓	✓	Space, Force, Time
ATTITUDES (EFFORT/ MENTAL)	attitudes	attitudes	
fighting-indulging resisting-yielding constricting-enduring withholding-accepting	fighting-indulging resisting-yielding		contending-indulging
EFFORT ELEMENTS	qualities / elements of movement	qualities	Effort variations
W firm-fine touch	light (1980) / light		increasing-diminishing pressure
T sudden-sustained	✓ ✓	✓	accelerating-decelerating,
S direct-flexible	✓ ✓	✓	directing-indirecting
F bound-free	✓ ✓	✓	binding-freeing
MEASURABLE-OBJECTIVE FUNCTION CLASSIFIABLE-SENSA- TION COMPONENTS	quantitative and qualitative movement		

(To be Cont'd.)

(Cont'd.)

LABAN's CLASSIFICATION	Preston (1963) Preston-Dunlop (1980)	North (1972)	Russell (1969)	Lamb (1965)/ Ramsden (1973)
INCOMPLETE EFFORTS/ INNER ATTITUDES	Effort attitudes	∴		
S & T "awake"	∴			
F & W "dreamlike"	∴	∴		
S & F "remote"	∴	∴		
W & T "near"	∴	W & T "rhythmic"		
S & W "stable"	∴	S & W & "unchanging"		
T & F "mobile"	∴	T & F & "change"		
DRIVES/MOVEMENT DRIVES	Effort drives	∴		
WTS "action drive" (basic effort actions)	actions	action-like drive		
SFT "vision drive"	visionary	visionary drive		
WSF "spell drive"	spell-like	spell-like drive		
WTF "passion drive"	passionate	emotional stressed drive		
ATTENTION – SPACE				Attending
INTENTION – WEIGHT				Intending
DECISION – TIME				Committing
PROGRESSION – FLOW		Flow – emotion/precision/ relationships		(Ramsden, 1973)
EFFORT GRAPH	∴	∴		& Shape graph*

(To be Cont'd.)

(Cont'd.)

LABAN's CLASSIFICATION	Preston (1963) Preston-Dunlop (1980)	North (1972)	Russell (1969)	Lamb (1965)/ Ramsden (1973)
BASIC EFFORT ACTIONS ("action drive")	✓			
thrusting		nouns & WST as mental and emotional actions = "externalized drives"	nouns	
floating				
dabbing				
pressing				
slashing				
wringing				
flicking				
gliding				
TRANSITIONS/MUTATIONS				
change of one element	gradual	transitions		
change of two elements	less gradual	changes		
change of three elements	abrupt			
RANKING	used in phrases (1980)	✓		
GRADING		exaggerated & lessened degrees neutral states of motion factors		
Complete Effort Action SWTF				

4. *Survey of Interpretations of Laban's Classification of BODY Movement*

LABAN's CLASSIFICATION	Preston (1963) Preston-Dunlop (1980)	North (1959, 1961, 1972)	Russell (1959)	Lamb (1959)
BODILY ACTIONS				
– the stance	5 body actions and stillness:	activities based on everyday actions:	body activities:	posture*: action involving a continuous adjustment of the whole body
– transference of weight	gesture	travelling	locomotion	
– steps (leaps, turns, runs)	stepping locomotion	turning opening & closing	elevation turns	gesture*: action confined to a part or parts of the body
– gesture (scooping/ gathering-strewing/ scattering; head and facial expression)	jumping turning stillness	jumping (1961) body parts used in body actions: gesture; steps; carriage (1972)	gesture rising, sinking opening, crossing, advancing, retreating	
WAYS OF USING THE BODY				
– upper or lower		body function and restriction, range; where movement originates (1972);		
– right or left				
– off or on the floor				
– symmetric or asymmetric	symmetry & asymmetry; body flow: simultaneous or successive	symmetry & asymmetry (1959); movement: successive or simultaneous; still-	symmetry & asymmetry; body flow: simultaneous or successive	
– simultaneous or successive		ness and movement simultaneously;		
– similar or different movements simultaneously		touching or join-		
– touch or grip		ing; melodic or chordic;		
– mono- & polylinear sequencing	mono- & polylinear movements (chordic)	shaping (1972)		

5. *Survey of Interpretations of Laban's Classification of RELATIONSHIP Aspects*

LABAN's CLASSIFICATION	Preston (1963) Preston-Dunlop (1980)	North (1959, 1961)	Russell (1959)
ADAPTATION TO PARTNERS			
– contrasting	doing the same, conversational,	meeting	near-apart
– leading & following	dancing together (1963)	parting	approaching-parting
– moving together	dancing to a partner (1980)	passing by	surrounding
		staying with (1959)	leading & following
			unison
		surrounding each other	canon
		leading & following	opposition
			harmony
GROUP FEELING			
– rising & sinking	group feeling & group	group ideas: converging &	group feeling:
– whirling around	composition: being part	dispersing, growing-shrinking,	unison rising &
– common meter	of group leading & adapting	surrounding, passing through,	sinking, circling;
– observation of and response to	mimetic group action	rising-falling, turning, mirror-	traveling, spiraling &
another group	composing & directing for a	ing, leading-following,	unwinding; passing on
	group; time, space, weight,	echoing, shadowing etc.	an action; common
	flow relationship.	(1961)	effort rhythm, etc.
GROUP FORMATIONS			
– row, circle, curve	as a unit, linear formations	significance of formations:	group formations:
– waxing & waning	solid group formations,	unity of circles, concentra-	possibilities of
– different levels	irregular formations,	tion of spiralling, tension of	lines
– symmetrical &	visual aids (1980)	line, adaptability of curving,	circles
asymmetrical		rigidity of block (1959)	blocks
			freer group shapes

Appendix III

Integration of Laban's Concepts into Other Theoretical Frameworks: Survey Tables

Laban's concepts and classification of movement have been increasingly applied as research instruments in several other disciplines, such as anthropology, choreology, psychology, and nonverbal communication. Particularly instrumental in paving the way for such crossfertilizations was Irmgard Bartenieff (1900-1981). On the basis of her broad background as a Laban-trained dancer and notator, as well as a trained physio-therapist, Bartenieff's individual and collaborative activities created several cross-disciplinary links between movement/dance and remedial work, and between dance and anthropological research. After her emigration from Germany in 1936, Bartenieff (together with Irma Otte-Betz) introduced Laban's notation to the U.S.A. and became a member of the Dance Notation Bureau in New York. In the 1960's, she developed Laban-Lamb-based methodologies with reference to teaching and therapy at the Albert Einstein School of Medicine, and at the Jacobi and Bronx State Hospitals in New York. In 1966, Bartenieff was appointed director of dance research of an ethnological project headed by ethno-musicologist Alan Lomax, and with assistant Forrestine Paulay she formulated a "choreometric" approach to the investigation of dance style and culture. The analysis of over 200 films from five continents resulted in seven choreometric profiles of dance characteristics and was published in Lomax's *Folk Song Style and Culture* (1968). Bartenieff's own investigations in fundamental exercises of movement training appeared as an appendix to her *Body Movement: Coping with the Environment* (co-written with Dori Lewis) in 1980. A summary of her life-long work, the book interprets Laban's concepts and exemplifies them through situations from everyday life, dance, martial arts, sport, and research.

The nucleus of what was to become in 1978 the Laban Institute of Movement Studies (LIMS) was the founding of the Effort/Shape division of the New York Dance Notation Bureau in 1965-66, headed by Bartenieff. (The Laban Institute, now the Laban-Bartenieff Institute, provides training in Laban Movement Analysis founded on Labanotation, Effort/Shape, and

Space Harmony, as well as Bartenieff's Fundamentals.) The Dance Notation Bureau Extension of The Ohio State University's Department of Dance organized two "Laban-analysis Research Workshops" (1973, 1976) which gathered movement and dance experts from both institutions under the direction of Lucy Venable. Its 1976 team (Odette Blum, Angelika Gerbes, Elizabeth Kagan, Janis Pforsich, Lucy Venable, and Irene Wachtel) designed a coding sheet for the distinction of ethnic, historical, and choreographic styles. Movement classification had been compiled from two complementary systems: Labanotation and Effort/Shape, with some parameters from North (1972) and the Bartenieff-Paulay choreometric project (1968). Several subsequent choreological projects used Labananalysis (Labanotation and Effort/ Shape), such as those of Elizabeth Kagan (1978), Suzanne Youngerman (1978), and Jill Gellerman (1978).

The integration of some of Laban's concepts with non-verbal communication theories has been spearheaded by Martha Davis. Initially Bartenieff's student and assistant, Davis was trained both in movement/dance and psychology; she founded the Institute for Nonverbal Communication Research in New York in 1978. Author of *Understanding Body Movment: An Annotated Bibliography* (1972) and co-author (with Janet Skupien) of *Body Movement and Nonverbal Communication: An Annotated Bibliography 1971-1981* (1982), in *Towards Understanding the Intrinsic in Body Movement* (1975) she draws a glossary of movement terms from Labanotation, Effort/Shape, and the Eshkol-Wachmann movement notation. Since 1983, Davis has also directed the "consensus project" of the Laban-Bartenieff Institute of Movement Studies, which is preparing a compendium of Laban-derived terms, their definitions, and special applications.

Freudian analyst Judith Kestenberg, who also studied with Lamb and Bartenieff, designed ways of observing infants by applying and expanding some Effort/Shape concepts in the context of the oral, anal and urethral developmental phases. Her three studies on the role of movement patterns in development — rhythms of movement, flow of tension and Effort, and the control of shape — were first published in the *Psychoanalytic Quarterly* 34 (1965). Cecily Dell's handbook *A Primer for Movement Description: Using Effort-Shape and Supplementary Concepts* (1970) has resulted from the work initiated by Bartenieff, also incorporating some of Kestenberg's concepts.

The survey charts below provide only an initial outline of how Laban's concepts have been integrated in other theoretical frameworks; it is expected that the LIMS compendium of terms and their application will present a comprehensive account of these transformations.

1. Survey of Integration of Laban's SPATIAL Concepts in Frameworks of Other Disciplines

	Kestenberg (1967) [Freudian Analysis]	Lomax-Bartenieff-Paulay, (1968) [Anthropology]	Dell (1970) [Handbook]	Davis (1975) [Nonverbal Communication]	OSU Coding Sheet (1976) [Choreology]
EXTENSION	wide to narrow big to small bulging to hollow		growing-shrinking reach-space near-far	size or range	use of kinesphere
ORIENTATION	horizontal plane= oral phase; Vertical plane= anal phase; Sagittal plane= urethral phase	use of directions and planes in activities and transitions between them	spatial orientation in 26 main directions	areas of space direction planal stress	use of kinesphere
SHAPE	shape flow (Lamb*)	shape of transition and activities: vague, angular, curved arc, round, looped; three-dimensional indefinite	gathering & scattering; concaving: sinking, narrowing, retreating. convexing: rising, widening, advancing.	type of path figures in space vague-clear direct-sinuous	spatial path spatial forms
PATH		simple reversal cyclic looped	spoke-like arc-like	type of path spatial transition	
HARMONY	Effort/Shape				Effort/Shape

2. *Survey of Integration of Laban's Concepts into Other Theoretical Frameworks*

EFFORT

Kestenberg (1967)	Lomax-Bartenieff-Paulay (1968)	Dell (1970)	Davis (1975)	OSU Coding Sheet (1976)
Flow of tension (can be independent of effort) forerunner of effort: mature effort	Energy of transition: quality held over, new quality; Energy in main activity: fleeting, . . . strength, speed, slow-fast, flow, jerky-smooth	assimilation of Laban-Lamb concepts and some Kestenberg-derived terms	includes quantitative and qualitative terms related to tension; weight, time	phrasing of Effort; range of Effort Elements

BODY

Kestenberg (1967)	Lomax-Bartenieff-Paulay (1968)	Dell (1970)	Davis (1975)	OSU Coding Sheet (1976)
	Most active body parts Number of parts moving Body attitude: trunk as one or two units	Body part involvement in movement Body attitude	includes multiple articulation of maintained and mobile aspects of body movement and position	Body actions; Body part relationships; Order of actions Body attitude

RELATIONSHIPS

Kestenberg (1967)	Lomax-Bartenieff-Paulay (1968)	Dell (1970)	Davis (1975)	OSU Coding Sheet (1976)
		Group relationships: group formation, types of relationships (orientation, toward-away, proximity, symmetry, opposition, synchrony, common focus, leading-following, "floor plans")		

Appendix IV

Annotation of Laban's Writings Used in the Research

1. Laban, Rudolf von, *Die Welt des Tänzers* (Stuttgart: Walter Seifert Verlag, 1920), 264 pp. and the table of contents.

Laban's first book conveys a sense about the artist and the budding theoretician who interprets all phenomena in dance-like terms. More than in his other texts, the style of writing reflects the symbolism in German literature of his time. The "Einführung" (Introduction) is followed by the "Erster Reigen: Über den Menschlichen Ausdruck" (First Reigen: About Human Expression), "Zweiter Reigen: Über den Tänzer" (Second Reigen: About the Dancer), "Dritter Reigen: Uber Tänzerische Erziehung und Kultur" (Third Reigen: About Dance Education and Culture), "Vierter Reigen: Über Tanz als Kunst" (Fourth Reigen: About the Dance as Art), "Fünfter Reigen: Über Reigengesetze" (Fifth Reigen: About Reigen Laws), and the final "Bausteine" (Buildingblocks). Between the introduction and the First Reigen, the third edition published in 1926 contains five photographs of "Rudolf von Laban Gruppe für Neuen Bühnentanz" (Rudolf von Laban Group for the new Theatredance). According to a personal communication from Lisa Ullmann, the photographs were taken at the summer workshop in Gleschendorf on the North Sea where Laban assembled his first dance group. In addition seventeen dance photo plates of Laban, Bereska, Wigman, Lenares, groups from Laban schools, and of wrestlers and a Persian dancer are included in the book. A color reproduction of Laban's "Entwurf einer Tanzszene" (Sketch for a Dance Scene) prefaces the title. References to this work are made throughout the manuscript and its intent is discussed on p. 51.

2. Laban, Rudolf von, "Kultische Bildung im Feste," *Die Tat*, (June 1920), pp. 161-168.

This is an early statement of belief about the social significance of festive activities, such as free exercises which can heighten an awareness of the body-mind unity in movement, and the participation in plays of ritualistic content.

3. Laban, Rudolf von, "Symbole des Tanzes und Tanz als Symbol," *Die Tat*, (1922?), pp. 669-675.

The article is based on the premise that the symbolism of dance develops from the symbolism of forms in motion. Discussions of numbers, proportions, form elements and polygons are complementary to those in *Die Welt des Tänzers* and *Gymnastik und Tanz*. Of particular interest is the section on "harmony of forms" including the discussion of "Eurhythmy" in which Laban claims the autonomy of dance.

4. Laban, Rudolf von, "Der Tanz als Eigenkunst," *Zeitchrift für Ästhetik und Allgemeine Kunstwissenschaft* (Stuttgart: Verlag Ferdinand Enkel, 1925, XIX Band), pp. 356-364.

The article points to the current renaissance of interest in dance and addresses views of dance as an independent art form throughout history. The primacy of dramatic, musical or pure movement structures in dance is also discussed. The essay shows not only Laban's thorough study of major primary sources, but also his cognizance of their cultural context and his critical view of some of the translations. Also well substantiated is Laban's belief (expressed in his later article "Dance in General" [see no. 29]) that besides data about historical facts, dance history should incorporate analyses of movement principles, the laws of harmony and theories, and methods of dance education.

5. Laban, Rudolf von, *Choreographie*: Erstes Heft (Jena: Eugen Diedrichs, 1926), 103 pp. and the table of contents; twenty-two illustrations.

A well-informed translation and annotation of this book is long overdue. In a concentrated form it provides insight into the forming of Laban's theoretical framework and his notation. Beside drawings of spatial forms and notation symbols, the book includes eleven photograph-plates of spatial scale performances in the icosahedron. The intent of the book is described on p. 51 and its content on p. 57. Numerous quotations and paraphrases of sections are used, particularly in Chapter I.

6. Laban, Rudolf von, *Gymnastik und Tanz* (Oldenburg: Gerhard Stalling Verlag, 1926), 176 pp. and the table of contents including the description of the appendix: "Anlage: Praktische Übungen" (Plan: Practical Exercises); the last page contains an announcement about the foundation of Laban's institute for further elaborations of his Choreography (dance notation).

The text and illustrations show which specific observations of human movement, within the context of gymnastics and dance, led Laban to formulate the fundamentals of his theories. The sections of the book consider "Gymnastische Grundbegriffe" (Basic Concepts of Gymnastic), "Bewegungskultur und Weltanschauung" (Movement Culture and the View of the World), "Anatomie als Grundlage der Bewegungsgesetze" (Anatomy as the Basis for Movement Laws), "Soziale Möglichkeiten" (Social Possibilities), "Bewegungskunst" (The Art of Movement), and "Abschluss" (Conclusion). The second edition of the book contains eight photograph-plates and 47 photographs of Laban's students and the work in their schools. The intent of the book is described on p. 51 and quotations and paraphrased sections are used throughout; the practical exercises from the appendix are presented in Chapter II, p. 95.

7. Laban, Rudolf von, *Des Kindes Gymnastik und Tanz* (Oldenburg: Gerhard Stalling Verlag, 1929), 135 pp. with four photo-plates and 34 photographs within the text (from children's classes in Laban schools).

Similar in content to *Gymnastik und Tanz*, the book is written as a long essay without separate chapters (there is also no table of contents). The emphasis of particular sections is, however, indicated by italicized sentences or paragraphs, such as *"The first written signs were images of gestures. A thousand undescribable things and exhilarations spoke from them not only a single sound, as word or a sentence"* (p. 34). The intent of the book is not a critique of current education but an insight into ways one could provide for the need of the growing child and maintain a healthy and aware "bodysoul" (p. 8).

8. Laban, Rudolf von, "Das Tänzerische Kunstwerk," *Die Tat*, (November 1927), pp. 588-591.

This is an important article outlining the main ideas Laban presented at the first German Dance Congress in 1927. The article is extensively paraphrased in Part One.

9. Laban, Rudolf von, *Schrifttanz: Methodik, Orthographie, Erläuterungen*. (Vienna: Universal Edition 9600, 1928; English and French editions — 9600 a, 1930), 20 pp.

This booklet is of historical importance because it is the first publication of the system of Kinetography as a handbook. Its content is referred to in Chapter III, (note 11). The quarterly *Schrifttanz* described it as "the handbook of Laban's dance notation giving a basic introduction to Kinetography. This handbook is indispensible to all who deal with notation" (See ads at the end of the 1929, 1930 and 1931 issues). The sequel of the booklet is *Kleine Tänze mit Vorübungen* (*Short Dances with Preliminary Exercises*), Universal Edition 9601; it contains a German-English-French text. The publication is described as the first collection which publishes complete dances in Laban's dance notation. The booklet contains three group and a solo dance by Laban and Bereska with music by Beethoven, Schumann, and Lavry, and one dance without music: "Slow Motion."

10. Laban, Rudolf von, "Grundprinzipien der Bewegungsschrift," *Schrifttanz*, Heft I, 1928, pp. 4-5.

A key article complementary to the booklet on the orthography and methods of Kinetography. Principles underlying the system are discussed and illustrated with simple drawings. Chapter III draws from it.

11. Laban, Rudolf von, "Die Entwicklung der Bewegungsschrift Laban," *Schrifttanz*, Heft II, 1928, pp. 27-30.

This article and its illustrations were part of Laban's lecture-demonstration at the second German Dance Congress in 1928. The presentation was illustrated with slides and practical examples. Chapter III draws from the article.

12. Laban, Rudolf von, "Tanzkomposition und Schrifttanz," *Schrifttanz*, Heft II, 1928, pp. 19-20.

The significance of notation for dance composition is discussed from several angles. A notated piece can show the composer's dependence on some dance traditions or some historical stylistic combinations. On the other hand, notation can also offer a survey of many possible movement combinations as material of dance expression facilitating a gradual path to free composition. Here lies the true value of script-dance, Laban maintains. Chapter IV (note 3) refers to the article.

13. Laban, Rudolf von, "Vom Tanzinhalt: Studien Über die Pole des Tanz-kunstwerkes," *Der Tanz*, Heft 1, 1928, pp. 2-3.

This article which discusses the perception of art in general and dance in particular has been extensively drawn from in Chapter IV (notes 9-10).

14. Laban, Rudolf von. "Choreographie und Theater," *Der Scheinwerfer*, Heft 11/12, 1928, p. 22.

Not unlike "Tanzkomposition und Schrifttanz," this article also discusses the significance of notation as well as dance theory for the development of dance composition. Chapter IV draws from it (notes 3, 12).

15. Laban, Rudolf von, "Probleme des Tanzes," *Schrifttanz*, Heft I, 1929, p. 19.

The information about this lecture-demonstration can be found in the section of "Verschiedene Mitteilungen" (Various Communications) of the magazine. The chart titled "Was Tut Not? Praktisch und Theoretisch" is discussed in Part One (note 57) and Chapter IV (note 1).

16. Laban, Rudolf von, "Über die Tänzerischen Berufe," *Der Tanz*, Heft 14, 1929, pp. 2-4.

Laban deplores the general lack of understanding and support for dance and deduces it to the poor and undifferentiated state of dance professions in general.

17. Laban, Rudolf von, "Das Choreographische Institut Laban," *Monographien der Ausbildungsschulen für Tanz und Tänzerische Körperbildung*, Band I. Liesel Freund ed. (Berlin: Leo Alterthum Berlag, 1929), pp. 11-14.

This manifesto contains three photographs and an example of a notated dance phrase. Part One, pp. 17-19 draws from this information.

18. Laban, Rudolf von, "Vom Sinn der Bewegungschöre," *Schrifttanz*, Heft II, 1930, pp. 25-26.

The article is an abridged version of Laban's lecture on the occasion of the founding of the first movement choir in Hamburg, published in a pamphlet titled *Tänzerische Zeitfragen* (Hamburg: Tanzbühne Laban, Sleipner Verlag, 1929). Fragments of the lecture are also published in *Gymnastik und Tanz* on pp. 132-136. Layman dance in movement choirs is seen as the chief means of body-mind education for the new era and is discussed for its socio-cultural significance.

19. Laban, Rudolf von, *Ein Leben für den Tanz* (Dresden: Carl Riessner Verlag, 1935); translated and annotated by Lisa Ullmann and published as *A Life for Dance* (London: Macdonald and Evans, 1975), 193 pp.; illustrated with Laban's drawings.

A sense of Laban the dreamer and story teller can be gained from this autobiographical text. Ullmann's annotations greatly interpret and clarify the narration so that the book may be seen as filling the gap of an outstanding Laban biography. Part One of this manuscript extensively draws from its text.

20. Laban, Rudolf, *Choreutics*, annotated and edited by Lisa Ullmann (London: Macdonald and Evans, 1966), 214 pp.; 97 figures.

After the introductory *Choreographie*, this is Laban's major work on his theory of space harmony. Although its Part I was written in English (1930) and subsequently annotated and edited by Ullmann, it does not make for easy reading, and many sections require additional interpretations; the survey in Part II of *Choreutics* was drawn from Gertrud Snell's notes (1929). While the intent of the book is described on p. 51, Chapter I draws extensively from the book for purposes of comparative analysis.

21. Laban, Rudolf and Lawrence, C.F., *Effort* (London: Macdonald and Evans, 1947), 88 pp.

The Effort theory is outlined here in the context of the author's concerns with the optimal realization of human potentials and its application to work processes. Chapter II of this manuscript discusses the presentation of the concepts.

22. Laban, Rudolf, *Modern Educational Dance* (London: Macdonald and Evans, 1948), 110 pp.

Germinal ideas of the sixteen basic movement themes starting from the awareness of the body, to force-space-time-flow components, to interaction with partners and groups are presented in Laban's brief formulations. Subsequent chapters dealing with the development of Effort capacity and the conception of the sphere of movement provide an additional view of the Effort and Space theories. The book is referred to in Chapter I, Chapter IV, and Chapter VI.

23. Laban, Rudolf, *The Mastery of Movement on the Stage* (London: Macdonald and Evans, 1950), 190 pp; *The Mastery of Movement*, second revised edition by Lisa Ullmann (ibid., 1960), 186 pp; *The Mastery of Movement*, fourth edition, revised and enlarged by Lisa Ullmann (ibid., 1980), 196 pp.

This is among Laban's most approachable texts. His intent to present a guide to stage practice as the forum for artistic enhancement of human activity in general has been carried out by a series of short movement sequences, "moves," and mime scenes which provide for the experimental understanding of the text. In revising it, Ullmann (1960) omitted the "on the stage" qualifier and broadened several sections of the book concerned with the Effort theory. In its fourth revised edition, she included marginal abstracts to most paragraphs and provided the originally planned kinetographic description of the "moves." Of particular interest is the appendix in which Ullmann used an unpublished manuscript written by Laban before 1950 titled "Rhythmic Control of Man's Activities in Work and Play." References to the book are made in three chapters of the manuscript: Chapter II, Chapter III, Chapter VI.

24. Laban, Rudolf, "The Work of the Art of Movement Studio," *Journal of Physical Education*, Vol. 46, No. 137, 1954, pp. 22-30.

The rationale for the work in the Studio (1946-1954) comes from the significance of the art of movement in education. Statements by Lisa Ullmann (director), Valerie Preston, Marion North, and Geraldine Stephenson (teachers) are included.

25. Laban, Rudolf, "A Letter to Guild Members," *The Laban Art of Movement Guild Magazine*, No. 15, 1954, pp. 4-9.

In this autobiographical account, Laban also refers to his so-called 'Archives' which were twice destroyed in the two world wars. The information about the reason for his exile from Germany is referred to in Part One.

26. Laban, Rudolf, "Foreword by Rudolf Laban," *Labanotation* by Ann Hutchinson, second edition (New York: A Theatre Arts Book, 1970), pp. XIII-XVI, (written by Laban in 1954).

Here Laban refers to written dance as "script-dance," which is the translation of the term "Schrifttanz" widely used in the '20's. Laban reiterates the information about his search for primary action signs in ancient cultures, as well as the matter of his debt to Feuillet's notation. He also clarifies the fact that instead of publishing a second volume of *Choreographie* he compiled in 1928 the "Method and Orthography of Kinetography Laban."

27. Laban, Rudolf, *Principles of Dance and Movement Notation* (London: Macdonald and Evans, 1956), 56 pp.

This is an important book for understanding Laban's view of notation as "motor symbols" which, when combined in various ways, can represent the elementary motor faculties of man; on the other hand, the rhythm and flow of the notation can capture the spiritual content of movement and dance. Chapter III refers to the book.

28. Laban, Rudolf, "Vorwort," *Abriss der Kinetographie Laban* by Albrecht Knust (Essen: Das Tanzarchiv Verlag, 1956), pp. IX-XI.

Laban pays tribute to Knust's major contributions in developing Kinetography as a fully fledged language of movement with its own logic and orthography, thus establishing dance notation as an independent profession. The account of shared interests in recreative group dance yields interesting information: it was in Knust's group of enthusiastic layman dancers that the name "movement choir" arouse. This preface was translated into English and reprinted in Knust's *A Dictionary of Kinetography Laban*, (1979) Vol. I., pp. XV-XVI.

29. Laban, Rudolf, "Dance in General," *Rudolf Laban Speaks about Movement and Dance*, selected and edited by Lisa Ullmann (Addlestone, Surrey: Laban Art of Movement Centre, 1971), pp. 56-68.

In this reprint of a lecture Laban gave in Dartington Hall (1939) in a history of dance series, he discusses the meaning behind various views of dance through the ages and also makes reference to some archetypal movement actions, such as turning, circling and hopping, inducing various moods in performers and viewers.

30. Laban, Rudolf, *A Vision of Dynamic Space*, compiled by Lisa Ullmann (London: Falmer Press in association with Laban Archives, 1984), 80 pp.

This is a long awaited publication based on holdings of the Laban Archives. A selection from Laban's two- and three-dimensional works, i.e., sketches, drawings, paintings, and models, is juxtaposed with quotations from mostly unpublished writings (1938-1950). Most of the works are reproduced in color. The book vividly exemplifies Laban's concept of space as being created through human movement in each of its phases from stillness to stir, rather than as an empty receptacle to be filled with motion. Chapter VI makes a reference to the book.

With permission of Lisa Ullmann, custodian of the Laban Archives, three unpublished manuscripts have been drawn from and quoted in this study:

31. A three-page manuscript (typed) titled by Ullmann: "Comments by R. Laban 1957."

It is written in the form of a letter and sections are reprinted in this manuscript in Part One and in Chapter VI.

32. "Film über die harmonische Bewegung des Menschlichen Körpers." 4 pp. (typed). Not dated; one may speculate that it was written in the late 1930's.

The translation of this film scenario has been revised by Lisa Ullmann, and it is reproduced in its entirety in Chapter IV.

33. "Raumspielpuzzle." 20 pp (typed); not dated; one may speculate that it was written in the late 1930's.

The manuscript outlining a "space-game-puzzle" has been extensively discussed in Chapter IV.

Appendix V

Annotated Bibliography of Selected German Sources

1. Bie, Oskar, *Der Tanz* (Berlin: Julius Bard Verlag, 1923), 394 pp.

This is a history of Western social and theatrical dance. References to Laban, Loheland, and Wigman from p. 382 are commented on in Part One.

2. Böhme, Fritz, "Vorstellung und Erlebnis im Tanz: 'Gaukelei,' 'Drosselbart,' 'Schwingende Landschaft,'" *Schrifttanz*, Heft II, 1930, pp. 37-39.

This essay on the theatrical dimensions of dance is exemplified in Laban's "Jugglery," Jooss' "Trashbird," and Wigman's "Swinging Landscape." While the latter is seen as a lyric-epic dance suite, the former two are considered as dramatic theatre dance works. The article is referred to in Part One.

3. Böhme, Fritz, "Laban's tänzerischer Nachwuchs," *Schrifttanz*, Heft IV, 1929, pp. 66-68.

The particular interest of this article lies in its summary of Laban's significance and the description of principal performance and choreographic characteristics of former Laban proteges Wigman, Jooss, Bereska, Loeser, Keith, Feist, Bodmer, Wulff, Frank and Algo.

Dance author and critic, Böhme, supportive of the new dance also wrote in 1949 "Rudolf von Laban und die Entstehung des modernen Tanzdramas" ("Rudolf von Laban and the Evolution of the Modern Dance Drama"), which has not yet been published.

4. Brandenburg, Hans, *Der Moderne Tanz* (München: Georg Müller, 1917 2nd. ed.; first published in 1913), 100 pp.

In this work, the beginnings of modern dance in Europe are discussed in a rhapsodic style. This is not actually a history but an account of the points of departure of various artists, such as the Wiesenthal sisters, Sent Maheza, Clotilde von Derp, Alexander Sacharof, and Gertrud Leistikow. It also presents a critique of pedagogical centers, such as the school of Elizabeth Duncan and of Jacque-Dalcroze. The second edition includes an expose on Laban's two programmatic issues: the "free dance," and explorations of "dance, word, sound." Early photographs are of particular interest. Information from the book is incorporated in Part One and Chapter III.

5. Brandenburg, Hans, "Erinnerungen an Laban's Anfänge," *Schrifttanz*, Heft IV, 1929, pp. 70-71.

This retrospective article furnishes some interesting information about the beginnings of Laban's search for notation. It is drawn from in Chapter III.

6. Brandenburg, Hans, "Laban als Stilreformer," *Singhor und Tanz*, December, 1929, pp. 297-298.

Paying tribute to Laban's 50th birthday, Brandenburg succinctly summarizes Laban's significance. The article is referred to in Part One.

7. Gleisner, Martin, *Tanz für Alle* (Leipzig: Hesse & Becker Verlag, 1928), 174 pp.

This book is a good resource for Laban's activities and the state of his theories by 1928. It also elaborates on movement choirs, on the prerequisites for choir leaders, and on choir repertory. Information from the book is drawn from in Part One and Chapter II.

8. Gleisner, Martin, "Schrifttanz und Laientanz," *Schrifttanz*, Heft II, 1928, pp. 20-22.

The significance of Laban's movement theory and notation for recreative dance is discussed and the advantages of creating dance literature (scores) are emphasized.

9. Gleisner, Martin, "Laban als Wegbahner des Tanzes für die Allgemeinheit," *Singhor und Tanz*, December, 1929, p. 301.

The author emphasizes Laban's contribution to the socio-pedagogical role of dance and lists his compositions for movement choirs. The article is referred to in part One.

10. Gleisner, Martin, "Laban als Schöpfer von Laientanz und Bewegungschor," *Schrifttanz*, Heft IV, 1929, pp. 69-70.

This article covers ground similar to Gleisner's *Singhor und Tanz* article, elaborating further on movement choirs and their cultural significance.

11. Jooss, Kurt, "Rudolf von Laban und das Ballett," *Singhor und Tanz*, December, 1929, pp. 296-297.

With a sense of objective distance, Jooss places Laban's work in the context of contemporary movements in music and art. He also discusses Laban's initial revolt against the artificial forms of ballet at the beginning of the century. Part One draws from the article.

12. Klingenbeck, Fritz, "Der Tanzende Festzug," *Schrifttanz*, Heft II, 1929, pp. 27-28.

This article provides an inside view of the technical possibilities and limitations which determined the movement style of Laban's pageant for the Craft Guilds of Vienna in the summer of 1929.

13. Klingenbeck, Fritz, "Kleiner Rückblick," *Singhor und Tanz*, December, 1929, p. 306.

This is a retrospective article honoring Laban's 50th anniversary. Beside the information concerning the emergence of Kinetography, Klingenbeck presents an insight into Laban's ways of working. Constantly pursuing new ideas, Laban would leave them to others to develop further, and it is as though Klingenbeck anticipated early-on his own claim in the 1980's to the invention of some principles of Laban's notation. The article is drawn from in Part One and Chapter III.

14. Klingenbeck, Fritz, "Schreiben und Lesen," *Schrifttanz*, Heft IV, 1929, pp. 76-77.

Klingenbeck discusses the importance of capturing the most significant features when notating a dance, arguing that too many details may hinder the ease of its reconstruction. He recommends phrasing of notation and an eventual inclusion of catchwords to enhance the expressive character of the notated piece. The article is illustrated with kinetograms (examples in notation); of particular interest is example (g) showing an attempt in notational shorthand.

15. Klingenbeck, Fritz, "Tanzschrift im Schauspiel," *Schrifttanz*, Heft I, 1931, p. 21.

In the Reinhard seminar for acting and directing, Klingenbeck introduced for the first time Laban's notation in the directing script of Maugham's *Victoria* (illustration is included) and for Shakespeare's *Twelfth-Night* produced in the style of the *commedia dell' arte*.

16. Klingenbeck, Fritz, "Technik und Form," *Schrifttanz*, Heft II, 1930, pp. 21-22.

The author argues that Laban's theory of harmony should become a bodily technique for dancers rather than a theoretical concept. By explaining in simple terms how Laban developed his spatial analysis of movement on the basis of ballet positions, Klingenbeck sees it as a link between "old" and "new" dance. The article also attempts to place Laban's "revolution *for* dance" in its historical context.

17. Klingenbeck, Fritz, "Was auschreiben und was nicht?" *Schrifttanz*, Heft II, 1930, pp. 48-49.

This article addresses key problems in notating dance pieces: Klingenbeck points to the distinction between the choreographic structure, the performer's interpretation, and the stylistic components. He discusses the difficulty of drawing border-lines between these three areas, emphasizing the importance of distinguishing the work from its personal interpretation by a performer. It would be absurd, he argues, to prescribe to somebody else idiosyncrasies such as either frequent movement initiations with an upbeat in the hips, shoulders, head and feet, or other minute impulses and variations. These characteristics are best captured on film. For the indication of stylistic components, Klingenbeck suggests pre-signs or key-signatures, such as the sharp or flat in music or a "b" indicating the ballet style. He hopes that further practice will discover other useful possibilities.

18. Klingenbeck, Fritz, "Laban Curriculum Vitae," Katalog für Rudolf Von Laban 1879-1958, Eine Ausstellung des Österreichischen Theatermuseums, 1980/81 (An Exhibition of the Austrian Theatre Museum), pp. 4-16.

Here Klingenbeck presents Laban as the most important dance reformer, dancer, choreographer, philosopher, and creator of a style which is still today, after 60 years, considered "new" by some choreographers. Inspite of its interesting documentation and illustrations, however, the write-up loses credibility because of sweeping and debatable statements such as the author's claims about the invention of basic principles of Laban's Kinetography.

19. Knust, Albrecht, "Laban als Erzieher," *Singhor und Tanz*, December, 1929, pp. 304-305.

This article is an excellent account of Laban as an educator in the 1920's. It also refers to Laban's differentiation of the three types of movers – high, medium, and deep dancers. Part One draws from the article.

20. Knust, Albrecht, *Abriss der Kinetographie Laban* (Hamburg: Das

Tanzarchiv Verlag, 1956), Text 227 pp; Examples 116 pp.

This was the basic textbook used in Europe in the 50's and 60's. Rules and examples of Labanotation are included whereever they differ from the writing conventions of Kinetography. (Different "dialects" of Laban's notation developed during World War II when communication among centres in Germany, England, and America was interrupted.)

21. Knust, Albrecht, *Handbook of Kinetography Laban* (Hamburg: Das Tanzarchiv Verlag, 1958).

This is the English translation of the above text book.

22. Knust, Albrecht, "The Roots of Laban Notation," *Dance Notation Record*, Vol. IX, 1958, pp. 8-10.

This write-up is a commemorative article aiming at an understanding of concepts and points of view which confronted Laban during his formulation of Kinetography. Knust also refers to his unfinished discussion with Laban about the exceptional nature of his notation which spread more successfully than the master's other inventions. The discussion about Jooss' and Bereska's efforts in reconciling Feuillet's and Laban's analyses of movement is referred to in Chapter III.

23. Knust, Albrecht, *Dictionary of Kinetography Laban (Labanotation)* Plymouth: MacDonald and Evans, 1979), Vol. 1, Text 420 pp. Vol. 2, Examples 162 pp.

The exposition of various groups of symbols and writing rules is illustrated with hundreds of examples. The section on the development of Kinetography (pp. 367-369) is informative for those interested in both the historical background of the system and the function of the International Council of Kinetography Laban, ICKL.

24. Lämmel, Rudolf, *Der Moderne Tanz: Eine allgemeinverständliche Einführung in das Gebiet der Rhythmischen Gymnastik und des Neuen Tanzes* (Berlin-Schöneberg: Peter J. Oestergaard Verlag, [1928]), 216 pp. followed by 96 pp. of photographs.

Although the year of publication is not given, the information in the preface indicates that it was 1928. Holding a Ph. D., the author had a particular interest in the development of progressive ideas in movement and dance education. Involved with the organization of the Dalcroze Institute in Hellerau, he was subsequently interested in the work of Laban and Wigman, among others. Incorporating their writings and personal interviews, the book is an important resource for the development of Modern Dance in Europe in the 1920's. Lämmel's own acknowledgement of sources, however, is not always complete.

25. Lewitan, Joseph, "Laban der Tanz-Tribun," *Der Tanz*, Heft 14, 1929, p. 6-7.

Founder, editor, and publisher of *Der Tanz* from 1927-1933, Lewitan's succinct eulogy at the occasion of Laban's 50th birthday is referred to in Part One.

26. Schikowski, John, *Geschichte des Tanzes* (Berlin: Büchergilde Gutenberg, 1926), 164 pp. followed by 33 illustrations.

Starting from dance manifestations of prehistoric times and surveying folk, social, and theatrical dance until the twentieth century, Schikowski presents a five-page discussion (pp. 137-141) on Laban as the creator and the founder of modern dance. It is referred to in Part One.

27. Schlee, Alfred, "Nicht Stehen Bleiben," *Singhor und Tanz*, December, 1929, p. 307.

The editor of *Schrifttanz*, Schlee emphasizes both achievement and difficulties Laban encountered while attempting to bring German dance to international recognition. He suggests that instead of paying tribute to Laban's past achievements, one should maintain close contact with Laban's work. Referred to in Part One.

28. Schlee, Alfred, "Wo Steht Laban? *Der Tanz*, Heft 14, 1929, pp. 4-5.

In this second article composed for Laban's 50th birthday, Schlee critically discusses Laban's points of view on dance and dance theory. Part One draws from the article.

29. Schuftan, Werner, *Handbuch des Tanzes* (Mannheim: Verlag Deutscher Chorsänger Verband und Tanzerbund, 1928), 170 pp.

This handbook considers theoretical and practical aspects of dance. Entries on Laban can be found in the historical survey on pp. 24-27 and in the section on dance notation, pp. 84-87. Biographical data are interwoven with Schuftan's interpretations of Laban's principles and evaluation of their educational value. Illustrations include excerpts from notation scores, such as of the *Titan* on p. 85. Part One refers to the book.

30. Schuftan, Werner, *Manuel de Danse* (Paris: Editions Edgar Malfère, 1938), 222 pp.

This is a revised version of the above handbook. Entries on Laban can be found on pp. 46-54 and 169-176, including an illustration of Laban's model for a dance theatre (p. 175).

31. Schuftan, Werner, "Laban's Bewegungsschrift," *Singhor und Tanz*, December, 1929, p. 302.

The article informs us that Laban's notation produced serious interest on the part of associations for reforms in industry; as a result, they requested presentations of the system and available literature.

32. Skoronel, Vera, "Laban," *Singhor und Tanz*, Heft IV, 1929, pp. 299-300.

Student of Laban and Wigman, Skoronel discusses both masters as prime movers of the European new dance.

33. Snell, Gertrud, "Tanzwissenschaft," *Schönheit*, Heft II, 1926, pp. 62-67.

Although appearing the same year as *Choreographie* and also using photographs from the book, this article contributes descriptions of Eukinetics which are referred to in Chapter I and Chapter II.

34. Snell, Gertrud, "Grundlagen einer Allgemeinen Tanzlehre, "Schrifttanz" Heft I, 1929, pp. 8-11.

This introductory article discusses Laban's attempt to provide a scientific foundation for the practical experience of movement and dance. Snell maintains that Laban succeeded in providing an analysis which is necessary for synthesis and free integration. Reference is made to the article in Chapter I.

35. Snell, Gertrud, "Grundlagen einer Allgemeinen Tanzlehre: II. Choreologie," *Schrifttanz*, Heft II, 1929, pp. 21-24.

Outlining two main areas of movement laws, (1). laws of form and (2). laws of expression, the article focusses on the former which is called choreutics. Chapter I draws from the article.

36. Snell, Gertrud, "Grundlagen einer Allgemeiner Tanzlehre: III. Eukinetik," *Schrifttanz*, Heft II, 1930, pp. 48-50.

As referred to in Chapter II this is an important article for the elucidation of Laban's theory of Eukinetics.

37. Terpis, Max, *Tanz und Tänzer* (Zürich: Atlantis Verlag, 1946), 130 pp.

Former student of Perrottet and Wigman, Terpis (dancer, choreographer, ballet master of the Berlin Opera, architect and writer) gives an excellent rendering of Laban's concepts of the dynamics of the late 1920's. His comment on the discrepancy between the limitations of Laban's writings, the depth of his insights, and the breadth of his teaching is insightful. The concise four-page write-up (pp. 93-97) is extensively drawn from in Part One and Chapter II.

38. Wagner-Regeny, Rudolf, "Neue Grundzüge der Musikalischen Theorie als Ergebnis der Schrifttanzforschung," *Schrifttanz*, Heft I, 1928, pp. 13-15.

This is an interesting essay on differentiating the horizontal and vertical structures of music and dance. The author believes that Laban's script-dance differentiates dancers from composers for dance, and also offers insight into the multitude of possible approaches to dance-music in general. The article is referred to in Part One and Chapter II.

39. Wigman, Mary, "Rudolf von Labans Lehre vom Tanz," *Die Neue Schaubühne*, 5./6. Heft, Dresden, September 1921 3. Jahrg., pp. 99-106.

In accordance with her subsequent writings this article offers insight into the changing directions and emphases of Laban's search in the 1910's. Besides giving an account of activities which she observed or took part in, Wigman, as early as 1921, gives an evaluation of the significance of Laban's artistic, pedagogical and theoretical points of view. The article is drawn from in Part One and Chapter I.

40. Wigman, Mary, "Rudolf von Laban zum Geburtstag," *Schrifttanz*, Heft IV, 1929, p. 65.

The article provides a vivid picture of Laban both as an ingenious improviser and experimenter and as a thorough researcher capturing the ineffable in dance by means of symbols. Chapter III.

41. Wigman, Mary, "Rudolf von Laban," *Singhor und Tanz*, December, 1929, p. 295.

This is actually a reprint of the article which appeared in *Schrifttanz*, Heft IV, 1929, paying tribute to the master on the occasion of his 50th birthday.

42. Wigman, Mary, *The Mary Wigman Book: Her Writings Edited and Trans-*

lated by Walter Sorell (Middletown, Conn.: Wesleyan University Press, 1975), 214 pp.

Although available in English, the book is mentioned here because it is an invaluable source for gaining insight into both Laban's beginnings in Switzerland and Munich, and Wigman's growth as a student and independent artist. Wigman's crayon portrait drawn by Laban in 1917 appears on its front page. Also of interest is a photograph of Laban with a long 'Assyrian' beard, ca. 1914. The book is drawn from in Part One.

43. Wulff, Käthe, "Aus Alten Briefen," *Schrifttanz*, Heft IV, 1929, p. 72.

Laban's former student and co-director of the Laban school in Basel excerpts information from her personal correspondence between 1914 and 1918. Plans for a dance building and Laban's intention to show her his manuscript of *Choreutics* are among interesting fragments of an unwritten Laban biography. Part One refers to this write-up.

Bibliography

Aubel, Herman und Marianne. *Der Künstlerische Tanz unserer Zeit*. Leipzig: Karl Robert Langewiesche Verlag, 1935.

Auerbach, Lotte. "My Memories of Laban," *The Laban Art of Movement Guild Magazine*, No. 51, 1973.

Bartenieff, Irmgard, Paulay Forrestine. "Choreometric Profiles," *Folk Song Style and Culture* by Lomax, Alan. Washington: American Association for the Advancement of Science, 1968.

Bartenieff, Irmgard. "The Root of Laban Theory: Aesthetics and Beyond," *Four Adaptations of Effort Theory in Research and Teaching*. New York: Dance Notation Bureau Publications, 1972.

Bartenieff, Irmgard. "Space, Effort and The Brain," *Main Currents of Modern Thought*, Sept.-Oct. 1974, Vol. 31, No. 1.

Bartenieff, Irmgard with Lewis, Dori. *Body Movement: Coping with the Environment*. New York: Gordon and Breach, 1981.

Bie, Oskar. *Der Tanz*. Berlin: Julius Bard Verlag, 1923.

Bodmer, Sylvia. "Harmonics in Space," *Main Currents of Modern Thought*. Sept.-Oct. 1974, Vol. 31, No. 1.

Bodmer, Sylvia. *Studies Based on Crystalloid Dance Forms*. London: Laban Centre for Movement and Dance, 1979.

Böhme, Fritz. "Vorstellung und Erlebnis im Tanz: 'Gaukelei,' 'Drosselbart,' 'Schwingende Landschaft'," *Schrifttanz* Heft II, 1929.

—. "Laban's Tänzerischer Nachwuchs" *Schrifttanz*, Heft IV, 1929.

Brandeburg, Hans. *Der Moderne Tanz*. München: George Müller, 2nd ed., 1917.

—."Erinnerungen an Laban's Anfänge," *Schrifttanz*, Heft IV, 1929.

—. "Laban als Stilreformer," *Singhor und Tanz*, December, 1929.

Braur, Fritz. "Einblick in die Deutsche Tanzkultur," *Der Tanz*, Heft 14, 1929.

Buytendijk, F.J.J. *Allgemeine Theorie der Menschlichen Haltung und Bewegung*. Berlin: Springer Verlag, 1956.

Cage, John. *Silence*. Cambridge, Mass: The Massachusetts Institute of Technology Press, 1967.

Cohen, Selma Jeanne. "Dance as an Art of Imitation," in Copeland, Roger and Cohen, Marshal ed., *What is Dance? Readings in Theory and Criticism*. New York: Oxford University Press, 1983.

Coton, A.V. *The New Ballet: Kurt Jooss and His Work*. London: Dobson, 1946.

Cunningham, Merce. *Changes: Notes on Choreography*. New York: Something Else Press, 1968.

—. "The Impermanent Art," in *Esthetics Contemporary*. Buffalo, NY: Prometheus Books, 1978.

Curl, Gordon. "Philosophic Foundations," I-VI. *The Laban Art of Movement Guild Magazine* Nos. 37-39, 40, 43, 1966-1969.

Davis, Martha. *Understanding Body Movement: An Annotated Bibliography*. New York: Arno Press, 1972.

—. "Movement as Patterns of Process," *Main Currents in Modern Thought*. September-October 1974, Volume 31, No. 1.

—. *Towards Understanding the Intrinsic in Body Movement*. New York: Arno Press, 1975.

Davis, Martha and Janet Skupien. *Body Movement and Non-verbal Communication: An Annotated Bibliography, 1971-1981*. Bloomington, IN: Indiana University Press, 1982.

Dell, Cecily. *A Primer for Movement Description: Using Effort-shape and Supplementary Concepts*. New York: Dance Notation Bureau Publication, 1970.

Feist, Herta. "Laban unserer Wegbereiter." Lecture given in Hannover, November 6, 1954 (Laban Archives)

Feuillet, Raul-Auger. *Chorégraphie ou l'art d'Ecrire la Danse*. New York: Broude Bros., 1968 (A facsimile of the 1700 Paris edition.)

Foster, John. *The Influences of Rudolf Laban*. London: Lepus Books, 1977.

Gassner, John. *Directions in Modern Theatre and Drama*. New York: Holt, Rinehart and Winston, Inc., 1966.

Gellerman, Jill. "The Main Pattern as an Indicator of Cultural Attitudes in Three American Hasidic Communities: A Comparative Approach Based on Labananalysis," in Woodruff, Diane, ed., Essays in Dance Research, *Dance Research Annual* IX, Committee on Research in Dance, 1978.

Gleisner, Martin. *Tanz für Alle*. Leipzig: Hesse Becker Verlag, 1928.

—. "Schrifttanz und Laientanz," *Schrifttanz*, Heft II, 1928.

—. "Laban als Schöpfer von Laientanz und Bewegungschor," *Schrifttanz*, Heft IV, 1929.

—. "Laban als Wegbahner des Tanzes fur die Allgemeinheit," *Singhor und Tanz*, December, 1929.

—. "Conversations between Laban and Myself in 1926," *The Laban Art of Movement Guild Magazine*, No. 65, 1980.

Goldberg, RoseLee. *Performance: Live Art 1909 to the Present*. New York: Abrams Inc., 1979.

Gordon, Donald E. *Ernst Ludwig Kirschner*. Cambridge, Mass: Harvard University Press, 1968.

Gropius, Walter & Ise, Bayer Herbert, eds. *Bauhaus 1919-1928*. Boston: Charles T. Branfort C., 1959.

Hildebrant, Hans. *Oskar Schlemmer*. München: Prestel Verlag, 1952.

Hodgson, John. in "Historical and Biographical Considerations," by Dunn, Margaret, *Laban Centenary Symposium Report*, 1979.

Holbrook, Jennifer K. "Laban, Wagner and the Gesamtkunstwerk," *Move-*

ment and Dance: Magazine of the Laban Guild, no. 70, 1983.

Innes, Christopher. *Holy Theatre: Ritual and the Avant Garde.* Cambridge: Cambridge University Press, 1981.

Janik, Alan and Stephen Toulmin. *Wittgenstein's Vienna.* New York: Simon and Schuster, 1973.

Jeschke, Claudia. *Tanzschriften: Ihre Geschichte und Methode.* Bad Reichenhall: Comes Verlag, 1983.

Jooss, Kurt. "Rudolf von Laban und das Ballett," *Singhor und Tanz* (December, 1929).

Jung, Carl G. *Man and his Symbols.* New York: Doubleday and Windfall, 1964.

Kagan, Elizabeth. "Towards the Analysis of a Score: A Comparative Study of *Three Epitaphs* by Paul Taylor and *Water Study* by Doris Humphrey," in Woodruff, Diane ed., Essays in Dance Research, *Dance Research Annual IX*, Committee on Research in Dance, 1978.

Kestenberg, Judith S. "The Role of Movement Patterns in Development, *Psychoanalytic Quarterly*, Vol. 36, 1967.

Kleist, Heinrich von. "Puppet Theatre," *Salmagundi*, N. 33-34, Spring-Summer, 1976.

Klingenbeck, Fritz. "Der Tanzende Festzug," *Schrifttanz*, Heft II, 1929.

—. "Kleiner Rückblick," *Singhor und Tanz*, (December, 1929).

—. "Schreiben und Lesen," *Schrifttanz*, Heft IV, 1929.

—. "Tanzschrift in Schauspiel," *Schrifttanz*, Heft I, 1930.

—. "Technik und Form," *Schrifttanz*, Heft II, 1930.

—. "Was Auschreiben und Was Nicht?" *Schrifttanz*, Heft II, 1930.

—. "Laban Curriculum Vitae," Katalog für Rudolf von Laban 1879-1958, Eine Ausstellung des Österreichischen Theatermuseums, 1980-81.

Knust, Albrecht. "Laban als Erzieher," *Singhor und Tanz*, December, 1929.

—. *Abriss der Kinetographie Laban.* Hamburg: Das Tanzarchiv Verlag, 1958.

—. "The Roots of Laban Notation," *Dance Notation Record*: Rudolf Laban Memorial Issue, Vol. IX, 1958.

—. *Dictionary of Kinetography Laban* (*Labanotation*).Vol. 1 and 2. Plymouth: Macdonald and Evans, 1979.

Koegler, Horst. *In the Shadow of the Swastika: Dance in Germany 1929-1936 Dance Perspectives 57*, Spring 1974.

Kostelanetz, Richard, ed. *Esthetics Contemporary.* Buffalo, New York: Prometheus Books, 1978.

Kuhn, Thomas S. *The Structure of Scientific Revolutions.* Chicago: Univery of Chicago Press, 1973.

Kuhn, Thomas S. "Second Thoughts on Paradigms," in Suppe, Frederick. *The Structure of Scientific Theories.* Chicago: University of Illinois Press, 1974.

Kurath, Gertrude and Marti, Samuel. *Dances of Anahuac.* Chicago: Aldine, 1964.

Laban, Rudolf von. *Die Welt des Tänzers.* Stuttgart: Walter Seifert Varlag, 1920.

—. "Kultische Bildung im Feste," *Die Tat*, Heft 3, 1920.
—. "Symbole des Tanzes und Tanz als Symbol," *Die Tat*, 1922 (?).
—. "Der Tanz als Eigenkunst," *Zeitschrift für Aesthetik Und Allgemeine Kunstwissenschaft*, XIX Band, 1925.
—. *Choreographie*: Erstes Heft. Jena: Eugen Diedrichs, 1926.
—. *Gymnastik und Tanz*. Oldenburg: Gerhardt Stalling Verlag, 1926.
—. *Des Kindes Gymnastik und Tanz*. Oldenburg: Gerhardt Stalling Verlag, 1926.
—. "Das Tänzerische Kunstwerk," *Die Tat*, November, 1927.
—. *Schrifttanz: Methodik, Orthographie, Erläuterungen*. Vienna: Universal Edition, 1928.
—. "Grundprinzipien der Bewegungsschrift," *Schrifttanz*, Heft I, 1928.
—. "Die Entwicklung der Bewegungsschrift Laban," *Schrifttanz*, Heft II, 1928.
—. "Tanzkomposition und Schrifttanz," *Schrifttanz*, Heft II, 1928.
—. "Vom Tanzinhalt: Studien uber die Pole des Tanzkunstwerkes," *Der Tanz*, Heft 1, 1928.
—. "Choreographie und Theater," *Der Scheinwerfer*, Heft 11/12, 1928.
—. "Probleme des Tanzes," *Schrifttanz*, Heft I, 1929.
—. "Uber die Tänzerische Berufe," *Der Tanz*, Heft 14, 1929.
—. "Das Choreographische Institute Laban," in *Monographien der Ausbildungs-schulen für Tanz und Tänzerische Körperbildung*. Band I. Berlin: Leo Alterthum Verlag, 1929.
—. "Vom Sinn der Bewegungschore," *Schrifttanz*, Heft II, 1930.
—. *Ein Leben für den Tanz*. Dresden: Carl Riessner Verlag, 1935. Translated and annotated by Lisa Ullmann and published as *A Life for Dance* by London: Macdonald and Evans, 1975.
Laban, Rudolf. *Choreutics*. Annotated and edited by Lisa Ullmann. London: Macdonald and Evans, 1966.
Laban, Rudolf and Federick, Charles Lawrence. *Effort*. London: Macdonald and Evans, 1947.
Laban, Rudolf. *Modern Educational Dance*. London: Macdonald and Evans, 1948.
—. *The Mastery of Movement on the Stage*. London: Macdonald and Evans, 1950.
—. *The Mastery of Movement*. Second edition revised by Lisa Ullmann. London: Macdonald and Evans, 1960.
—. *The Mastery of Movement*. Fourth edition revised and enlarged by Lisa Ullmann. London: Macdonald and Evans, 1980.
—. "The Work of the Art of Movement Studio," *Journal of Physical Education*, Vol. 46, No. 137, 1954.
—. "A Letter to Guild Members," *The Art of Movement Guild Magazine*, No. 15, 1954.
—. "Foreword by Rudolf Laban," in *Labanotation* by Ann Hutchinson. New York: New Directions Publishers, 1954.

—. *Principles of Dance and Movement Notation*. London: Macdonald and Evans, 1956.

—. "Vorwort," *Abriss der Kinetographie Laban* by Albrecht Knust. Essen: Das Tanzarchiv Verlag, 1956.

—. "Dance in General" in *Rudolf Laban speaks about Movement and Dance*. Selected and edited by Lise Ullmann. Addlestone, Surrey: Laban Art of Movement Centre, 1971.

—. *A Vision of Dynamic Space*. Complied by Lisa Ullmann. London: Falmer Press in association with Laban Archives, 1984.

—. Unpublished manuscript from 1957, Laban Archives.

—. "Film über die Harmonische Bewegung des Menschlichen Körpers." Unpublished manuscript, Laban Archives.

—."Raumspielpuzzle." Unpublished manuscript, Laban Archives.

Lamb, Waren. *Posture and Gesture: An Introduction to the Study of Physical Behavior*. London: Duckworth & Co., 1965.

Lämmel, Rudolf. *Der Moderne Tanz*. Berlin-Schöneberg: P.J. Oestergard Verlag, [1928].

Lange, Roderyk. "Albrecht Knust — An Appreciation," *Dance Studies*, Vol. 1, 1976.

Leicht, Urs, ed. *Jooss: Dokumentation von Anna und Herman Markard*. Köln: Ballet-Bühnen-Verlag Rof Garske, 1985.

Lewitan, Joseph. "Laban der Tanz-Tribun," *Der Tanz*, Heft, 14, 1929.

Lomax, Alan, Bartenieff Irmgard, Paulay Forrestine. "Dance Style and Lange, Roderyk. "Albrecht Knust — An Appreciation," *Dance Studies*, Vol. 1, 1976.

Lewitan, Joseph. "Laban der Tanz-Tribun." *Der Tanz*, Heft, 14, 1929.

Lomax Alan, Bartenieff Irmgard, Paulay Forrestine. "Dance Style and Culture," *Folk Song Style and Culture*. Washington: American Association for the Advancement of Science, 1968.

Maletic, Vera. "On the Aisthetic and Aesthetic Dimensions of the Dance: A Methodology for Researching Dance Style," Ph.D. diss., The Ohio State University, 1980.

Mauldon, Elizabeth. "Oskar Schlemmer — Rudolf Laban: Similarities and Differences." *The Laban Art of Movement Guild Magazine*, No. 54, 1975.

Merleau-Ponty, Maurice. *Phenomenology of Perception*. Translated from French by Colin Smith. London: Routledge & Kegan Paul, 1962.

Mikunas, Algis. "The Primacy of Movement." *Main Currents in Modern Thought*, Vol. 31, No. 1, Sept.-Oct. 1974.

Milburn, Patrick. "Movement and the Idea of Organism," *Main Currents in Modern Thought*, Vol. 31, No. 1, Sept.-Oct. 1974.

North, Marion. *A Simple Guide to Movement Teaching*. London: Marion North, 1959.

—. *Composing Movement Sequences*. London: Marion North, 1961.

—. *Personality Assessment Through Movement*. London: Macdonald & Evans, 1972.

—. "The Language of Bodily Gesture," *Main Currents in Modern Thought*. Vol. 31, No. 1, Sept.-Oct. 1974.

Noverre, Jean Georges. *Lettres sur la Danse*. Paris: Éditions Lieutier, 1952 (first published in 1760).

Ohio State University. "A Summary of the 1976 Labanalysis Workshop: June 21-July 2, 1976," Columbus, OH: Dance Notation Bureau Extension. The Ohio State University.

Otte-Betz, Irma. "The Work of Rudolf Laban," Part I-III. *Dance Observer*, Dec., 1938, Jan., 1939, March, 1939.

Patterson, Michael. *The Revolution in German Theatre 1900-1933*. Boston: Routledge & Kegan Paul, 1981.

Preston, Valerie. *A Handbook for Modern Educational Dance*. London: Macdonald & Evans, 1963.

Preston-Dunlop, Valerie. *A Handbook for Dance in Education*. London: Macdonald & Evans, 1980.

—. "Choreutics: The Study of Logical Spatial Forms in Dance," *Dancing and Dance Theories*, 1979.

—. "The Nature of the Embodiment of Choreutic Units in Contemporary Choreography," Ph.D. Thesis, University of London, Goldsmith's College, 1981.

—. "Going for a Walk with a Line," *Movement and Dance: Magazine of the Laban Guild*. No. 69, 1982.

Prevots, Naima. "Zürich Dada and Dance: Formative Ferment," *Dance Research Journal*, 17/1, Spring/Summer 1985.

Ramsden, Pamela. *Top Team Planning: A Study of the Power of Individual Motivation in Management*. London: Cassell/Associated Business Programs Ltd., 1973.

Redfern, H.B. *Concepts in Modern Educational Dance*. London: Kimpton, 1973.

Richter, Hans. *Dada: Art and Anti-Art*. London: Thames and Hudson, 1965.

Russell, Joan. *Creative Dance in the Secondary School*. London: Macdonald & Evans, 1969.

Salter, Alan. "An Art of Movement," *Laban Centenary Symposium Report*, 1979.

Salter, Alan. "Movement and Mind," *Movement and Dance: Magazine of the Laban Guild*. No. 73, 1984.

Saltzman, Eric. *Twentieth Century Music: An Introduction*. New Jersey: Prentice-Hall, 1967.

Schikowski, John. *Geschichte des Tanzes*. Berlin: Büchergilde Gutenberg, 1926.

Schlee, Alfred. "Nicht Stehen Bleiben" *Singhor und Tanz* (December, 1929).

—. "Wo Steht Laban?" *Der Tanz*, Heft 14, 1929.

Schlemmer, Oskar. *The Letters and Diaries of Oskar Schlemmer*. Tut Schlemmer ed. transl. by Winston Krisham. Middletown, Conn: Wesleyan University Press, 1972.

Schuftan, Werner. *Handbuch des Tanzes*. Mannheim: Verlag Deutscher Chorsänger Verband und Tanzerbund E.V., 1928.
—. "Laban's Bewegungschrift," *Singhor und Tanz*, December 1929.
—. *Manuel De Danse*. Paris: Éditions Edgar Malfère, 1938.
Shawn, Ted. *Every Little Movement: A Book About François Delsarte*. Pittsfield, Mass: Eagle Printing Co., 1954.
Sheets-Johnstone, Maxine. "On the Nature of Theories of Dance," *Dance Research Collage*. ed. Rowe, Patricia A. and Stodelle, Ernestine. New York: Committee on Research in Dance, 1979.
Siegel, Marcia. "Waiting for the Past to Begin," *Arts in Society*, Vol. 13, No. 2, Summer-Fall 1976.
Snell, Gertrud. "Tanzwischenschaft," *Schönheit*, Heft II, 1926.
—. "Grundlagen einer Allgemeinen Tanzlehre," *Schrifttanz*, Heft I, 1929.
—. "Grundlagen einer Allgemeinen Tanzlehre: II. Choreologie," *Schrifttanz*, Heft II, 1929.
—. Grundlagen einer Allgemeiner Tanzlehre: III. Eukinetik." *Schrifttanz*, Heft II, 1930.
Snell-Friedburg, Gertrud. "The Beginnings of Kinetography Laban," *The Laban Art of Movement Guild Magazine*, No. 63, 1979.
Straus, Erwin W. *Phenomenological Psychology*. New York: Basic Books, 1966.
Terpis, Max. *Tanz und Tänzer*. Zürich: Atlantis Verlag, 1946.
Thornton, Sam. *A Movement Perspective of Rudolf Laban*. London: Macdonald and Evans, 1971.
Tompkins, Calvin. *The Bride and The Bachelors: Five Masters of the Avant Garde*. Harmondsworth, Middlesex: Penguin Books, 1977.
Ullmann, Lisa. *Some Preparatory Stages for the Study of Space Harmony in the Art of Movement*. a 1971 reprint of six articles published in *The Laban Art of Movement Guild Magazine*, 1952-1955.
—. "What Notated Movement can tell," *Dance Studies*, Roderyk Lange ed., Vol. 1., 1976.
Wagner-Regeny, Rudolf. "Neue Grundzüge der Musikalischen Theorie als Ergebnis der Schrifttanzforschung," *Schrifttanz*, Heft I, 1928.
Warner, Mary Jane and Frederick E., editors. *Labanotation Scores: An International Bibliography*. an ICKL publication, 1984.
Winearls, Jane. *Modern Dance: The Jooss-Leeder Method*. London: A & C. Black, 1958.
Wigman, Mary. "Rudolf von Labans Lehre vom Tanz," *Die Neue Schaubühne*, 5./6. Heft, September 1921, 3 Jahr.
—. "Rudolf von Laban zum Geburtstag," *Schrifttanz*, Heft IV, 1929.
—. "Rudolf von Laban." *Singhor und Tanz*, December 1929.
—. *The Mary Wigman Book*. Edited and translated by Walter Sorell. Middletown, Conn: Wesleyan University Press, 1975.
Wulff, Käthe. "Aus Alten Briefen," *Schrifttanz*, Heft IV, 1929.
Youngerman, Suzanne. "The Translation of a Culture into Choreography:

A Study of Doris Humphrey's *The Shakers* based on Labananalysis," in Woodruff, Diane ed., Essays in Dance Research, *Dance Research Annual IX*, Committee on Research in Dance, 1978.

Index of Names and Sources

Algo, Julian, 22, 43 n34.
America/U.S.A., 22, 36, 37, 115.
Angiolini, 154.
Appia, Adolf, 32.
Arbeau, Thoinot, *also* Tabourot, Jehan, *Orchesography*, 155.
Arp, Hans, 40 n17.
Art of Movement Studio, 25, 26, 65, 81 n48, 83 n91; 181. Addlestone (1954), 25, 38, 82 n84; Certificate, 25; Diploma, 25; Manchester (1946), 25, 38, 82 n84.
Ascona, Lago Maggiore, Switzerland, 6, 14, 19, 27, 37.
Aubel, H. and M., *Der Künstlerische Tanz Unserer Zeit*, 29.
Auerbach, Lotte, 23; "My Memories of Mr. Laban," 47 n111.
Austria, 9, 13.
Austro-Hungarian Empire, 4.

Balkans, 4.
Ball, Hugo, 7, 40 n17.
Bartenieff, Irmgard, Dombois, vi, 42 n32, 56 n10, 82 n84; 181, 216; *Body Movement: Coping with the Environment* (with Dori Lewis), 215; "Choreometrics," *see also* Lomax and Paulay, 215, 217-218; "The Root of Laban Theory: Aesthetics and Beyond," vi, 239.
Bauhaus, 21, 33, 34, 36.
Bayreuth, 19.
Beauchamps, 114, 115, 122, 155, 163, 166.
Bereska, Dussia, 6, 9, 18, 22, 37, 40-41 n18; 98, 99, 122, 181,

219, 222 n9.
Berlin, 17, 33, 37.
Berlin Dance Notation Bureau, The, 42 n32.
Berlin State Opera, 21.
Berlin University, 17.
Bewegungschöre Laban, 15, 44 n65.
Bibliothèque de L'Opéra, 5.
Bie, Oskar, *Der Tanz*, 27, 47 n118, 229/1.
Blaine, Vera; 146 n4.
Blasis, Carlo, 155; *Traité Elémentaire Théorique et Pratique de l'Art de la Danse*, 154.
Blaue Reiter, Der, 34.
Blum, Odette, 216.
Bode, Rudolf, 36, 165, 166.
Bodmer, Sylvia, vi, 9, 42 n34; 69, 181; "Harmonics in Space," vi, 239; *Studies Based on Crystalloid Dance Forms*, 56 n10.
Böhme, Fritz, "Laban's Tänzerischer Nachwuchs," 22, 41-42 n32, 46 n102; 229/2, 3. "Vorstellung und Erlebniss im Tanz", 31, 48 n137.
Bosnia, 4.
Brandenburg, Hans, 3, 8, 31, 160, 168 n37; "Erinnerungen an Laban's Anfänge," 119, 129 n32; 230/5; "Laban als Stilreformer," 12, 31, 44 n50; 48 n135; 230/6; *Moderne Tanz, Der*, 27, 33, 39 n6; 40 n15; 47 n116; 48 n140; 119, 130 n34; 229-230/4; *Sieg des Opfers, Der*, 8.
Bratislava, 4.
Braur, Fritz, 32.

Brecht, B., 32.
Brecht-Weill Theatre, 32.
Brücke, Die, 34.
Buber, Martin, 40 n17.
Budapest, 4.
Burg Lauenstein, 19.
Buytendijk, F.J.J., 189, 192, 193, 194, 195, 196, 198; *Allgemeine Theorie der Menschlichen Haltung und Bewegung*, 190.

Cage, John, 141-142; *Silence*, 142, 146 n18.
Cannstadt, 19.
Cassierer, Paul, 40 n17.
Center for Integrative Education, 189.
Central Europe, v, 3, 4-5, 32.
Chicago World's Fair (1933-1934), 5.
Choreographisches Institute Laban, 16, 57; Berlin (1927), 18, 37, 122; merger with Dance Department of Folkwangschule Essen (1929), 18, 19, 38; prospectuses, 88, 106 n23; 109. Würzburg (1926), 17, 37, 97.
Cohen, Fritz, 19, 183
Cohen, Selma, Jeanne, "Dance as an Art of Imitation," 184, 185 n37.
Confucius, 155.
Congress of Aesthetics in Paris (1937), 24, 38.
Coton, A.V.; *The New Ballet*, 158.
Craig, Gordon, 32.
Cunningham, Merce, 141, 163; *Changes: Notes on Choreography*, 142-143, 146 n19.
Curl, Gordon, vi, 158; "Philosophical Foundations," 167 n29.
Czechoslovakia, 4.

Da Vinci, Leonardo; Golden Section, 158.

Dadaism, 7-8, 33-36, 40 n18; 142; Cabaret Voltaire events, 7; *Kaufleute, Die*, 40 n18; *Noir Kakadu*, 40 n18.
Dalcroze, Émile-Jacques, 6, 36, 160, 178, 230 n4; 234 n24.
Dance Notation Bureau in New York, 42 n32; 115, 189, 215.
Dance Notation Record, 3, 131 n43.
Dance Observer, 30.
Dance Research Collage, 152 n1.
Dance Studies, 128 n13.
Dartington Hall, 19, 24, 38, 57, 98, 181, 226 n29.
Davis, Martha, vi; *Body Movement and Nonverbal Communication: An Annotated Bibliography 1971-1981* (with Skupien, Janet), 216; "Movement as Patterns of Process," vi, 240; *Towards Understanding the Intrinsic in Body Movement*, 216; *Understanding Body Movement: An Annotated Bibliography*, 216.
Dell, Cecily; *A Primer for Movement Description: Using Effort-Shape and Supplementary Concepts*, 216, 217-218.
Delsarte, François, 5, 73, 119, 154, 155, 166.
Derp, Clotide von, 229 n4.
Desaix, 155.
Descartes, René, 194; *Meditations of First Philosophy*, 162.
Dessau, 33, 34.
Deutsche Gesellschaft für Schrifttanz, 16, 122, 129 n14.
Deutscher Tänzerbund, 21.
Diaghileff, Serge; Ballet Russe, 36.
Dietrich-Eckhard Theatre, 23, 24.
Dresden, 34.
Duchamp, Marcel, 141-142, 146 n16; "Musical Erratum," 142; *Three Standard Stoppages*, 146 n16.

Duncan, Elizabeth, 230 n4; School in Grunewald, 36.
Duncan, Isadora, 22, 36, 154, 165, 166.

École des Beaux Arts, 5.
Egk, Werner, 24.
Einstein, Albert, 166.
Eshkol-Wachmann Movement Notation, 216.
Esmé Church Theatre School and Children's Theatre (Bradford), 26, 38.
Essen, 17, 18, 19, 37.
Expressionism, 22, 32, 33, 34, 35, 36, 40 n18, 216.

Feist, Herta, 9, 31, 42 n32.
Feuillet, Raoul, Auger, 5, 63, 75, 115, 122, 155, 161, 162, 163, 166, 225 n26; *Chorègraphie ou L'Art de Décrire la Danse*, 5, 63, 114, 155, 161.
Fokine, Michel, 22, 36, 129 n14.
Folkwangschule in Essen (Dance Department), 18, 24, 98.
Foster, John, *The Influences of Rudolf Laban*, vi, 240.
Frank, Edgar, 9, 32, 42 n32.
Freud, Sigmund, 161.
Futurists, 33, 142.

Gelb-Goldstein study, 194.
Gellerman, Jill, 216, 240.
Gerbes, Angelika, 216.
German Dance Congress, First (Magdeburg, June, 1927), 10, 13, 14, 15, 21, 29, 34, 37, 121.
German Dance Congress, Second (Essen, June, 1928), 12, 16, 37, 113, 128 n5.
Germany, 8-24.
Gleisner, Martin, 9, 15, 28, 43 n34; 181; "Laban als Wegbahner...," 14, 44 n58; 230/9; "Schrifttanz

und Laientanz," 122, 131 n50; 230/18; *Tanz für Alle*, 28, 47 n122; 96, 97, 106 n16; 230/7.
Gleschendorf, 19.
Goebbels, Dr., 23, 24.
Graff, Kurt, 19.
Graham, Martha, 165, 166.
Gropius, Walter, 34.
Günther, Dorothee, 24.

Hamburg Dance Notation Bureau, 42 n32.
Hamburg's Movement Choirs Rudolf von Laban, 17.
Herzegovina, 4.
Hitler, Adolf, 23, 29.
Hodgson, John, vi, 240.
Holbrook, Jennifer K., 33; "Laban, Wagner and the Gesamtkunstwerk," 48 n143.
Hollywood, 22.
Humphrey, Doris, 165, 166.
Hungary, 4.
Husserl, Edmund, 162, 189.
Hutchinson, Ann; *Labanotation*, 115, 123, 129 n25; 131 n43.

I Ching, 142.
Ibsen, Henrik, 32.
Institute for Nonverbal Communication Research, 216.
International Dance Competition in Paris (1932), 21, 34, 38.
International Dance Festival (Berlin, 1937), 23.
Italy, 9.
Ivers, Suzanne, 18, 21.

Jessner, Leopold, 33.
Joos, Kurt, 9, 12, 18, 19, 22, 31, 33, 34, 35, 38, 41-42 n32; 57, 64, 98, 99, 122, 181; "Rudolf von Laban und das Ballett," 12, 22, 31, 44 n51; 46 n101; 48 n135; 231/11; *The Green Table*, 21, 34,

38; *Tragödie*, 42 n34.
Joos: Dokumentation von Anna und Hermann Markard, 41 n32; 48 n148.
Joos-Leeder School of Dance, 19, 24, 38, 57, 98.
Joyce, James, 40 n17.
Jung, Carl Gustav, 36, 157, 179.

Kagan, Elizabeth, 216, 241.
Kaiser, Gerg, 32, 33; *Gas I and II*, 33.
Kammertanzbühne Laban (Chamber-Dance-Theatre-Laban), 9, 17, 37.
Kandinsky, Vassily, 34.
Kant, Immanuel, 194.
Keith, Jens, 9, 22, 42 n32.
Kestenberg, Judith, 82 n84; 216, 217-218; "The Role of Movement Patterns in Development" (*Psychoanalytic Quarterly* 34, 1965), 216.
Kirchner, Ernst, 34.
Kleist, Heinrich von, 165.
Klingenbeck, Fritz, 12, 121, 130 n43; 231/12-15; 232/16-18; "Kleiner Rückblick," 12, 44 n49; 130 n43; 231/13; "Laban Curriculum Vitae," 130-131 n43; 232/18; "Schreiben und Lesen," 129 n14; 231/14.
Knust, Albrecht, v, 9, 17, 23, 31, 42 n32, 123, 126, 181, 226/28, 232/19, 233/20-23; *Dictionary of Kinetography Laban (Labanotation)*, 129 n25; "Laban als Erzieher," 15, 20, 44 n63, 46 n92; "The Roots of Laban Notation," 121, 122, 130 n43, 131 n47.
Koegler, Horst, 24; *In the Shadow of the Swastika: Dance in Germany, 1927-1936*, 24, 39 n4.
Kreutzberg, Harold, 24.
Kuhn, Thomas, 151.

Kurath, Gertrude, 185 n32.

Laban, Azra von, 42 n32.
Laban, Rudolf von:
— articles: "Choreographie und Theater," 139, 141, 146 n3,12; 222/14; "Choreographische Institute Laban, Das," 17-19, 45 n78&79; 223 n17; "Comment by R. Laban, 1957," v, 32, 48 n139; 182, 184n 25; "Dance in General," 183, 185 n33-35; "Entwicklung der Bewegungsschrift Laban, Die," 113-114, 128 n5; 116, 129 n21&22; 222/11; "Film ueber die Harmonische Bewegung des Menschlichen Körpers," 143-146; 146 n22; "Foreword by Rudolf Laban," 26, 114, 128 n9; "Grundprinzipien der Bewegungsschrift," 115, 129 n17-19,23,24,26; 222/10; "Kultische Bildung im Feste," 14, 44 n59; 219 n2; "Letter to Guild Members, A," 23, 25, 47 n109; "Probleme des Tanzes", 13, 44, n57; 139, 146 n1; 223/ 15; "Raumspielpuzzle" ("Spacegamepuzzle"), 35, 48 n141-3; 146 n14; 227/33; "Symbole des Tanzes und Tanz als Symbol," 113, 128 n1; 139, 146 n7; 219-220/3; "Tanz als Eigenkunst, Der," 55, 56, n16; 63, 153, 154-5, 167 n3, 12; 220/4; "Tänzerische Kunstwerk, Das," 10-11,37, 44 n47; 221/8; "Tanzkomposition und Schrifttanz," 139, 140, 146 n3,11; 222/12; "The Dancer's Script," 122, 131 n55; "Uber die Tänzerischen Berufe," 182, 184 n28; 223 n16; "Vom Tanzinhalt: Studien über die Pole des Tanzkunstwerkes," 139, 140, 146 n9; 222/13; "Work of the

Art of Movement Studio, The,"
25, 47 n113; 225/24.
– books: *Choreutics*, 24, 51, 53,
54, 57, 58, 59, 65, 73, 77, 78,
79 n2, 7; 80 n13, 21, 34, 38, 39,
42; 81 n51,55; 82 n72, 83, 92,
93; 84, 86, 88, 89, 90, 91, 92,
97, 98, 105, 107 n61, 63; 127,
128 n10; 129 n28; 132 n74; 147
n21; 156, 158, 159, 167 n20, 21,
36; 168 n54; 176, 181, 184 n7,
15, 26; 200 n54, 61, 63; 201
n66, 67, 70, 72, 73; 224/20;
237/43; *Choreographie*, 5, 9, 12,
16, 24, 51, 54, 56 n14, 57, 59,
65, 68, 69, 70, 78, 84, 85, 86,
87, 88, 89, 90, 91, 92, 93, 105,
106 n3, 7, 14; 107 n51, 52, 62,
63; 109, 115, 119, 120, 122,
129 n16; 130 n38-40; 133-137,
139, 146 n2; 162, 163, 165, 168
n47, 51, 56; 173, 176, 184 n1,
11; 220/5; 225/26; *Effort* (with
Lawrence), 51-52, 97, 100, 107
n31, 40, 42, 47; 110-112;
Gymnastic und Tanz, 9, 21, 51,
65, 84, 85, 86, 87, 90, 92, 106
n4, 6, 8; 107 n53; 109, 113, 128
n4; 126, 132 n75; 141, 146 n13;
167 n9, 17, 25; 168 n40, 46, 49;
220-221/6: *Kindes Gymnastik
und Tanz, Des*, 9, 51, 87, 113,
128 n3; 221/7; *Language of
Movement: A Guide Book to
Choreutics*, 51, 176; *Ein Leben
für den Tanz*, 3, 27, 38, 233/19;
(*see also A Life for Dance*); *A
Life for Dance*, 3, 4, 5, 9, 10,
21, 22, 39 n1, 8, 9, 13; 41 n27,
28, 29; 43 n34-40, 42, 43; 44
n45, 46, 60, 61, 66, 67; 45 n70;
46 n95, 96, 98; 48 n133, 141,
142, 147; *Mastery of Movement,
The*, 66, 81 n48; 86, 92, 95, 100,
106 n13, 107 n39, 41, 43, 46,

48, 49, 58, 59; 110-112, 124,
125, 127, 128, 132 n63, 68, 69,
71, 78, 80; 138, 141, 173, 174,
179, 184 n8, 14; 192, 200 n29,
30; *Mastery of Movement on the
Stage, The*, 26, 52, 100, 110-112,
124, 132 n60, 67; 138, 141,
161, 173, 179, 224/23; *Modern
Educational Dance*, 26, 52, 58,
79 n11; 82 n79; 85, 86, 89, 92,
100, 110, 111, 112, 138, 140,
146 n8; 176, 179, 203, 224/22;
*Principles of Dance and Move-
ment Notation*, 38, 52, 115, 122,
123, 129 n20, 23, 29; 130 n42;
131 n52; 132 n70; 139, 146 n6;
154, 167 n8; 183, 185 n30; 225/
27; *A Vision of Dynamic Space*,
182, 184 n24; 226/30; *Welt des
Tänzers, Die*, 7, 9, 27, 37, 51, 59,
80 n12, 24; 84, 85, 87, 88, 90,
92, 93, 109, 131 n55; 132 n72;
160 n1, 5; 167 n1, 11, 19, 27, 31,
35; 168 n39, 42, 48, 55; 184 n5,
23; 199 n11, 16; 200 n23, 26;
219/1.
– choreographic works: *Agamemnon's Tod*, 15, 33; Agamemnon,
10; *Alltag und Fest*, 15; *Casanova*,
9; Casanova, 10; *Dämmernde
Rhythmen*, 15; *Don Juan* (Gluck),
10; *Epische Tanzfolge*, 9; *Erde,
Die*, 8; *Faust Part II*, 9, 33;
*Festzug des Handwerkes und der
Gewerbe* (Pageant for the Crafts
and Trades), 14, 15, 35, 37;
Gaukelei, 9, 31, 42 n34;
Geblendeten, Die, 9; *Grünen,
Die*, 8; *Kleine Tänze mit
Vorübungen*, 222/9; *Lichtwende*,
15; *Nacht, Die*, 9, 33; *Narrenspiegel*, 9, 34; *Prometheus*, 9;
Ritterballet, 9; *Schwingende
Tempel, Der*, 9; *Spielman, Der*,
8, 37; *Vom Tauwind und der*

Neuen Freude, 23; *Titan, The*, 15, 17, 122, 130 n43.
Laban Archives, vii, 25, 26.
Laban Art of Movement Centre, The, U.K., vii, 25, 38, 58, 181; General Information, 58, 79 n9; 92; Summer Schools, 26.
Laban Art of Movement Guild, The, 23, 26, 158.
Laban Centre for Movement and Dance at the University of London Goldsmith's College (U.K.), vii, 26.
Laban Diploma; Courses, 18; Examinations, 19.
Laban Institute of Movement Studies, New York (LIMS), 42 n32; 215, 216.
Laban School in Hamburg, 126.
Lamb, Warren, 25, 78, 82 n84; 165, 168 n58; 180, 181, 203-213, 216; "Action Profile," 165, 168 n58; 180, 181, 203; *Posture and Gesture*, 82 n84; 168 n58.
Lämmel, Rudolf, 3; *Der Moderne Tanz*, 4, 7, 39 n2, 6; 41 n25; 233/25.
Langer, Hans Claus, 23.
Lawrence, D.H., 40 n17.
Lawrence, Frederic Charles, 25, 38, 52, 99.
Lederer, Maja, 6, 7, 41 n18.
Leeder, Sigurd, 19, 24, 99.
Leistikow, Gertrud, 229 n4.
Lenares, Maja, 219.
Lewitan, Joseph, 4; "Laban der Tanz-Tribun," 29, 47 n125; 234/25.
Ling Physical Education Association, 24.
Lipps, Theodor, "Theory of Empathy," 159.
Loeser, Ruth, 9, 18, 22, 42 n34.
Loheland, 27, 36, 165.
Lomax, Alan, 215; *Folk Song Style*

and Culture, 215.
London, 24.
Lucian, 153.

Maheza, Sent, 229 n4.
Main Currents in Modern Thought (Fall, 1974), vi.
Maletic, Ana, 39 n4; 49 n18; 81 n61; 106 n29, 30; 146 n4.
Manchester Dance Circle, 181.
Mandelieu, 19.
Mannheim, 14, 15.
Mannheim National Theatre, 9, 14, 15.
Marck, Franz, 34.
Martin, John, "metakinesis," 159.
"Mary Wigman: When the Fire Dances Between Two Poles" (A. Fuller-Snyder and A. Macdonald producers), 40 n46.
Mauldon, Elizabeth, "Oskar Schlemmer − Rudolf Laban: Similarities and Differences," 34, 48 n146.
Mensendieck, Bess, 36, 165.
Merleau-Ponty, Maurice, 162, 189-199; *Phenomenology of Perception*, 190, 194.
Milburn, Patrick, 189; "Movement and the Idea of Organism," 199 n4.
Mlakar, Pia and Pino, *The Devil in the Village*, 42 n32.
Moekle, Jan, 183.
Moll, Edward, Dr., 128 n14.
Monte Verità in Ascona, Switzerland, 6, 7, 40 n17; "Schule für Kunst" ("School for the Arts"), 7, 37, 40 n17.
Morel (Monsieur), 5.
Movement and Dance: Magazine of the Laban Guild, vi, 26, 40 n16.
Müller, Hedwig, "Joos and Expressionism," 35, 48 n148.
Müller, Lotte, 42 n34.

Munich, 5-6, 14, 34, 37.

Nazism, 19, 23, 36, 181; National Socialism, 35; Nazi Germany, 3.
Neue Schaubühne, Die, 39 n7.
Niedecken-Gebhard, Hans, 21, 24.
Nietzsche, Friedrich, 23, 155; *Thus Spake Zarathustra*, 23, 155-156.
Nolde, Emil, 6, 34, 35.
North, Marion, vi, 25, 181, 203, 225/25; 204-213; *Composing Movement Sequences*, 203; *Personality Assessment through Movement*, 203, 204-213; "The Language of Bodily Gesture," vi, 244.
Noverre, Jean George, 155, 163; Ballet d'Action, 154; *Lettres sur les Arts Immitateurs en General et sur la Danse en Particulier*, 154.
Oedekoven, Henry, 40 n17.
Ohio State University, The (U.S.A.); College of the Arts, vii; Department of Dance; 183, 215.
Olympic Games (1936), 23.
Orff, Carl, 24.
Otte-Betz, Irma, 215; "The Work of Rudolf Laban," 30, 47 n127; 181, 184 n22.

Palucca, G., 24.
Paris, 5-6, 33, 37, 38.
Partsch-Bergsohn, Isa, 80 n31.
Paulay, Forrestine, 215, 217-218; *see also* Bartenieff & Lomax.
Pavlova, Anna, 21, 129 n14.
Perrottet, Suzanne, 6, 7, 8, 36, 37, 40 n18; 181.
Pforsich, Janis, 216.
Piscator, Erwin, 32, 34.
Plato, 176; Platonic solids, 67; *Timeaeus*, 155, 158.
Plauen, 17.
Poszony, 4, 37.

Preston, Valerie, 25, 181, 225/24; *A Handbook for Modern Educational Dance*, 203, 204-213; *see also* Preston-Dunlop.
Preston-Dunlop, Valerie, 56 n10; 182, 203, 204-213; "Choreutics; The Study of Logical Spatial Forms in Dance," 166, 169 n61; "Going for a Walk with a Line," 166, 169 n62; 175; *Handbook for Dance in Education*, 203, 204-213.
Prevots, Naima; "Zürich Dada and Dance," 35, 48 n151.
Priest, Helen, 30, 42 n32.
Prussian Academy of Arts in Berlin, 36
Prussian Theatres, 21, 36.
Pythagoras, 158.

Ramsden, Pamela, 181; *Top Team Planning*, 165, 168 n59.
Redfern, Betty, *Concepts in Modern Educational Dance*, vi, 244.
Reichsbund fur Gemeinschaftstanz, 23.
Reinhardt, Max, 32, 34, 183; *Grosses Schauspielhaus*, 34.
Richter, Hans, F.; *Dada: Art and Anti-Art*, 35, 39 n4.
Robst, Herman, 9, 18, 19, 43 n34.
Russell, Joan, 181; *Creative Dance in the Secondary School*, 203, 204-213.

Sacharof, Alexander, 229 n4.
Saint Gallen, library of, 114.
Saint Leon; *La Sténochoreographie ou l'Art d'Écrire Proprement la Danse*, 154.
Salter, Alan, "Movement and Mind," vi, "An Art of Movement," 36, 48 n157, 244.
Scheinwerfer, Tanz Sonderheft, *Der*, Essen, 39 n4.

Schlemmer, Oskar, 21, 34; *Gesture Dance*, 34; *Letters and Diaries of Oskar Schlemmer*, 46 n94; *Space Dance*, 34.

Schikowski, John, 3; *Geschichte des Tanzes*, 6, 27, 31, 40 n15; 47 n119, 120; 48 n136; 234/76.

Schlee, Alfred, 4, 35, 234 n27&28; "Nicht Stehen Bleiben," 12, 44 n48;234/27;"Wo Steht Laban?," 23-29, 47 n123; 234/28.

Schoenberg, Arnold, 35, 36.

Schönheit, Die, 39 n4.

Schrifttanz Quarterly Magazine, 1928-1931, 3, 4, 12, 17, 37, 39 n3, 4; 115, 122.

Schrifttanz: Methodik, Orthographie, Erläuterungen (*Script-Dancing: Methodics, Orthography, Explanations*), 16, 115, 128 n11;132 n56;133-137, 138.

Schuftan, Werner, 3, 28, 234 n29; 235 n30&31; *Handbuch des Tanzes*, 28.

Shawn, Ted, *Every Little Movement*, 73, 82 n73.

Siegel, Marcia, 183, 184, "Waiting for the Past to Begin," 184.

Siimola, Aino, 9, 43 n34.

Singhor und Tanz, 3, 39 n4.

Skoronel, Vera, "Laban," 235/32.

Snell, Gertrud, 9, 16, 18, 19, 43 n34; 56, 57, 70, 99, 118, 121, 181; 224/20; "Grundlagen einer Allgemeinen Tanzlehre," 57, 79 n1; 235/34; "Grundlagen einer Allgemeiner Tanzlehre: II Choreologie," 82 n70; 98, 106 n25; 235/35;"Tanzwisenschaft," 58, 79 n6; 98, 106 n26; 235/33; "The Beginnings of Kinetography Laban," 118,120,121, 131 n46. (Snell-Friedburg)

Sonner, Rudolf, *Musik und Tanz*, 114, 128 n13.

Sorell, Walter, ed. and transl., *The Mary Wigman Book*, 237/42.

St. Denis, Ruth, 36, 155.

Staffelberg, 24, 38.

Stanislavsky, Konstantin, 32.

Steiner, Rudolf, 36, 16, 178.

Stephenson, Geraldine, 181, 225/ 24.

Stratton, G.M., 194.

Straus, Ervin, 189-190, 192, 193, 194, 195, 197, 198; *Phenomenological Psychology*, 189, 193.

Strindberg, Arthur, 32.

Surrealists, 33, 142.

Switzerland, 5-8, 13.

Taeuber, Sophie, 8, 35.

Tanz, Der, 4, 23, 28, 29, 223 n16.

Tanzbühne Laban (Dance-Theatre Laban), 9, 17, 18, 37.

Tanzschule Joos-Zentralschule Laban, 19; prospectus, 109.

Tat, Die, 43 n44.

Taylor, Paul, 183.

Terpis, Max, v, 30, 95, 96; *Tanz und Tänzer*, 30, 47 n128, 129; 95, 96, 106 n11, 17, 18.

Thornton, Sam, *A Movement Perspective of Rudolf Laban*, vi, 245.

Toller, Ernst, 33; *Man and Masses*, 33.

Turner, 181.

Toscanini, Arturo, 21.

Ullmann, Lisa, 3, 19, 24, 25, 26, 45 n80; 69, 83 n91; 94, 96, 97, 181, 203, 204-208, 223/19; 224/20, 23; 226/30; "Letter to Kurt Joos," 97, 106 n22; "Milestones in Laban's Life," 3, 39 n3; "My Apprenticeship with Laban," 20, 21, 46 n93; 94, 106 n8, 17, 21; "Some Preparatory Stages for the Study of Space

Harmony," 56 n10; 58, 79 n8; "What Notated Movement Can Tell," 128 n13. annotated and edited *Choreutics*; compiled *A Vision of Dynamic Space*; revised *Modern Educational Dance* (third ed.), *Mastery of Movement on the Stage* (second ed.); revised and enlarged its fourth edition; selected and edited *Rudolf Laban speaks about Movement and Dance*; translated and annotated *A Life for Dance*.

Venable, Lucy, 216.
Verkauf, W., 7.
Vienna, 14, 15, 36, 38.
Vietta, Egon, 31.
Vigano, 154.

Wachtel, Irene, 216.
Wagner, Richard, 9, 21; *Gesamtkunstwerk*, 6, 40 n16, 32, 33; *Tannhäuser*, 9, 21.
Wagner-Regeny, Rudolf, 15, 36, 48 n155; 106 n29.
Wagner, Siegfried, 21.
Wedekind, Lotte, 9, 43 n34.
Weill, Kurt, 32.
Weimar, 33, 34.
Wertheimer, Max, 194.
Weybridge, Surrey, 26, 38.
Wieland, 153.
Wiener-Neustadt, Austria (military academy), 5, 37.
Wiesentahl sisters, 229 n4.
Wigman, Mary, 3, 6, 7, 8, 13, 16,

19, 20, 21, 22, 24, 27, 29, 30, 31, 33, 34, 35, 36, 37, 40 n18; 64, 77, 119, 160, 166, 181, 219, 234/24; 235/32; *Mary Wigman Book, The*, 16, 19-20, 22, 30, 40 n17; 45 n73; 46 n89-91, 106; 47 n130, 131; "Rudolf von Labans Lehre vom Tanz," 7, 8, 39 n7; 41 n20, 29, 31; 46 n104; 77 n81; 236/39; "Rudolf von Laban zum Geburtstag," 6, 22, 41 n19, 21; 119, 129 n31; 160, 168 n38; 236/41; "Swinging Landscape," 31.
Wilckens, Frederich, 9.
Winearls, Jane, *Modern Dance: The Joos-Leeder Method*, 99.
Wir Tanzen, 23, 39 n4.
World Wars: I, 7, 31, 34, 35, 36, 37; II, 3, 21, 24, 38.
Wulff, Käthe, 6, 8, 13, 22, 40 n18; 237/43; "Aus Alten Briefen," 5, 39 n12, 13; 44 n55.
Wundt, Wilhelm, 153, 157.

Yugoslavia, 4, 9.
Youngerman, Suzanne, 216, 246.

Zentralschule Laban (Central-School Laban): Berlin, 1927, Essen, 1929, 18, 57; Hamburg, 1923, 14, 37, 42n32; Würzburg, 1926, 17; Prospectuses, 88, 109.
Zirkus Busch (Hamburg), 15.
Zirkus, Schumann, 34, 222 n9.
Zorn, *Grammatik der Tanzkunst*, 154.
Zürich, 7, 35, 37, 40.

Index of Concepts

Actions, *see* Body and Effort.

Aesthetic, 18, 143, 158, 158, 161, 163, 182; aesthetic theory of Empathy, 159.

Affinities, 77-79, 82 n84; 107 n50; 168 n58; 172; correlation of space and dynamics, 54; *see also* Effort-Shape.

Analysis, 124, 125, 126, 141, 155, 166, 172-173, 176, 183, 189, 220; and synthesis of movement, 57; *see also* Classification.

Architecture, 5, 33; circus 11; theatre 5, 11.

Art(s), 5, 26; of acting 33, 161, 179; of Africa, Asia, Australia, 162; criticism, 163, 183; drawing, 20; of Europe, 162; film, 33, 143-146; movements in the arts, 32-34; of performing, 7, 26, 32; poetry, 6, 20, 30, 113, 155, 162; of Polynesia, 162; speech, 14.

Art of Movement/*Bewegungskunst*, 25, 33, 113, 154, 221.

Asymmetry, 52-54, 84, 125, 140; *see also* Symmetry.

Attitudes, *see* Effort.

Ausdruckstanz, 35, 40 n18.

Balance, 11, 53, 65, 87-174, 197-198; laws of, 87; as simple form of harmony, 84, 87; tensions, 75; *see also* Equilibrium.

Ballet, 5, 9, 12, 16, 21, 32, 59, 63, 68, 101, 163-164, 165, 166, 176; *battu, fouetté, glissé*, 97, 103, 178; notation, 68; old b., 69, 81 n50; 85, 119; origins of, 161;

positions, 12, 85, 120; theory of, 59, 63, 162; tradition, 12, 155, 177.

Body, 84, 85, 88, 95, 96, 133, 138, 173-175, 212; actions, 77, 123-125, 126, 173-174, 212; articulation and notation, 123-125, 163-164; awareness, 14; carriage, 26, 59; bilateral extension/structure, 74, 116; body-mind (unity or dichotomy), 14, 15, 36, 100, 153, 162, 165, 171, 173, 179, 199, 219; "bodysoul" 221; centre of, 58-58, 64, 65, 66, 68, 73, 74, 75, 165, 177; centre of gravity/weight, 55, 58-59, 64, 65, 73, 74, 84, 85, 87, 98, 119, 127, 164, 165, 196; classification of b. movement, 124-125; b., flow: successive-simultaneous sequencing, 116, 119, 125; functions/movement of the joints: bending-stretching/contraction-extension, twisting/rotating, 22, 64, 74, 75; b. as an instrument of expression, 94, 173, 199; lived, phenomenal body, 189-199; parts, 104; periphery, extremities, 66, 73, 75, 161; positions and counter-positions, 59, 87; proportions, 77, 87, 158; structure, 67, 73, 74, 157; support 74; symmetries (three: r.-l., f.-b., u.-d.), 60, 66, 69, 74, 116; three types of movers, *see* Harmony; upper-lower, 60, 123, 124, 125; vertical extension/structure, 64; body wave, 66.

Body culture, 11 12, 160, 165; body dance culture, 27.

Central (path), 64, 65, 68, 75, 76, 87, 98, 105, 177; guidance, 96; initiation, 165; undulating, 99.
Choir, 8, 9;*see also* Movement choir.
Choreography (as composition), 9, 10, 17, 18, 21, 31, 139-147, 182; Laban's 30, 31-32, 35; for layman, 8; military, 4; new choreography, 12, 16; as new dance, 57; notes and sketches, 8; structure, 31; study of, 11; *see also* Composition.
Choreology, 7, 10, 11, 13, 17, 18, 98, 140, 151, 172, 178; laws of, 18; sources and origins of, 156-163.
Choreosophy, 10, 13, 155-156.
Choreutics, 18, 19, 29, 45 n80; 57-58, 64-73, 75-77, 79, 87-89, 98, 109, 118, 127, 140, 156, 160, 166, 172, 175-178, 179, 199; choreutic forms, 88-89, 207; origins and applications of, 57-58; choreutic research (future), 159, 182; root of the term, 176.
Classification, 51, 52, 54, 93, 126, 124, 126, 172-177, 181, 184; *see also* Analysis.
Composition, 7, 10-14, 15, 18, 19, 57, 64, 115, 139-147, 155; analysis of, 166; C. by chance (Duchamp, Cage, Cunningham, 142, 143; chance game 35; forms of, 7; form movement choirs, 230; partner dance, 140; solo – group dance, 9, 16, 139-140; "space-game-puzzle," 141; *see also* Choreography.
Concept(s), 22, 27, 96, 119, 172; of affinities, *see* Affinities; of Effort, *see* Effort.
Crystallization, Crystalline forms, 60, 67, 68, 75, 176, 189; five polyhedra/Platonic solids, 67, 158, 176; polyhedral scaffoldings, 85, 204; structures, 157.
Cube, 60, 67, 68, 74, 75, 176.

Dance, 53, 172, 193, 198, 220; absolute d., 6, 7, 8, 28, 31, 40 n15; 141; academy, 21; aesthetics, 18; anthropology/ethnography, 183; art of, 9-14, 18, 22, 139, 141, 156, 168 n58; chamber d., 9, 14, 29; choral d., 14; comedy, 9; company, 6; concepts, 35, 96, 141; critic (ism), 11, 17, 27, 183; dance-drama, 8, 9, 10, 15, 31, 140; dance-music relationship, 159-160; play, 9, 17; dance-sound-word/*Tanz-Ton-Wort*, 6, 7, 27, 33, 37, 230; description, 171, 172; design, 11; education, pedagogy, 8, 13, 18, 19, 21, 25, 26, 28, 100, 113; experience, 156; ethnic/folk d., 4, 26, 37; film d., 143-146; "free dance," 6, 27, 31, 36, 40 n15; 100, 160, 166, 230; group d., 5, 9, 14, 16; history, 18, 27, 186, 220, 226; insights, 51; language of, 11, 12 (grammar & syntax), 115; for layman, 9, 13-14, 28, 139; modern d., 9, 12, 21, 27, 28, 171; new dance, 32, 57, 68; new dance notation, 29, 122, 163-164; operatic d., 19; organizations, 12; period d., 26; poem, 14; performance, 11, 32; pure d., 11; recreational, 12, 32; research, 172; rhythm, 160; science of, 13, 139, 183, *see also* Choreology; schools (Laban), 6, 17, 19, 30; sense, 163, 191; social d., 11, 12, 16. solo d., 14, 16; structures, 11; suite, 31; sword d., 4; theatre d., 5, 9, 11, 12, 15,

17, 18, 31, 160, 161; theory, 31, 51, 163, 170, *see also* Theory; writer, 11, 30.

Design (Winearls), 98.

Dimensional planes, 60, 82 n78; 88; "door," "table," "wheel," 74, 76, 80 n19; vertical, horizontal, sagittal, 60, 62 Fig. 3; 74: three dimensional planes, 85, 178.

Direction(s), 58-63, 74-75, 85, 90, 143, 196; counter-d., 65, 74, 176; diametral, 58, 74, 75, 82 n78; 85, 127, 177; diagonal/oblique, 54, 55, 60, 64, 68, 74, 84, 85, 87 (deflected), 118, 127, 164, 166, 175, 177, 197; dimensional, 59-60 (deflected), 64, 68, 74, 84, 85, 118, 127, 164, 166, 175, 177, 192; four-diagonal cross, 85, 175; horizontals, 55; levels 58-63; orientation, systems of, 58-63, 74-75, 85, 90, 117-118, 129 n25; 164, 176-177, 208, 217; six-diametral cross, 85; three dimensions, 118; three-dimensional cross, 58, 74, 85, 118, 175, 196; twenty-six space directions, 74, 85, 117, 203; vertical(ity), 54, 55, 127, 173, 174.

Dodecahedron, 67, 176.

Drama, 11, 26, 154, 160; *see also* Dance.

Droit/straight, 63-64, 75, 85; *see also* Form.

Dynamic(s), 51, 54, 55, 77, 91, 93-97, 109, 136; accent(s), 127, 174; actions, 78, 98; agglomeration, nucleation/Ballung, 93; Anschwung-Ausschwung, 95, 96, *see also* Swing; Anspannung-Abspannung/tension-release, relaxation, 22, 94, 95, 160; dynamic characteristics of deep. medium, high movers, 77, 92,

208; concept of, 97; d. content of form, 54, 93; contraction-release (Graham), 165; d. crystallization, 198; dynamosphere, 78, 92; d. expression in dance, 18; energy, *see* Energy; force, *see* Force; impulse, *see* Impulse; d. intensity, nuance, stress, range, 78, 79, 92, 95, 96, 121, 165; d. laws of harmony, 156; of movement in space, 11, 118, 195; d. process of movement, 171; proportionality of force, time, space, flux, 94; qualitative-quantitative aspects, phenomena, 94, 101, 127; d. qualities, 78, 121; regulators of intensity: force, space, time, flux, 64, 78, 84, 91, 93, 104; secondary tendencies, 78; spatial dynamism, 11; thrust, 84, 95, 96; d. traits, 91; tension, tensility/Spannung, 53, 93, 96, 127, 174; d. transformation, 182; weight 127, 174, 179, *see also* Effort; weightless, 84.

Effort, 26, 97, 99-112, 156, 172, 174, 178-180, 209-211; actions, eight basic, 98, 180, 211; assessment tests, 82 n84; attitudes (inner, mental): indulgence in — fighting against, 10, 100, 101, 192; attitudes toward space, weight, time, flow, 102, 179, 209; combination of two qualities, incomplete efforts, inner attitudes, 102, 210; combinations of three qualities, drives, 102-103, 210; combinations of four qualities, complete effort actions, 103, 211; concept of, 99-101, 156, 160, 174, 178, 189, 192, 199; e. cube, 107 n50; e. elements, 101, 118, 157,

160, 179, 192; grading, 211; e. graph. notation, 26, 78, 127, 128, 180, 210; movement sensations, 100; motion factors (four), 100, 179, 192; mutations/transtitions, 104, 211; phases of attention, intention, decision, precision, corresponding to thinking, sensing, intuiting, feeling, 100, 103, 157, 179; psychosomatic experience, 100; quantitative – qualitative/measurable – classifiable components of e., 100, 101, 104, 128, 156; term "effort" 99, 106 n30; e. theory 101-104, 128, 178; *see also* Effort-Shape.

Effort-Shape, 78, 180, 208; Effort/Shape, 215-217; *see also* Affinities.

Energy, 139, 173, 178, 179, 192, 193; components (Winearls), 99; muscular e., 124; *see also* Force.

Equilibrium, 52-55, 64, 65, 68, 74, 84, 88, 95, 164, 174, 197; *see also* Balance and Stability.

Eukinetics, 18, 19, 45 n15; 29, 57, 97-99, 109, 118, 140, 160, 166, 172, 178-179; as choreographic theory, 98; four primitive modes of expression, 98; eight qualities, 99; root of the term, 97; as theory of expression, 97.

Eurhythmy, 36, 160; Eurhythmicist, 161, e. methods; principles of e., 139.

Expression, expressive, 11, 12, 16, 18, 19, 26, 32, 64, 67, 79, 96, 98, 99, 100, 114, 119, 127, 139, 141, 154, 155, 157, 159, 160, 163, 171, 172, 173, 179, 189-199; Eukinetics as theory of expression, and of expressive qualities in dance, 97, 178; Effort as theory of expressive qualities

in human exertion, 97, 106 n22; facial e., 124; power(s) of e., 7; spatial e., 124.

Extension, 63-64, 74, 86, 94, 119, 176, 177, 204, 217; e. – contraction of kinesphere, 64, 197; narrow – wide, 64; *see also* Size and Metrics.

Feminine – masculine: characteristics of scales, 69-70; dance for males, 10-11.

Festival(s), 6, 11, 14, 15, 17, 23, 28, 33.

Flow, 14, 30, 53, 55, 96, 104, 105; body flow: successive – simultaneous, 125; Effort f., 101, 102-103; as flight, fluency, fluidity, flux, 54, 68, 93, 95, 96; in notation, 116, 125, 129 n29; 127-128.

Force, 54, 96, 98, 119, 163, 171, 174, 209; form building f., 67; nuances of, 95, 160; polarities/contrasts, 93-94.

Form, 11, 14, 15, 18, 54, 57, 67, 93, 143; choreutic forms, 88-89; dimensionality of f.: linear, plane-like, plastic, 64, 85; elements of form, 54; modes of f., 63-64; *see also* Shape.

Gathering – scattering, 66, 68, 80 n48, 68, 124, 138, 212.

Gedankenreigen, 7

Gesture, 14, 31, 33, 54, 95, 153, 154, 160; of admiration, adoration, 11, 198; benediction and submission, 198; of environment/ *Umweltsgebarde*, 191; expressive g., 161; power of g./*Gebärdenkraft*, 6, 161, 190-192.

Golden section, laws of: 68, 81 n55; 87, 88, 158.

Gymnastics, 13, 14, 16, 17, 22, 36,

51, 139, 141, 153, 161, 165, 220-221; expressive (Bode), 166; martial arts, 161; rhythmic, 4, 13,154,166; sport,161; systems, 36, 165.
Guidance: central — peripheral, 96; centrifugal — centripetal, 96.

Harmony, harmonics, harmonious, harmonic, 25, 26, 53, 58, 77-79, 116, 179,208,217; contrapuntal movement,66, 87; as correlation/ relationship of dynamic stress and spatial patterns, 26, 77-79, 83 n91; 91; as manifest in movement qualities of deep, medium, high movers, 77, 92, 155; directional h. 57, 117; dynamic laws of h., 156; dynamosphere and kinesphere, 208; harmonic/ logical order, 67; laws of h., 87, 161; h. laws of form 57, 157; harmonious movement (also disharmonious), 11, 19, 57, 66, 78, 87, 98; "harmony of movement," 58; perception of, 157; h. principles, 75, 177, *see also* Principles; harmonic relations in space, 65, *see also* Choreutics and Space Harmony; h. regularity, 143; simplest forms of, 53, 58, 65, 87, 160; h. structure of scales, 68-70, *see also* Scales; theory of, *see* Theory.
Holistic (views of movement), 78, 94, 100, 153, 156, 157; comprehensive 118.

Icosahedron, 34, 60, 67, 74, 76, 88, 120, 143,158, 159, 176.
Improvisation, 6, 10,12,19, 20, 30, 139, 141.
Impulse, 96, 97, 121.
Intentionality, 125, 178, 190, 191, 199, 200 n21.

Inclinations: steep, flat, flowing, 69, 70, 76, 88, 89, 120.

Kinesphere 59, 64, 66, 74, 78, 86, 119, 177, 196, 197, 204.
Kinetic: aspect, 79; components, 104; content of form, 54, 93, 109; k. energy, 97, 118.
Kinetography Laban, 16, 21, 26, 29, 37, 52, 115, 122, 139, 166; International Council of, (ICKL), 132 n59; root of the term, 114, 128 n11; *see also* Labanotation and Notation.

Labananalysis, 216.
Labanotation, 16, 52, 115, 166: *see also* Kinetography and Notation.
Lability/*Labilitat*, 52, 53, 55, 66, 68, 74, 78, 79, 84, 94, 95, 116, 118, 127, 135, 164, 177, 197; *see also* Mobility.
Language (of movement and dance), 11, 140; grammar and syntax of 12.
Law(s), 8, 65; artistic l., 10; of choreology, 18; of movement and dance 21, 22, 118, 139; Delsarte's laws and orders of movement, 73,154; of harmony, 30, 156, 161; fundamental laws (opposition and sequence), 65; of proximity,78; sequential laws, 70, 73, 87, 88; of structuring movement, 57, 116, 161; *see also* Harmony and Principles.

Metric(s): content of form, 54, 64, 93; metrics (wide-narrow), 95; *see also* Extension.
Mime, 4, 11, 30, 31, 100, 140, 154, 161, 179; mimetic dance, 140; pantomime, 145.
Mobility, 52, 53, 68, 74, 76, 79,

84, 118, 127, 135, 166, 174, 176, 177, 197, 198; mobile chord, 66; m. equilibrium, 74; *see also* Lability.

Monolinear, 116-117, 123, 175; *see also* Successive.

Motility, 63, 189-192, 199, 200 n21.

Motor, motoric: elements, 118; energy, 140; powers, 30, 36; principles, 118.

Movement, 162-166; conscience, 32; description, 171-172; education, 26, 36, *see also* Dance education: elements, 171; expressive m., 67; factors, 179; functional m., 11; fundamental facts of 32; harmony, 25, 26, 79, 182, *see also* Harmony; initiation, impulse, 30, 55, 166; lived, living movement, 189-199; m. memory, 20; motivation for, 52, 179; principles of, 171, 220; properties of, 93; qualities of, 55, 102-104, 162, *see also* Effort; range (natural), 60; research, 25, 115; rhythms, 52; sense of, 11, 31; stillness – movement, 52, 53, 68; systematization of, 171-172; m. themes (sixteen basic), 140; three types of m.: impulse-tension-swing, 96-97, *see also* Dynamics.

Movement Choir/*Bewegungschor*, 9, 14-17, 20, 23, 28, 29, 31, 36, 44 n62; 122, 126, 130, 132 n73; 223, 226/28; 230-231; centers of, 19; choral movement, 15; leaders of, 23, 122, 126; m. ch. symphony, 15; *see also* Dance for layman.

Music, 6, 7, 11, 18, 23, 26, 33, 113, 127, 142, 155, 160, 162, 166; accompaniment, 8, 9, 15; atonality, twelve tone system, 22, 36; composer, 28; music-dance relationships, 159-160, 163; harmony, 22, 69, 70, 116, 159-160, 176; notation, 114, 121, 155, 164; percussion, sound, 7, 14, 15, 28; theory, 58, 176; visualizations, 166; Waltz and polka, 121; Western m., 163.

Notation, 5, 7, 9, 12, 13, 15, 16, 17, 18, 19, 30, 51, 58, 68, 78, 113-138, 139, 141, 155, 163-164, 172, 173, 183; of bodily articulation, 123-125; categorization of group formations, 123; choreography, 13, 114, 119, 155, 156, 162; drawings of floor patterns, 120; *Körperkreutz* – bodycross script/writing, 120, 123; Methodology, 123; Orthography, 123; principles (1928), 115-118, 121; principles of Beauchamps-Feuillet notation, 122, 163; publication of *Schrifttanz*, 122; relationships, 125-126; Schrifttanz/script-dance vs. Tanzschrift/dance-script, 114, 115, 128, 129 n14; 155; swallow-tail writing, 120; universality of Laban's notation, 118; *see also* Kinetography, Labanotation, Scores.

Observation, 25, 26, 51, 54, 125, 133, 154, 173, 203.

Octahedron, 60, 67, 68, 74, 75, 176.

Opera, 7, 11, 14, 19, 21, 33.

Oral tradition of Laban-based teaching, vii, 68, 81 n48, 61; 83 n91.

Ouvert/open, 63, 75, 85; *see also* Shape.

Pageant, 14, 15, 24, 35.

Path, 64, 96; *see also* Shape.
Perception, 22, 63, 127, 156,
157, 159, 171, 189-190, 191;
theories of, 161; of time, 94;
Vollsehen, total perception, 140.
Peripheral (path), 64, 68, 75, 76,
87, 98, 105, 177; peripheral
guidance, 96; undeviating p., 99.
Phrase, phrasing, 20, 94, 95-96,
103; phrases of action: preparation, contact, release, 126.
Planes, *see* Dimensional planes.
Plastic/three-dimensional, 11, 54,
66, 84, 116, 161, 164.
Play, 7, 11, 14; dance pl. 16, 17,
19; movement pl., 15.
Polarities, 104, 140, 193; polar
attitudes: indulgence in − fighting against, 100; asymmetry-
symmetry, 52; bound-loosened,
released, 93, 109; disequilibrium-
equilibrium, 52; of Effort
elements, 101; in Effort-graph,
101; extended-narrow, 78, 93,
109; fast-slow, 78, 93, 109;
hate-love, 101; mobile-rigid, 78,
93, 109; mobility-stability, 52;
movement-stillness, 52, 53; near-
far, 64, 86, 93, 109; weak-strong,
78, 93, 109.
Polylinear, 116-117, 123, 175;
see also, Simultaneous.
Posture-gesture (Lamb), 82 n84;
165.
Principles, 74, 94, 126, 160, 171,
183; of complementarity, 69, 73,
177; of counter-movement/
opposition/tension, also con-
tapuntal, 59, 65-66, 68, 73, 75,
87, 119, 141, 177; of eurhythmy,
139; harmonic p., 75, 76, 177,
see also Laws: of Laban's notation, 19, 54, 115-118; motor
p., 118; of parallelism, 70, 73,
76, 77, 87, 177; of proportional-

ity, 139; of regularity, 139; of
sequence, 65-66, 68, 165; of
stability-mobility, 52, 53; of
symmetry, 139; of tension-
relaxation, 94; *see also* Laws.
Proportionality, 94, 100, 139, 158,
160.

Reigen, 7, 9; *Reigenwerk*, 33.
Relationships, interaction, 30, 125-
126, 137, 138, 140, 141, 174,
196, 213; between directions, 58;
group, r., 26, 140, 213; of movement components, 94; partner
r., 140, 213; in scales, 75.
Rhythm, 14, 27, 55, 95-97, 99-100,
160, 164; components of, 160;
course in, 19; elements of, 160;
of exertion and recovery, 26;
Greek rhythms, 95, 174; occupational, 15; rhythmic chain, 69;
rhythmic content of form, 54,
93; rhythmology, 145; of scales,
70, 73; space/spatial rh., 10, 60,
63, 86, 95, 113, 116, 117, 174;
time/temporal rh., 92, 95, 116,
117, 127, 136, 174; of tension-
release/relaxation 94-97; weight
rh., 95, 174.
Rings, 57, 60, 76, 88, 175-178,
206-207; logical order of, 178;
mixed four-, seven-rings, 77;
numerical relations 69, 76; two-
three-four-rings, 70, 72, 77.
Ritual (istic), 14, 20, 22, 37, 155,
156, 160-161, 219; r. traditions,
4.
Rond/circular, 63, 75, 85; *see also*
Shape.

Scales, 34, 35, 57, 60, 67-77, 89,
116, 122, 158, 176-178, 206-
207; A and B, transversal standard scales, 57, 69-72, 76-77, 87,
89, 120, 177, 178; axis (structur-

al, diagonal) of scales, 69, 75, 76, 81 n64; 178; Axis scale, 57, 70, 72, 76, 89; definition of, 75; Diagonal scale, 68-69; Dimensional/defence/swing scale, 67-68, 75, 161; Equator scale, girdle, 57, 70, 76, 89; inclinations, *see*; Inclinations; logical order of, 178; numerical relationships between directions, 69, 76; Primary, peripheral standard scale, 69, 76, 81 n64, 89, 178; steeples, 70, 76; volutes, 57, 70, 76.

Scores, 15, 16, 17, 23, 126, 141, 182; *see also* Notation.

Shape, 53, 54, 63-64, 75, 127, 143, 157-159, 174, 176, 177, 205, 217; Arabic numerals, 63, 96, 161; of body carriage (pin, ball, wall, screw), 26, 63, 86; chordal − sequential forms/shapes, 174; dimensionality of sh.: one-two-three dim./linear, plane, plastic, 63, 64; Effort-Shape, 78; Effort/Shape, 82 n84; formal elements: *droit, ouvert, rond, tortillé*, 63-64, 75, 85-86, 161, 162, 177; fundamentalform elements, 158; of gesture, 26, 75; Greek alphabet, 63, 161; of path, 63, 89; patterns; air, floor, 63; perception of, 63, 159; shape-flow, 82 n84.

Simultaneous, 63, 116, 125, 174.

Sign, *see* Symbol.

Size, 63-64, 74; *see also* Extension.

Space, spatial, 134, 140, 162-164, 173, 174, 175-178; s. chord, 66, 84, 116, 174; direction, 11, *see also* Direction; extension, size, *see* Extension; general, infinite s., 59, 89, 203; s. intent, 68, 76; s. interrelationships, 58; s. laws, 140; lemniscate, 146, 147 n21; s. levels, 77; lived space, 189-199; s. order, 12, 16, 58; s. orientation, 59, 90, *see also* Directions; s. planes, *see* Three-dimensional Planes; s. relationships, 65; s. rhythms, 60, 63; spatiality, 79, 140, 189-199; sphere of movement, *see* Kinesphere; perceived s., 189; s. theories, 33, 57, *see also* Theory and Choreology.

Space Harmony, 6, 7, 24, 57, 58, 64-73, 90, 119, 172, 175-178, 206; origins and application of the term, 58; *see also* Choreutics.

Speed, *see* Time.

Stability/*Stabilitat*, 52-55, 66, 74, 76, 79, 84, 94, 95, 116, 118, 127, 135, 164, 166, 175, 176, 197, 198, 204; *see also* Balance and Equilibrium.

Style, 9, 10, 12, 16, 19, 22, 31, 32, 33, 116, 118, 125, 126, 161, 162, 166, 172, 175, 176, 180, 181, 183-184; Apollonian and Dionysian, 12; of Laban's teaching, 20.

Successive, 63, 116, 119, 125, 174.

Swing, 22, 54, 55, 77, 84, 95, 96-97; Anschwung-Ausschwung, 69; figure eight swings, 96; as a metaphor for harmonious movement, 161; s. scale/sequence, 22, 67.

Symbol, Sign, 155, 158, 159, 183; alphabet, 63, 118, 158, 161; graphic sy., 155; inner symbol as *Erlebnis*, 191; movement sy., 20, 54, 63; movement-dance notation signs and symbols, 16, 20, 54, 63, 78, 113, 114, 116-117, 119, 120, 122, 123-125, 143; numerals, 63, 96, 161; pre-signs, 121; runes, 155; signs for qualitative interpretations, 121;

symbolic, 140, 159, 182 (forms).
Symmetry, 52-54, 65, 84, 87, 125, 139, 160, 173; bodily symmetries, 60; *see also* Asymmetry.

Tableaux vivants, 5.
Technique, 7, 12, 18, 19, 20, 35, 64; "free dance technique," 100; *see also* Training.
Tetrahedron, 59, 67, 88, 176.
Theatre, 15, 18, 25, 31, 154, 161, 183; in the round, 5, 28, 34; proscenium, 11; set design, 5; total theatre, 34, 36; *see also* Dance.
Theory, 8, 13, 17, 18, 22, 156; contemporary dance th., 141; crystallographical and geometrical th. of space, 157, 176; of dance, 18, 163, 166, 175; of directions, 57; dynamic vs. static from theory," 54; of Effort, 128, 178, 224; of harmony, 11, 18, 19, 29, 30, 121, 141; "Laban's

theory," 12, 28, 29, 30; of movement harmony, 116; of perception, 161; of space harmony, 118, 156, 157, 224.
Time, 162-164, 173-174; aspects of, 126-127; duration, 94, 117; t. factor (Eukinetics), 98; motion factor time (Effort), 101-103; linear time, 163; qualitative dimension of, perception of, 94; t. rhythm, 95, 117, 127, 136; speed, 96, 99, 127; tempo, 127; temporal sequence, 54, 116; temporality, 189-199.
Tortillé/wavy, twisted, 63, 75, 85; *see also* Shape.
Transversals, 64, 65, 75, 76, 88, 177; *see also* Inclinations.
Training, 18, 26, 32, 52, 57, 94, 95; *see also* Technique.

Work, industry, 14, 16, 25, 32, 36, 100, 154; "industrial movement research," 52; work study, 25, 26.